Good Fat, Bad Fat

How to lower your cholesterol and reduce the odds of a heart attack

This book can save your life—
A simple plan for anyone who can count to 10
What's fact and what isn't?
Answers about antioxidants
Recipes and tips for enjoyable eating

William P. Castelli, MD
& Glen C. Griffin, MD

FISHER
er
BOOKS™

Publishers	Bill Fisher	**Book Design**	Deanie Wood
	Helen Fisher		Anne Olson
	Howard Fisher	**Cover Design**	Randy Schultz
Managing Editor	Sarah Trotta	**Cover Photo**	© Robert Llewellyn / SuperStock, Inc.
Editors	Sarah Trotta	**Recipe Development**	Helen Fisher
	Bill Fisher		
	Alison Fisher	**Nutritional Analysis**	Miriam Fisher

Published by
Fisher Books, LLC
5225 W. Massingale Road
Tucson, Arizona 85743-8416
(520) 744-6110
www.fisherbooks.com

Fisher Books is a member of the Perseus Books Group.

Printed in U.S.A.

Printing 10 9 8 7

Library of Congress Cataloging-in-Publication Data

Castelli, William P.
    Good fat, bad fat : reduce your heart-attack odds / William P. Castelli, Glen C. Griffin.
        p. cm.
    Includes bibliographical references and index.
    ISBN 1-55561-117-6
      1. Hypercholesteremia—Prevention. 2. Myocardial infarction—Prevention. 3. Lowfat diet—Recipes. 4. lipids in human nutrition.
I. Griffin, Glen C. II. Title.
RC632.H83C37   1997
616.1′2305—dc21   96-37278
                                                     CIP

CONTENTS

HEART INSURANCE?

If you could buy heart insurance, would you? Your heart is far more complex than any machine, car, computer, or other equipment you may use. In fact, chances are that your heart has already outlasted several cars and computers.

How much longer will it keep going?

Your heart didn't come with a 10-year warranty or a lifetime guarantee. But you can insure your heart, if you wish. By paying a monthly premium, an insurance company will pay your survivors when your heart quits. Nice for them. But what about you?

What if you could get heart insurance to keep your heart running longer? Well, that's what this book is all about—a way to extend the life of your heart. We're going to help you know how to increase the quality of your heart's service to you. What's more, you can really enjoy life and eating tasty foods without killing yourself and others in your family with too much fat and cholesterol.

ABOUT THE AUTHORS

William P. Castelli, M.D.

Doctors everywhere know Bill Castelli as the soft-spoken expert who crusades all over the world teaching about the dangers of bad fat. Castelli has a particular interest in sharing all that he knows.

Because of his family history, Castelli might have gotten heart disease before the age of 50, as every other member of his parents' families did. Castelli's brother, a heavy smoker, had an early heart attack in his 40s. Sadly, he never stopped smoking and died of heart disease at 67 convinced that his brother Bill would find a cure for heart disease so he wouldn't have to quit. Bill also watched his mother die of heart disease at 64, his father at 73 as well as most of his aunts and uncles. His wife Marge recalls that "The year Bill and I were married, everyone in his family seemed to be dying."

Well, Castelli was determined this wouldn't happen to him. He never smoked, unlike his brother and Winston Churchill, whom he otherwise always admired. A great influence on Castelli was his experience doing autopsies in Belgium as a student of Dr. Eugene Picard (see page 12). The connection between eating and health couldn't have been clearer to the young student. Castelli knew he didn't want coronary fat plaques to interfere with his life—or end it.

So years later, when Castelli learned his own cholesterol level was at a high of 270, he set a goal to get it down and control it so he wouldn't be plagued with heart disease.

No more cream. No more rich cheese. Very little meat. Much more fish and seafood. Regular, vigorous exercise. After Castelli rigidly limited the amount of bad fat and cholesterol he ate, his cholesterol levels came down. Yet, because of the set of genes he inherited from his parents, his regular walking program and habit of eating very little fat was not enough. He also needed the help of lipid-controlling medications, which he continues to take faithfully.

Now his cholesterol level runs about 190, with an HDL level of 60, giving a ratio of 3.2. Bill Castelli provides an admirable model of what he teaches others to do.

Long before others recognized that high triglycerides, low HDL levels and cholesterol/HDL ratios over 4 are major risk factors for heart disease, Dr. Castelli warned us about them.

In his clear, deliberate way, Castelli continues to unravel difficult problems and to patiently explain the truths he has sorted out from research done by others or that he has discovered himself to doctors, patients, committees, panels, reporters and critics. Truly a modern pioneer, Bill Castelli is responsible for helping millions live happier, healthier lives.

William P. Castelli, M.D., is the medical director of the Framingham Cardiovascular Institute. Before retiring from the U.S. Public Health Corps in 1995, he directed the famed Framingham Heart Study for 16 years. Before that, he was laboratory director of the long-term study for 14 years.

Castelli is also an adjunct associate professor of medicine at Boston University. He lectured at Harvard Medical School for 34 years and at the University of Massachusetts School of Medicine for 15 years. He has received the prestigious Meritorious Service Medal from the U.S. Public Health Service and honorary degrees from Northeastern University and Framingham College, among many other awards. He lectures in many countries around the world, including France, Russia, England, Australia, Japan, Germany, Norway, Spain, Canada and the United States. He makes frequent appearances on television and radio to discuss heart health.

Bill Castelli and his wife Marge have three children and five grand-children who love to play with his collection of electric trains. He and his wife live in Marlboro, Massachusetts.

Glen C. Griffin, M.D.

Growing up, Glen Griffin had no idea that hamburgers, French fries, eggs, doughnuts, ice cream, cheese and other high-fat foods were forming fat plaques in his coronary arteries. He was in a very high-risk group for having a heart attack, but didn't know it until much later. The first clue he had was a 1980 lab report saying his triglycerides were over 1000. While this didn't sound too good to him, none of the physicians he consulted seemed concerned because his total cholesterol level appeared normal at 160.

He cut down on the fat he was eating, documented everything he ate and checked his blood triglyceride level every day. Although he reduced his sky-high triglyceride level somewhat, Griffin found the recommended way to track his fat intake was a nuisance. He realized that if it was a bother keeping track of the percentages of fat calories he was eating, others were probably having the same problem. A simpler system was obviously needed.

Soon after, the authors developed a simple plan to make eating a pleasure while limiting saturated-fat intake to a 10- or 20-gram budget a day. Just as they were putting the finishing touches on their work, Griffin started feeling a little tightness in his chest every morning while running. He thought he was just "out of shape," but, in fact, he was a massive heart attack waiting to happen.

Each of his parents had had such fat-plugged coronary arteries that they had undergone open-heart bypass surgery. When he saw the fat plaques blocking his own parents' coronary arteries during their surgeries, Griffin knew he didn't ever want to go through their ordeal. He started eating more fish and did without eggs, butter, sausage or bacon. While he thought he was on a good program to prevent a heart attack, he wasn't! He was still eating too much ice cream, cheese and fish and chips—all loaded with fat.

In 1989, it was discovered that fat plaques plugged his coronary arteries almost completely, despite the measures he had taken since 1980 to combat heart disease. Griffin still remembers the cardiologist's words: "You have a 98% blockage. Even if the paramedics had been a block away when this major artery shut off, they would have brought you in dead-on-arrival."

Now he would undergo bypass surgery as well. He was a little frightened, as most people are who face heart surgery—especially with vivid memories of having watched the surgery performed on his parents years before. The good news is that he recovered from his open-heart surgery, "thanks to an excellent surgical team and lots of prayers."

Now he takes every opportunity to teach people the simple system of cutting down on bad fat that he and Castelli created to replace the complicated instructions patients are usually given.

On his first day of medical school, Glen Griffin set himself the goal of taking the gobbledygook out of complicated medical writing. He achieved his goal though years of medical practice, by writing books and syndicated newspaper columns, then as the editor-in-chief of *Postgraduate Medicine,* editorial director of McGraw-Hill Healthcare Publications and now as chairman of Griffin Communications.

An inventor and efficiency expert, Griffin created a drive-up-to-your-own-room medical clinic that was featured on the front page of the *Wall Street Journal,* on CNN and in *USA Today.*

He is a clinical professor of family medicine at the University of Utah and teaches residents at the Utah Valley Regional Medical Center. He has appeared on radio and television talk shows, helping people learn how to enjoy eating without killing themselves and their families with bad fat.

Glen and Mary Ella Griffin have six children and 14 grandchildren. They live in Mapleton, Utah.

What Can I Believe?

(WITH SO MUCH CONFUSING INFORMATION)

"Everyone has to die sometime. I'd rather eat what I want and die from a heart attack than suffer with something like cancer!"

The skeptic's conclusion might seem logical, but it isn't.

The first thing wrong with this reasoning is that many die of heart attacks at a very young age. So, someone who wants to die of a heart attack instead of cancer may find himself dying in the prime of life.

The next fallacy is that most people who have heart attacks *don't* die from them.[1] Usually they go through considerable pain and misery, spend time in intensive care and frequently suffer the trauma of heart surgery. Then, at best, there are major limitations on what they can do; at worst, a complete change of lifestyle.

The misinformed skeptic was probably rationalizing an unwillingness to give up a habit of eating fat-loaded food. She was not alone in being confused. So much information and misinformation make it hard for anyone to know what to believe.

"A professor says on the Internet that the cholesterol campaign is a myth and we should all eat more fat."[2]

"If you're a senior citizen with coronary-artery disease, don't bother to go on a low-fat diet."[3]

"A report in the *New England Journal of Medicine* says . . . "

"And today's newspaper says a study in the *Journal of the American Medical Association* concludes . . . "

Every time you pick up a newspaper or magazine, turn on the news, attend a lecture, listen to a talk show or scan the Internet, you are overwhelmed with data. Some of it is very convincing. Then you read a few lines (never the complete story, of course!) about *another study* which completely contradicts what you thought you had just learned.

The result is information chaos. It can't all be correct—it isn't all correct. What *can* you believe?

People are so confused with conflicting conclusions that they assume no one knows what is really true. Sadly, such confusion sometimes becomes a rationalization for doing things that will cause you problems.

Much of what is written about health is totally useless for public consumption. Some well-intended scientific writing is so complicated that it requires decoding by experts. It should be written simply so it can be understood. And some medical writing is just plain wrong. So much information and misinformation make it hard to know what to believe. Some of the problems include:

- Incorrect conclusions from bad science.
- Mistakes from poor study design.
- Studies based on false assumptions.

Many are honest mistakes. Even so, flaws sometimes creep into conclusions because of a doctor's or researcher's desire for recognition, a financial interest in the outcome or the speaking fees that come from presenting the *other side* of a position.

When misinformation is reported as fact by journalists eager for an interesting story, a new health myth is created.

Sorting out the truth is not even easy for experts. Sorting out facts from misinformation is even more difficult for those who are not real experts. We can either stay confused or do our best to come up with the best information we can possibly get.

Almost everyone knows too much cholesterol is a principle cause of heart attacks. Not everyone knows that when they eat saturated fat their bodies make cholesterol.

Saturated fat is usually a bigger problem than the cholesterol we consume.

Saturated fats are the characteristically *hard* fats found mostly in animal products such as lard, butter and fatty meat as well as in vegetable oils such as coconut and palm.

We usually consider all saturated fats as *bad* fats—and most are. Some saturated fats may turn out not to be as harmful as others. For the sake of simplicity, we suggest for the time being that all saturated fats be considered essentially the same.

Some people are still hiding their heads in the sand, like those who refused for decades to admit that smoking causes lung cancer, heart disease and emphysema. To help counter at least some of this confusion, we wrote this book to help you learn the best information about how you can prevent heart attacks.

We don't have all the answers, but we have a lot of them. If you follow a simple plan, you can go a long way toward reducing the odds of having a heart attack. At the same time, you can help your friends and family—especially the children and young adults who are important in your life.

Some Helpful Information

- Saturated fats are bad fats.

- Trans-fatty acids are also bad fats (even though they are unsaturated fats)

- So the total bad fat one eats is a total of the grams of saturated fat and the grams of trans-fat.

- Our advice is to limit the bad fat to 20 grams a day for healthy people and to 10 grams a day for people who have had a heart attack, heart surgery, elevated triglycerides, a ratio over 4 or an LDL over 130.

- It isn't easy to know how much trans-fat there is in food because there's is no requirement to label trans-fatty acids in food products at this time. (And no one is labeling or telling how much trans fat is in their products).

- Trans-fat is produced when unsaturated fat is hydrogenated—turning it into a solid.

- Until the amount of trans-fat in a product is put on labels, a helpful rule of thumb (a pretty good estimate) can be to consider that in most hydrogenated food products the trans-fat probably equals the saturated fat on the label.

- Thus, when you are wondering how much "bad fat" there is in a product like salad dressings, margarine, table spreads, cream cheese and other hydrogenated food products, we suggest checking the amount of saturated fat listed on the label and doubling that number. In other words, if there is 1 gram of saturated fat per tablespoon of a product, there is probably another 1 gram of trans-fat, giving a total of 2 grams of bad fat.

NOTES

1. About 15% of people die from their first heart attack, so 85% of people do not die from their first encounter with serious heart disease, they live. Half of the 85% who don't die still have serious problems: their heart function is so poor that their quality of life decreases greatly. Many cannot continue working at their usual jobs or do many of the important day-to-day activities they are used to doing. To make it worse, 50% of those who have had one heart attack have another one, many from blockages not visible on angiography. New blockages are often caused by clots which occur in rather small fat-rich plaque lesions that suddenly rupture. (However, these fatty deposits (lesions) reverse rapidly when people go on a lowfat diet.)

2. We completely disagree.

3. We completely disagree.

How You Can Change the Risky Odds

One out of every two.

That's how many people die of a heart attack or stroke. Not a comforting thought! Does this seem too far in the future to think about? Look at it from a different perspective. What if the odds were one in two that:

- your home would burn down?
- you would get a brain tumor?
- you were going to be in critical care after being shot?

You wouldn't like those odds. You would do whatever you could to keep these bad things from happening. More and more people are cutting their risks of a heart attack by eating less bad fat and exercising more.

But think about having dinner with some friends. Unless you and your friends change their eating habits and stay with a program of consuming less saturated fat, half of your group will probably die because of blockages in vital arteries supplying blood to your heart, brain or other vital organs.

There's more bad news.

Plaques of bad fat have probably already started to form inside the small arteries that supply blood and oxygen to your heart muscle.

Because your heart pumps blood all the time, what difference does it make if one of these little coronary arteries gets plugged? Can't the heart muscle get its oxygen and other nutrients from the blood it's pumping inside itself?

The answer is "No." Blood and oxygen cannot get to the muscle of the heart through your heart's inner lining. The only way your heart muscle can get nourishment is through the small coronary arteries on the surface of your heart that go to each area of heart muscle.

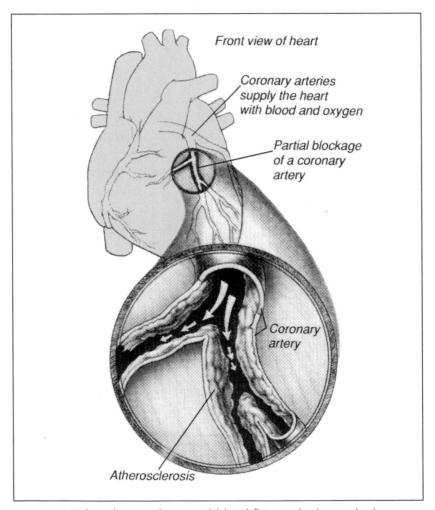

Front view of heart

Coronary arteries supply the heart with blood and oxygen

Partial blockage of a coronary artery

Coronary artery

Atherosclerosis

Figure A. *When there is decreased blood flow to the heart, the heart muscle may be damaged.*

What Is a Heart Attack?

Let's go back to the plugging of these little lifeline arteries, which look like small strands of spaghetti. Over the years, fat deposits collect in these little arteries like calcium and grease deposits on the inside of water pipes. As the deposits build up, shown in Figure A, the passageway for blood and oxygen gets smaller and smaller.

If the flow becomes partially restricted so the heart muscle doesn't get enough oxygen, brief episodes of discomfort occur in the chest, called *angina*. This pain is sometimes a *crushing* feeling. Other times it may be more like a *tightness* or a disconcerting *pressure*. Sometimes angina pain may be felt in the left or even the right arm, the jaw, the back or the abdomen. There also may be shortness of breath and/or dizziness, sweating or nausea.

People with angina eventually learn that a particular strenuous activity, excitement or stress brings on discomfort. Most find that rest and calming influences usually make the angina disappear in a few minutes. A small tablet of nitroglycerin dissolved under the tongue usually helps by dilating the coronary blood vessels, thereby increasing the blood flow and relieving the discomfort.

Fortunately, episodes of angina are relatively short, but when a clot forms in a coronary artery filled with plaque, the problem multiplies. If a complete blockage occurs in one of these little arteries, the result is severe damage to the heart muscle. This is a heart attack—a *myocardial infarction.* A severe crushing pain occurs in the mid chest as this happens. Pain often progresses down the left arm. This pain doesn't go away with rest or nitroglycerin. Heart-attack pain lasts for at least a half hour and often longer.

As oxygen is cut off to an area of heart muscle, another bad thing can occur. Something may go wrong with the heart's electrical system. The steady electrical impulses that kept the heart beating smoothly are replaced with a wild twitching rhythm called *ventricular fibrillation.* This irregular and inefficient rhythm doesn't let the heart pump the blood the way it is supposed to and that creates a life-and-death situation. Electrical shock may be required to restore a normal heart beat, but that does not always work.

At this point, time is of the essence. Every minute counts. When someone has a heart attack, it is vitally important to recognize what is happening and immediately get expert help. Calling 911 in most locations in the U.S. will usually get paramedics on their way in moments. This rapid-response team can provide oxygen and medications on the spot and from there the patient can be transported quickly to a coronary-care unit. If 911 is not an option or if an ambulance has to travel a long distance, it may be better to get to the hospital in the fastest way possible. Some people don't make it.

If the heart can be kept going, medications usually help strengthen the heart enough so little-by-little the body can re-route blood to the damaged heart muscle through other tiny vessels. Amazingly, this re-routing process, called *collateral circulation,* keeps many heart-attack victims alive. Sometimes the resulting collateral circulation is pretty good. More often it isn't anywhere near what it used to be. Patients in this situation are reminded of this from time to time by recurrent angina pain.

We usually don't have to sit back and just hope the body will create its own collateral circulation. Plugged arteries can be opened up with precision instruments which are snaked up through the aorta and into the plugged coronary artery from an artery in the thigh. You may be able to watch on a video screen as the surgeon performs one of the various *angioplasty* procedures in which a tiny balloon or instrument pushes, drills or blasts through the blocked passage. Think of angioplasty as something like unclogging drainage pipes with a rooter machine. To keep an artery open, a tiny steel device called a *stent* is often slipped into the artery. Amazing!

When there is considerable blockage, another way to get blood to the heart muscle is to make a new passageway around the blockage during bypass surgery. The surgeon makes a graft from an artery that previously supplied blood to the person's breast or from a vein from one of the person's legs. In each case the body creates collateral circulation for these areas which are not as critical as the heart. While the heart is stopped to put these grafts in, the blood is bypassed through large tubes into an artificial pump that keeps the blood going to the brain, lungs and the rest of the body during the surgery. With the heart stopped, the graft is stitched in, forming a new passageway for blood to flow around each blocked coronary artery. After the heart is restarted, the pump is disconnected and blood once again flows to the damaged heart muscle.

Sometimes it is even possible to put in bypass arterial grafts without stopping the heart. Imagine micro-stitching these little arteries while the heart is still pumping! Instead of making a large incision in the chest, a surgeon can sometimes work on the heart through tiny portholes in the skin and chest wall, called *keyhole surgery*. While problems sometimes occur, this marvelous technology is usually highly effective.

Sadly, even after such marvels of modern surgery, people sometimes don't change the lifelong patterns that led to the plugging of their coronary arteries. Not smart! Or, perhaps in some cases, *not informed.* Certainly anyone who has undergone bypass surgery or angioplasty or had a heart attack, should immediately change his or her lifestyle patterns that contributed to these blockages.

What are you doing now to keep your coronary arteries from becoming plugged?

Even if you haven't ever had a heart attack, angioplasty or bypass surgery, the question still applies. It's good that modern technology is available if you need it, but it's even better to prevent your arteries from getting plugged up in the first place.

Everyone who has a car knows it's much easier, less costly and less upsetting to prevent problems than to repair them. What about our hearts? We can prevent much of the plugging that occurs in coronary arteries. In fact, people in most parts of the world *don't* get heart attacks. You can be among those who don't—even living in a culture in which much of the population will spend time in coronary-care units because of fat-plugged coronary arteries.

Even if you already have some fat plaques in your coronary arteries, you have a choice every day whether to let the fat plugging get worse, stay the same or do something that has a good chance to make it regress.

You can personally significantly decrease the odds of a heart attack. It requires changing eating and exercising habits. We tell you how in this book.

A heart attack is no fun. It's gruesome! Don't fall for the line that you might as well eat lots of fatty junk and die pleasantly from a heart attack. Think about recurrent angina pain. Think about being in an intensive-care unit. And think about having heart surgery—even with the most modern techniques. Then realize you may be able to about avoid all these things.

Instead of rationalizing reasons to keep on eating fat, every morning ask yourself, "What can I do today to prevent more fat from plugging my coronary arteries?"

If you want to have clean and open coronary arteries, you can.

It's simple, but not easy.

If you want to change the odds, start living more like the people who almost never have heart attacks. To begin with, that means watching your diet.

Among the leading industrialized nations, the Japanese have the fewest heart attacks. Other cultures with historically little coronary-artery disease include other Asians, Eskimos, Africans, Mediterraneans and Latin Americans.

The people among these cultures who get heart attacks tend to live and eat the way most people in *our* culture eat. Of course, we are not suggesting you move somewhere far away. Just take a look at the eating patterns and lifestyles of people who do not get fat plaques in their coronary arteries—called *atherosclerosis*—and the eating patterns and lifestyles of those who do.

Saturated Fat is One of the Principle Culprits

As you may already know, meat and other animal fats, lard, butter, whole milk, ice cream, egg yolks, cheese and many other things contain saturated fat. Tropical oils such as coconut, palm and palm-kernel also contain lots of bad fat. These oils are in many of the things you eat, such as baked goods and especially junk food.

Most youngsters in our culture grow up eating hamburgers, fries and shakes—to say nothing of butter, cheese, bacon, sausages, fried foods and fatty meats. It's not just the kids. Although some change is going on, most people in our culture eat way too much saturated fat. People anywhere in the world who eat the same way as people in North America also have very high heart-attack rates.

So, what about people who don't get heart attacks?

Around the world, people eat vastly different foods with some interesting basic similarities. Each diet is built on some type of grain—wheat in the United States, Canada and Russia; rice in Japan and the orient; and corn in Mexico, Central America and much of Latin America.[1] Many also eat fish and seafood to complement the grains with essential amino acids.

Compare this eating pattern with the vast quantities of meat, eggs and whole-milk products that are a major part of the typical diets of people who *do* have heart attacks.

Another consistent dietary factor among many cultures with low heart disease is that, for the most part, ***they are not milk-drinkers.*** Cream, regular whole milk, cheese and ice cream contain butterfat.

"Wholesome milk is an essential food. Isn't it necessary in our diet?" you may wonder. Most of us have grown up learning and believing this is true. Commercials keep shouting at us to drink more milk to be healthy. No one denies that milk contains many good nutrients, especially for infants and young children. The problem is the butterfat in whole milk, cream, ice cream and cheese that is a significant contributor to clogging coronary arteries. Maybe that's one reason why only 2% of the people in the world drink milk after they are weaned.[2] Good evidence suggests it isn't coincidence that the traditional Japanese, Eskimos and others who don't have heart attacks usually don't drink milk or eat very much cheese or ice cream.

This doesn't mean we shouldn't drink any milk or eat any milk products, but after the milk-drinking years of childhood, a better choice is to use fat-free (nonfat) milk, yogurt and dairy products.

Another thing about the Japanese, Eskimos, people from the Pacific islands and other cultures where heart attacks are rare or non-existent, is that many of them get much of their protein from fish and seafood.

The traditional diets of most Africans and Latin Americans don't contain much bad, saturated fat. (Except for the cattle-producing countries of Argentina and Uruguay where meat consumption is high.) The beans and corn eaten so abundantly in Latin America provide valuable complex carbohydrates and protein.

Although people in the Mediterranean countries consume some saturated fat in lamb, yogurt and cheese, their cooking oil is primarily olive oil instead of animal fat. Olive oil contains mostly mono-unsaturated fat which seems to have some additional benefits.

There is absolutely no question about the correlation between saturated fat, plaque formation in coronary arteries and heart attacks. While almost everyone knows this now, it was not always so clear.

Let's roll back the calendar to 1952 and eavesdrop on a conversation while a Belgian pathologist, Dr. Eugene Picard, was performing an autopsy with the assistance of a young medical student:[3]

"They're coming back," Dr. Eugene Picard announced as he examined the inside of a dead man's coronary arteries.

"What's coming back?" asked the student.

"The fat plaques. Just look at the atherosclerosis plugging up this 52-year-old man's coronary arteries. This is why he died of a heart attack. We have not been seeing coronary-artery *plaques* for a long time."

"What do you mean?" asked the student.

"They disappeared by 1942 and they've been gone for about ten years. Now they have started to come back. We saw them before the war in three-quarters of the people we autopsied. They were almost always there in the older people. Then they started to go away and not many seemed to die of heart attacks. The people lived longer and when they died, for whatever reason, their arteries were open and clear."

Why did the fat plaques go away in Belgium during those horrible years of World War II? Something interesting happened. People couldn't get the rich foods they were used to eating—especially meat, butter, cream and milk. Troops came to the farms and took the livestock away for their own use. The Europeans, rich and poor alike, were *deprived* of meat, butter and cream. They had no choice. They lived on plain, ordinary foods like grains, vegetables and fruits. Fat plaques disappeared by 1942—and so did heart attacks—until after the war when the people were once again able to eat lots of fatty foods.

How early do fat plaques start being deposited in a person's coronary arteries? Is this something that just starts to happen when a person is old? This answer is of great significance because we think we can help children and young adults beat the odds of a heart attack, as well as ourselves.

Plaque buildup begins in childhood and in the young-adult years. This became evident when autopsies were performed on American troops killed in the Korean War. The average age of the young men killed in that war was 22 years and three-fourths already had fat streaks in their coronary arteries. Recent studies have confirmed this.

Think about these fat plaques every time you or family members eat greasy hamburgers, fries, doughnuts, butter and other things loaded with fat. And keep in mind that as this fat goes in, your body makes cholesterol and triglycerides. Little by little these add to deposits in your coronary arteries that may cause a lot of grief.

If you, or someone in your family, eats like a typical North American, odds are almost 50-50 that you will die of a heart attack or stroke. This is true for men *and* women. Because of the myth that women don't get coronary-artery disease, their symptoms are often not taken seriously—even by physicians. This is tragic because **women are at serious risk of heart disease, especially after menopause.** In fact, **coronary-artery disease is the leading killer of women over 65.** Five times more women die of heart disease than of breast cancer. **Every day more women than men in North America die of heart attacks.** Vital statistics show 49% of women still die of atherosclerotic vascular disease (includes coronary-artery disease, stroke, peripheral vascular disease, aneurysms, etc.) compared to 42% of men dying of these causes.[4]

No one likes lousy odds in a bet, yet sometimes people don't pay much attention to poor odds when it comes to themselves or their health. Too many people think "It won't happen to me." We hope you won't kid yourself with this misdirected reasoning. Plugged-up coronary arteries *can* happen to you. So can an untimely massive heart attack or stroke.

You can significantly change the odds.

NOTES

1. These grains provide essential building blocks called essential *amino acids.* Besides eating grain, to make a *complete protein,* people need other essential *amino acids* found in legumes such as beans. Fortunately, when both grains and legumes are eaten regularly (not necessarily in the same dish or even in the same meal), a balance occurs so a complete protein results. Fish and other seafood also supply the essential amino acids. Seafood or a combination of grains and legumes, are good low-saturated-fat sources of the essential amino acids. It shouldn't be surprising that these are the main diet components for people living in cultures where heart attacks do not occur—or occur rarely.

2. According to Frank Oski, M.D., the editor-in-chief of *The Yearbook of Pediatrics.*

3. The student was William P. Castelli.

4. Because hormonal replacement therapy markedly reduces the risk of these devastating causes in women who are no longer producing enough estrogen to be protective, we strongly recommend that these women be on on-going hormonal replacement therapy in addition to the other things we suggest.

Do You Know
Your Ratio & Cholesterol
& Triglyceride Levels?

"How do I know how much fat has already been deposited inside my coronary arteries?" you may wonder.

Most people don't think about this until something happens to them. They may experience a tightness, heaviness, some unusual discomfort (rarely would it be called a pain) in their chest, or just get very short of breath. Eventually, they realize they have to get medical care.

A doctor usually begins by doing a simple electrocardiogram on you. Twenty-five percent of heart attacks are *silent* but show up on a routine electrocardiogram. If the resting electrocardiogram is normal, the next step is to do a treadmill test. An electrocardiogram is done while you exercise. For people who can not exercise, some doctors will inject a medicine, dipyridamole (Persantin®), which makes your heart race.

If your heart arteries (coronaries) are clogged, when your heart rate increases, not enough blood will be delivered to your heart muscles. This changes your electrocardiogram in a characteristic way described as the ST (part of the tracing) depression or elevation. At this time, thallium or some other isotope may be injected into your arm vein and the heart will be scanned to see what part of your heart muscle is not receiving blood. Most people return about 2 to 4 hours (or longer) after the first scan to see if the blood-flow "deficit" is permanent.

If the deficit is permanent, it could mean the part of the heart muscle that was not receiving blood may have died. In any event, it usually means that a blockage exists in one of your coronary arteries and so doctors go to the next step to find out where the blockages are and how much. This requires that a catheter be inserted into an artery in your groin and run up the big arteries in your stomach and chest to the arteries of the heart. A radio-opaque dye is injected which allows your doctor to see where the blockages are.

A new procedure called *Ultrafast CT* (Computerized Tomography) scan only takes 6 minutes while you are lying down. With this test, doctors can see many of the deposits located on the arteries of your heart. An even newer procedure using Magnetic Resonance lets doctors look inside your arteries without having to use a catheter.

However, this is only part of the story when you realize that your first or next heart attack doesn't usually come from big blockages in your arteries that reduce blood flow, but rather from deposits of soft fat, usually in the valleys between the large blockages. These soft deposits are covered by only a thin layer of cells. This layer ruptures and causes a massive blood clot to form, producing a heart attack. We are only beginning to find ways to see these deposits before they grow into the kinds of deposits that block blood flow. When people lower the bad kind of cholesterols, or the bad triglyceride-rich particles in their blood, the first particles to shrink are these soft plaques.

Is there an easier way to see these soft or large plaques forming inside your coronary arteries? Not directly, but we may get a clue by doing a scan (ultrasound or Ultrafast CT) to see if plaque is forming in the big arteries—the *carotids*—that carry blood to your brain. "So what?" you may be thinking. "What does plaque in one's carotids have to do with plugging in a person's coronary arteries?"

Exciting pioneering work at Framingham shows that 76% of people older than 65 already have lesions in their carotids big enough to show up on a scan. Some of these lesions are just a thickening of the artery wall and others are deposits of fat. If there is plaque in your carotid arteries, we can be almost certain there is plaque in your coronary arteries.

We believe scanning testing for arterial plaque will become a very helpful and widely used procedure as time goes along. At this point, *carotid scans* are not a routine procedure for those with suspected coronary-artery disease.

Get a Blood Test

There is something everyone can and should have checked right now—how much fat is floating around in your blood. A set of blood tests (called a *lipid panel*) tells about the risk of your coronary arteries getting plugged up.

Do You Know Your Cholesterol and Triglyceride Numbers?

We say *numbers* instead of *number* because there are 18 different kinds of cholesterol—most bad, some good—and a very important ratio.

It all begins by having your total cholesterol and HDL cholesterol measured. These two cholesterol measures can be done without fasting (non-fasting). Doctors and patients should never again waste their time or money measuring the total cholesterol alone.

Look first at your total cholesterol. Is it under 150mg/dl (3.8mmol/L)? If so you should get your 2 miles in a day and eat a low-fat diet so you lower your risk of colon cancer, gall-bladder disease, or breast cancer. Your chances of getting a heart attack are slim.

If your total cholesterol reaches 150 (3.8) then you must make a simple ratio. Divide the total cholesterol by the HDL cholesterol. Suppose your total cholesterol was 200 and your HDL cholesterol was 50, your ratio would be 4.

$$\frac{\text{Total cholesterol}}{\text{HDL Cholesterol}} = \text{Ratio}$$

If your ratio is higher than 4 you are continuing to increase the deposits of fat in your arteries. You need to start your diet and exercise program to lower this ratio to under 4 to stop the progression of the cholesterol sludge in your arteries.

If you have had a heart attack, stroke or some artery blockage and want to shrink the deposits of fat you have to get your ratio under 3. But in order to know whether you have a nasty LDL cholesterol problem, a nasty triglyceride problem or both we need to do further testing.

If your total cholesterol reached 150 and your total cholesterol/HDL cholesterol ratio was 4 or higher you must have your blood fats retested after fasting 12 to 14 hours, where we measure the total cholesterol, HDL cholesterol and triglycerides.

If your total cholesterol is 150 or higher and your total/HDL cholesterol ratio is 4 or higher, look at your triglyceride number. If it is under 150 (1.7) you have nasty LDL. You have too much LDL cholesterol for the HDL cholesterol you have.

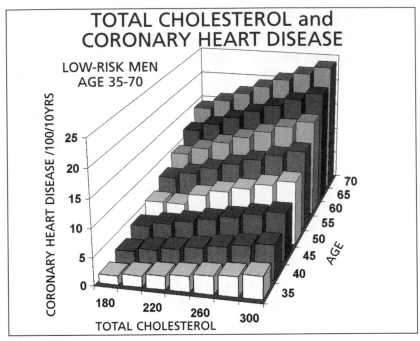

Figure B

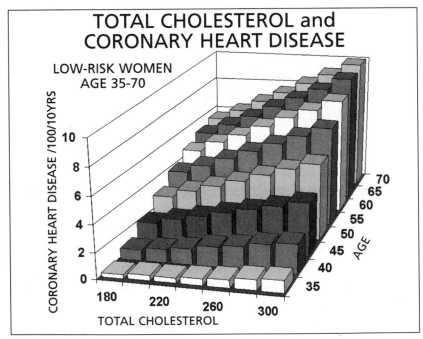

Figure C

If your triglyceride is 150 or higher with that bad ratio over 4 you have high triglyceride *and* low HDL cholesterol, the hallmark of Reaven's Syndrome X, Kaplan's deadly quartet, Williams' Dyslipidemic Hypertension, Defronzo's insulin-resistance syndrome, or the Polymetabolic Syndrome (see page 26).

Much of our knowledge of how cholesterol relates to coronary-artery disease comes from studies like the Framingham Heart Study and a few other well designed clinical trials. As you can see in *Figures B* and *C,* at virtually any age the heart-attack rate rises 2% for each 1% the level of total cholesterol in the blood goes up. This is even true for people over 65.

The average total cholesterol level of a man in the Framingham Heart Study who had a heart attack in the first 16 years of the study was 244. Now, some 33 years later, that level is about 225. In general, the higher this total cholesterol is, the more likely a person is to have a heart attack.

Some people in the Framingham Study who had high cholesterol levels didn't have heart attacks. The trick is to know where you stand if you have a high (or even not so high) total cholesterol level. Are you headed for a heart attack—or will you escape?

The Framingham Heart Study

An ongoing in-depth study was begun in 1948 with 5127 men and women in the town of Framingham, Massachusetts to evaluate the risk factors of coronary-artery disease. The test subjects represented one half of all the healthy adults—men and women—in that town. From then till now, they have been examined and checked every two years. Since then, other generations of Framingham people have joined the study. In a way, this study is a "gift" from the people of Framingham to the world.

Heart attacks, deaths and laboratory data have been carefully followed, providing valuable information about the risk factors related to coronary-artery disease. After careful analysis of the data from Framingham, as well as collaborative studies from across the U.S., Finland and other countries, there isn't any question that high cholesterol levels result in more heart attacks. Summing up these results shows that a 1% rise in cholesterol increases the chance of coronary artery disease by 2% in both men and women.

Co-author William P. Castelli was the Medical Director of the Framingham Heart Study of The National Heart, Lung and Blood Institute from 1979 until 1995.

Total Cholesterol Doesn't Tell Everything

The answer begins by knowing your cholesterol numbers. But your blood level of *total cholesterol* provides only one clue about what your body does with the saturated fat and cholesterol you eat. It's just *one* clue because there are 18 different kinds of cholesterol and other fats (lipids) in the blood—and they are *not* all bad. As we will show, measuring total cholesterol, HDL cholesterol and triglycerides allows us to make a good estimate of how you are doing.

A home cholesterol test kit or a cholesterol "screening test" at a shopping mall only measures *total cholesterol.* Although these tests may help to identify people with a very high total cholesterol, they miss people at risk whose cholesterol level may seem OK. We advise against relying on these simpler tests because they do not provide all of the information you and your doctor need. When your total cholesterol is between 150 and 300 (and that is about 90% of the people 30 years or older), we can't tell whether you are in the group to get a heart attack or stay free of an attack.

Most doctors follow the guidelines recommended by the National Cholesterol Education Program which recommend that everyone start by measuring their total *and* HDL cholesterols. Both tests can be done without fasting, so this is a very convenient way to start.

Now you can look at the major fat-containing players in your blood:

- total cholesterol
- LDL cholesterol
- HDL cholesterol
- triglycerides

Good (Healthy) Cholesterol (HDL)

One of the things a good group of blood tests will tell you is your level of good cholesterol, called *HDL,* short for *High Density Lipoprotein.* (The *H* in HDL can remind us this is *Healthy* cholesterol.)

Bad (Lousy) Cholesterol (LDL)

There is a harmful cholesterol called *LDL,* short for *Low Density Lipoprotein.* (The *L* in the LDL can be a reminder this is *Lousy* cholesterol.) See *Figure D.*

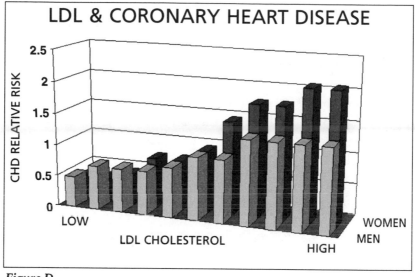

Figure D

If you don't have a vascular or heart problem and no other risk factors, get your LDL cholesterol under 160 (4.1).

If you are free of clinical disease but have two other risk factors (Family history of heart disease under age 55, hypertension, cigarette smoking, diabetes, HDL less than 35) then you need your LDL under 130mg/dl (3.4mmol/L). If you have had a heart attack or other vascular problem you must get your LDL under 100 (2.6).

Triglycerides

Most (about 70% in North America) of the triglycerides, a different kind of fat than cholesterol, are carried in small particles in your blood. These particles can also be deposited on the walls of your arteries. Because these particles also contain cholesterol, they add to the burden of cholesterol in your blood. These particles increase in our blood when we eat too much saturated fat and cholesterol and get fat.

Triglycerides are the most common form of fat in the diet—and in the human body. Too much of these fats put a person at risk for *pancreatitis*—inflammation of the pancreas—as well as increased risk of getting a heart attack.

Triglycerides are carried in the very-low-density lipoproteins (VLDL), which we can add to the other *lousy lipoproteins*.

High triglycerides can cause plugged-up coronary arteries even if the cholesterol levels are normal.

In addition, with high triglycerides, our blood is more likely to clot, our insulin goes up, our HDL cholesterols fall and our blood pressure goes up.

Another type of triglyceride-rich particle also can go up in our blood from eating too much refined carbohydrates (white flour, sugar), and while there is less tendency for these larger particles to be deposited in our blood vessels, they are usually associated with an increased tendency of our blood to clot. They also are associated with a fall in HDL cholesterol.

If your triglyceride is 150 or higher at the same time your HDL is 45 or less, you have the small triglyceride particles and a fast road to vascular disease; whereas if your triglycerides are high with high HDL cholesterol, you have the larger, somewhat less dangerous kinds of triglycerides. The large kind of triglyceride particles are also increased by drinking too much alcohol, taking estrogen, or taking the resin medicines Colestipol® or Questran®. The relationship of the risk of high triglyceride levels and a low HDL level is shown in *Figures E* and *F.*

This brings up another problem. Not everyone, even good health-care professionals and official organizations, understands the seriousness of high triglycerides. *Figure G* shows a definite relationship between high triglyceride levels and coronary-artery disease. Dr. Castelli tracked triglyceride data carefully over many years in the Framingham Heart Study and the evidence leaves no doubt.

The higher the level of triglycerides in the blood, the higher the heart-attack rate in every study. No matter what anyone may say to the contrary, people with high triglycerides—even with normal cholesterol levels—can and do have heart attacks from plugged-up coronary arteries.

Dr. Griffin knows this from the personal experience of having had bypass surgery after a 98% blockage in one coronary artery and an 80% in another, resulting from high triglycerides with a perfectly normal *total cholesterol* level.

Sooner or later, the danger of high triglycerides will be universally recognized. While the *official* word is that triglycerides *may be* a problem, there is absolutely no question about it. High triglycerides *are* a big problem.

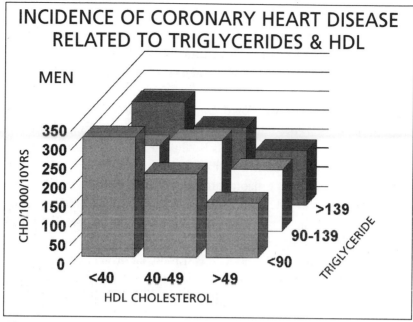

Figure E

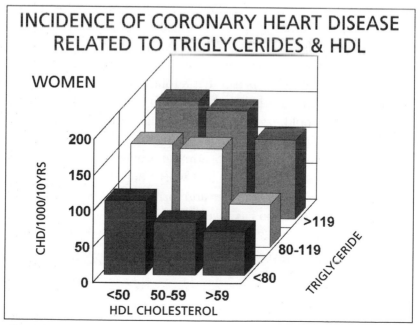

Figure F

The Cholesterol Ratio

This leads to another number we want you to know. We're not going to expect you to remember many numbers, but this one is important. It is your *ratio*—which is simply your *total cholesterol* divided by your *HDL* level.

A safe *ratio* is 4 or less. Anything higher means your risk for having a heart attack goes up. In fact, *Figure H* clearly shows, the higher the ratio, the greater the risk. This is why the ratio is so important.

As the solid evidence at the Framingham Heart Study has shown over many years, what someone's total cholesterol happens to be does not tell the full story. The significance of high total cholesterol really depends on how high or low the HDL cholesterol is in a person. As we explained, HDL is the *Healthy* or good cholesterol. The good thing is that if a person has enough HDL, it is somewhat protective against the damaging effects of an elevated LDL or total cholesterol. As is conclusively evident in *Figure F,* the higher a person's HDL level, the lower the incidence of a heart attack.

On the other hand, if a person has a very low HDL level, even with a normal cholesterol level, they may be at considerable risk. This means that someone with a very low HDL may be at even greater risk than someone who has a higher total cholesterol level but who also has a relatively high HDL level. The only time we don't care about your HDL or your ratio, is if your total cholesterol is *under* 150.

For example, let's say a person has a total cholesterol level of 170, considered by many to be perfectly normal. If that person has an HDL level of 32, she would have a dangerously high ratio of 5.3, meaning the person is at great risk for accumulating fat plaques and having a heart attack. (If you are in Canada, Europe or anywhere else where the mmol/L numbers are used, the ratio works out exactly the same— $4.2 \div 0.78 = 5.3$). Conversion tables and formulas are on page 32.

Suppose another friend has a seemingly normal total cholesterol of 180 and an HDL level of 30. The ratio is 6—even higher than the previous example. Both persons need to get on aggressive programs to help get their lipids under control.

Everyone agrees that an HDL level should at least be above 35, but not everyone understands the importance of the relationship of the HDL to the total cholesterol, which you can see in *Figure J.*

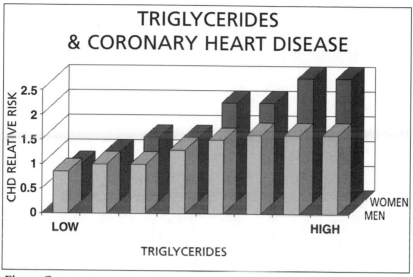

Figure G

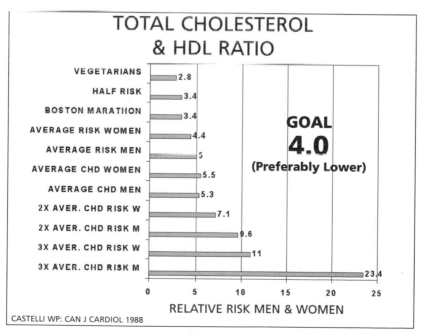

Figure H

Consider a friend with a total cholesterol of 250—well into the range that most people consider as being in a high-risk range for having a heart attack. Most of the time, this would probably be so. Now suppose this friend's HDL level was 65—quite a bit of *Healthy* cholesterol. The ratio comes out to be 3.8, which means your friend is really *not* at high risk. She has enough good HDL cholesterol to help protect her against the high levels of the bad cholesterol.

Understanding the relationship of HDL to total cholesterol explains why well-intended guidelines, based only on knowing a person's *total cholesterol,* do not provide enough information.

Many people believe anyone with a total cholesterol level under 200 is safe and not at risk. Surprisingly, the word in the original guidelines describing cholesterol levels under 200 was *"desirable."* At first, these guidelines went on to say that those with cholesterol levels between 200 and 240 are *borderline-high.* Just suppose a person has a total cholesterol level of 210 and an HDL level of 30. Dividing 210 by 30 gives a ratio of 7. There is nothing *borderline* about this person's risk, he is in a high-risk range.

Syndrome X

Here is a little more information about the "Deadly Syndrome X" (first mentioned on page 21), a combination of high triglycerides, low HDL (sometimes increased LDL), increased blood pressure, an increase in many clotting factors, increased uric acid and a blood sugar that starts to climb, often along with weight gain. This is often noticed as a *spare tire* spread around the middle. Anyone with an elevated triglyceride level and low HDL level should watch for weight gain and symptoms of diabetes (increased thirst, hunger and frequency of urination) or a gradually increasing fasting blood-sugar level.

Syndrome X is of such concern that a fasting blood-glucose level over 100 should be taken seriously in those with high triglycerides and a low HDL. To make this combination of difficult problems even worse, insulin levels rise in these people, putting them on the fast track to diabetes. When there has been a gain in weight, often trimming off just 15 pounds will make a big difference. Controlling each of the factors in this killer syndrome is extremely important.

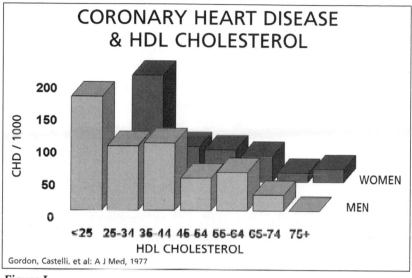

Figure I

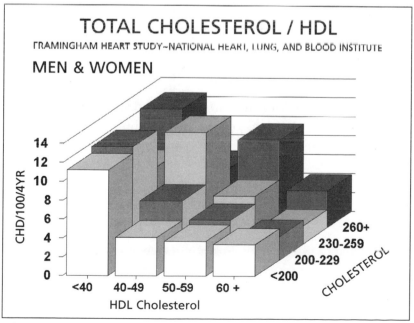

Figure J

The relationship of the risk of high triglyceride levels and a low HDL level is shown in *Figures D* and *E*.

Think how much money would be saved if we could discover all the people at risk for heart attacks and get them on the sensible program we are presenting in this book. The costs of intensive care in a coronary-care unit, angiography and angioplasty or open-heart bypass surgery for those who get coronary disease far exceed the costs of tracking down those at risk, helping them change their lifestyles and giving them lipid-lowering medications.

Let's talk about the people in your own home. We are going to help you—and every member of your family—decrease the risk of a heart attack. Here are the few easy numbers we want you to remember. Beyond remembering these numbers, we want you to get your numbers at these levels:

Total cholesterol	**150 or less is ideal**; if yours is above 150, you need to look at your total-to-HDL cholesterol ratio
Ratio of total cholesterol/HDL	**Less than 4** (less than 3 for those with vascular or heart disease)
LDL	**130** (or 100 for those who have vascular or heart disease)
Triglycerides	**150** (or 100 for those who have vascular or heart disease)

Now you know what your numbers are supposed to be. What are you going to do with this important information?

Making Sense of the Official Guidelines

Under the earlier *official* National Cholesterol Education Program guidelines, if your total cholesterol was over 240 or if you were in a *borderline* group between 200 and 239 and had two risk factors, you may have been sent to have your LDL checked.

Your chance of coronary-artery disease and a heart attack increases significantly if you have any two of these risk factors:

- you are a male (or a female over age 50)
- you have high blood pressure
- you smoke
- someone in your family has had a heart attack under the age of 55
- your HDL cholesterol is under 35
- you have diabetes mellitus
- you are overweight

If your LDL was under 130, you were probably told you are at low risk and to follow a prudent diet, exercise and not to smoke.

If your LDL was over 160, you were probably told this is really bad and were instructed to go on a low saturated-fat, low-cholesterol diet as we suggest!

You've just read a lot of numbers. As *Figure D* clearly shows, there isn't any question that the higher the LDL, the higher the risk of coronary-artery disease. Almost everyone agrees that keeping your LDL under 130 is good and that an LDL over 160 is way too high.

What about the people in between? We are concerned about the many people who are lost in the confusion.

You can see how much better and simpler it is to follow our suggestions about using your total cholesterol, ratio and triglyceride level to know how much risk you are at now and along the way. Where did these other confusing guidelines come from?

For a long time almost no one paid much attention to someone's cholesterol level—unless it was over 300, which was far too high.

To put this in perspective, when you were born, your total cholesterol level was about 70. Then, when you started eating, it went up to about 150 by your first birthday. As children in North America keep eating lots of fat, their average cholesterol goes up to about 160. This level usually then stays about the same until a person is about 17. Then, in cultures like ours, the level usually starts going up again until it reaches an average adult level of about 210 to 220. This *average* level is far from healthy.

Most people around the world don't have cholesterol levels this high. People in parts of the world who don't eat as much bad fat and who don't get coronary-artery disease have total-cholesterol levels at or under 150. Of the 5.7-billion people on the earth, 4 billion are not at any risk for the heart disease that kills half of North Americans. The average cholesterol of the people in central China is 125. The Masai in Africa have an average cholesterol of 135. In Latin America, outside the big cities, the average cholesterol is 140. Unfortunately, only 5% of North Americans over age 30 have a cholesterol level under 150.

And while most adults around the world have cholesterol levels under 150, half the children in the United States and Canada already have a cholesterol level higher than that.

You can see how the cholesterol problem became compounded when few were paying attention to a person's cholesterol unless it was over 300. We know from studies like the Framingham Heart Study that most people in our population who get a heart attack have a cholesterol level between 200 and 250. Remember, this is what has been called a *borderline* range.

But back to the origin of the guidelines. Although obviously well-intended, they did not go far enough. At a time when few physicians knew what levels of cholesterol were cause for concern and most people knew next to nothing about the part played by the saturated fat they were eating, something certainly had to be done.

So, The National Heart, Lung and Blood Institute, part of the National Institutes of Health, formed a group called *The National Cholesterol Education Program* to get the message to the public. The first thing they set out to do was to decide what cholesterol levels were too high. Then this panel began a major campaign all over the country so everyone would understand they needed to know their blood cholesterol level.

The National Cholesterol Education Program provided a great service in making people aware of the dangers of elevated cholesterol and in bringing cholesterol-screening campaigns to towns all across the United States. This was a very important preventive health measure. We believe they should have gone a little further.

We realize that with the average cholesterol level in the U.S. running between 210 and 220, it would have been hard for the panel to announce guidelines saying that over half the population was at high risk, which was the actual truth.

The National Cholesterol Education Program was designed to uncover the bulk of people who would get coronary-artery disease unless they made drastic changes. As we pointed out, half the people who have heart attacks have a total cholesterol level under 225. More people with a cholesterol level of 225 get heart attacks than at any other level! In North America, 35% of the heart attacks occur in people who have a cholesterol level under 200. So, as helpful as the official guidelines have been, they have missed a lot of people who are at risk.

Our recommendations go beyond those of *The National Cholesterol Education Program's* expert panel. We commend them for making the bold recommendations they did at the time—and the steps taken to improve them.

Obviously, judgment calls had to be made on the recommended numbers (levels). The economic and social impact of these decisions and recommendations probably weighed on the minds of the panel members as they made these decisions. These are very important considerations. Just imagine the economic effect that the panel's recommendations have already made, such as the costs for the testing equipment and supplies, as well as the technicians, physicians and others involved in obtaining and interpreting the results.

The impact on the food industry is mind-boggling. A drastic cut in the saturated fat we eat has affected almost every aspect of the food industry from production to groceries, markets, restaurants and especially the big fast-food business.

What is the Best Triglyceride Level?

Probably because of the economic reasons, the panel's current official policy is that any level of triglycerides under 200 is considered *normal.* This recommendation is better than saying that triglyceride levels under 250 are normal, which was the *original* official recommendation. A level of 200 is still too high. Sooner or later it will be generally accepted that triglyceride levels should be under 150, with possibly a few exceptions.

The foregoing material summarizes the Second Report of the National Cholesterol Education Program Expert Panel on the Detection, Evaluation and Treatment of High Blood Cholesterol in Adults (Adult Treatment Panel II). *JAMA* 1993; 269(23):3015-3023

CONVERSION TABLES BETWEEN WAYS OF REPORTING CHOLESTEROL, HDL & TRIGLYCERIDE LEVELS

CHOLESTEROL CONVERSIONS

mg/dl	= mmol/L	mg/dl	= mmol/L
120	3.1	270	7.0
130	3.4	280	7.2
140	3.6	290	7.5
150	3.9	300	7.8
160	4.1	310	8.0
170	4.4	320	8.3
180	4.7	330	8.5
190	4.9	340	8.8
200	5.2	350	9.0
210	5.4	360	9.3
220	5.7	370	9.6
230	5.9	380	9.8
240	6.2	390	10.1
250	6.5	400	10.3
260	6.7		

HDL CONVERSIONS

mg/dl	= mmol/L	mg/dl	= mmol/L
20	0.52	55	1.42
25	0.65	60	1.55
30	0.78	65	1.68
35	0.90	70	1.81
40	1.03	80	2.07
45	1.16	90	2.33
50	1.29		

TRIGLYCERIDE CONVERSIONS

mg/dl	= mmol/L	mg/dl	= mmol/L
100	1.1	500	5.6
150	1.7	600	6.8
200	2.3	700	7.9
250	2.8	800	9.0
300	3.4	900	10.2
350	4.0	1000	11.3
400	4.5	1500	16.9
450	5.1	2000	22.6

The formulas for converting the way triglyceride levels are reported in the United States to the SI (Systeme International d'Unites) unit system used in many parts of the world are as follows:

mg/dl of triglyceride X 0.01129 = mmol/L of triglyceride—and:

mmol/L of triglyceride x 88.496 = mg/dl of triglyceride

A Simple Bad-Fat Budget

CAN YOU COUNT TO 10 (OR 20)?

You probably know someone who should be eating less bad fat.

Most of us think we are doing pretty well ourselves, especially if we have cut back on fried and greasy foods. Yet, without continuous conscious effort, the grams of fat we eat everyday add up like taxes or the numbers on a gas pump.

People have no idea how much bad fat they are eating. Even though we can avoid eating too much obvious fat, bad fat hides in many food products.

Fat is an essential part of our diet. We need some fats, but not much—certainly not anywhere near the amount most people in our culture eat every day.

"So," you are thinking, "you're going to give me another complicated formula to figure how much fat I can have based on the calories I eat."

Wrong!

Even though the official recommendations are not as complicated as they may first seem, monitoring and calculating fat intake that way is a tedious nuisance. Most people just don't do it.

We developed an incredibly easy way to accomplish what the complicated formulas *try* to do. As we explained in an article in a prominent medical journal,[1] "It seems to us that for simplicity, consistency and better compliance, there should be a specific limit on the number of grams of saturated fat to be eaten each day."

Keeping track of a daily limit or budget of bad fat is so easy that anyone who can count to 20 can do it. If you are in a high-risk group (like both of us!), you can still follow our plan, except you only need to count to 10.

It's that simple.

33

All you need to do is put yourself on a budget—*a bad-fat budget.*

Bad fat means a total of s*aturated fat* and *trans-fatty acids* which we will talk more about later.

How much *bad fat* are we talking about? If you are in a high-risk group as we are or already have coronary-artery disease, peripheral vascular disease, an aneurysm or have had heart surgery, your budget is 10 grams of bad fat a day—no higher! If you're not in a high-risk group, your budget is 20 grams of bad fat a day. Don't be like most North Americans who currently eat 40 to 50 grams of bad fat per day.

Just count the grams of bad fat you eat during a day. Quit when you've hit your limit!

There are some exceptions—but not many. A person doing heavy outdoor work in a Minnesota winter, for example, needs to consume more saturated fat on those days. Most of us will be much healthier on a rather simple daily budget of limited saturated fat.

Perhaps surprisingly, a 20-gram-per-day bad-fat budget fits the recommended needs of most people, including children over the toddler age. The major exception is that people at high risk should limit their bad-fat intake to 10 grams a day.

This doesn't mean everyone must eat exactly the same thing. That's not our plan. You have lots of choices. People with exactly the same amount of money to budget never spend it exactly like their neighbors. Some choose to splurge a large chunk of their money all at once—and have little left for other things. Others spend their money more sparingly, spreading it out.

The same thing happens with bad-fat budgets. You can splurge sometimes—but when you do, if you are going to stick to your budget, it means putting limits on other things you eat. Of course, whether we're talking about bank-account or bad-fat budgets, some people entirely blow them. There are consequences in both cases.

Budgeting bad fat really gives you many choices. Don't even think of this plan as a "diet." Because it isn't. We don't even like the word "diet." You won't have to follow a particular menu plan and we don't expect you to eat exactly what we eat. In fact, each of our families has different favorite foods. Your family does too. We are going to help you figure out how to enjoy most of your favorite meals without as much bad fat as you've probably been feeding yourself and your family.

Putting yourself on a 10- or 20-gram budget of bad fat means taking charge and being in control—the same type of control it takes when you put yourself on a budget to make your money work more effectively. Many good foods contain little or no fat and there are wonderful ways to prepare tasty food without much bad fat. This includes many of your favorite recipes and dishes that can be modified to reduce the fat greatly. You and your family won't feel deprived. This plan is not going to be the torture like each of us once thought it would be. You'll find yourself enjoying some exciting foods and maybe even preparing them.

On the other hand, budgeting the fat you eat to stop fat plaques from forming in your coronary arteries, means not eating some things you may really like, if they are filled with bad fat. Look at butter: there are 7 grams of saturated fat in each tablespoon, so even small amounts can quickly blow your budget. Butter tastes better than the other spreads you have tried, but some spreads with little or no saturated fat taste pretty good.

When blowing a budget, it's possible to consume as much as 24 grams of saturated fat in one meal by eating a greasy double hamburger with cheese, fries and a milkshake made with real ice cream. That's as much bad fat as a half stick of butter! The next time you think about ordering one of these All-American meals, think what it would be like to eat 1/8 pound of butter! That's a big bad-fat overload.

The good news is that you don't have to give up all fast foods because of your new budget. In fact, we'll explain how you can fix these things so they are not overloaded with fat. Such a meal won't be fat-free, so you'll still need to keep count. There are ways to keep enjoying those favorites—at home and even at some fast-food places.

After hearing how much fat is in a typical fast-food hamburger meal, you may wonder how much bad fat your children and teenagers are eating each day. It's not too hard to guess that every day most kids are consuming a lot of bad fat. As you can imagine, many of their favorite fast foods are very unhealthy.

School lunches are loaded with fat! Most schools serve more foods with saturated fat today than ever before. This is happening for two reasons. One is the idea that to get students to eat school lunches, they must be offered everything from greasy burgers and fries to pizza with sausage. The other reason is that even before this idea caught on, and before anyone knew that bad fats were such a serious problem, government surpluses of subsidized dairy products such as butter, cheese, milk and ice cream were given to schools at little or no cost. Such programs were undoubtedly begun with good intentions, but now we know that the tons of bad fat being fed every day to school children will cause big health problems later on. Who knows how much bad fat the average child or teenager is consuming each day?

Most adults probably eat around 40 or 50 grams of bad fat in a day—some as much as 100 grams. That's too much! Besides the long-range effects of eating all this bad fat, it causes us to not feel as good as we do when we eat a reasonable amount of fat.

A budget of 20 grams of bad fat a day for those who are not known to be at risk and a 10-gram-a-day budget for those who are at risk is going to mean some changes.

You choose. The consequences of this choice are similar to the consequences of the choice to smoke or not to smoke. We hope you will choose not to smoke—and not to eat too much bad fat.

Limiting Your Saturated-Fat Intake

Our 10- and 20-gram budget numbers didn't just pop out of the air; they are based on the best information we have right now. *The National Cholesterol Education Program's* expert panel recommends that the first step in a heart-disease-prevention diet be reducing the amount of total fat we eat from 40% of our needed calories to 30%. This is total fat. To keep things simple, we are talking only about saturated fat.

The panel's recommendation is that the first step is to limit the saturated fat to 10% of the needed calories in a day. After all, not many people count calories—or even know how many calories they are supposed to be eating! Who wants to calculate how many grams of fat to eat, based on each gram of fat producing 9 calories?

If you do all the calculations for those who are "supposed" to be consuming around 2000 calories or a little less, it comes out to the 20-gram-a-day budget for bad fat we recommend for most people. You'll notice that this 20-gram-per-day budget is listed on all the standard FDA (U.S. Food & Drug Administration) food labels (for those who are supposed to be on 2000-calorie diet).

As a second step (after limiting total fat to 30% of our calories), the panel recommends limiting saturated fat to supply 7% of the needed calories per day for those at high risk, which figures out to be between 12 and 16 grams a day. Our recommendation for those at risk is slightly less—a 10-gram-per-day budget of bad fat. This includes both *saturated fat* and *trans-fatty acids* which are in hydrogenated food products such as margarine and shortening. If mayonnaise and salad dressing are prepared with hydrogenated ingredients, they also will contain trans-fatty acids. Figure there is as much bad trans-fatty acids as there are saturated fats in these hydrogenated products.

So, that's the number part of the budget. It's simple.

Keeping Track of Bad Fat

When we first set up our program, we had people keep track of how much cholesterol, total fat grams and saturated fat grams they were eating. Keeping track of three sets of numbers wasn't really necessary. People needed to be taught how to budget the bad-fat grams they would eat each day, along with a few basic principles about limiting the amount of cholesterol and other fat they would be eating.

How do you get started? For a while, start each day with a piece of paper or an index card and write down the grams of bad fat you eat each meal.

How will you know how much bad fat there is in the things you choose to eat? Most packaged foods you buy have a nutrition label that lists grams of saturated fat per serving and the serving size.[2] Also, take some time to study the tables in the back of Chapter 12 which list the grams of saturated fat in common foods. The great recipes in Chapter 15 also tell you exactly how many grams of saturated fat (and the exact amount of cholesterol) are in each serving. This is what you want to know and record.

As you go through the day, jot down the grams of *saturated fat* and *trans-fatty acids* in everything you eat. This may be one of the most important things you can do to help your heart. It may be a bother and you may be tempted to forget it after a day or two. We encourage you to keep it up long enough to get an idea about how much bad fat is in the food you eat—and to establish a healthy eating pattern.

After you've done this for a while and you get used to your daily bad-fat budget, it will come more naturally. Eventually it will be like driving a car. You just do it without having to think about braking, shifting or slowing up before turns and traffic signals. You'll get a feeling for what you can eat and what you shouldn't—without writing everything down and adding it up.

By the way, no one is checking on what you're doing day by day—you are on the honor system. It's a good idea to show your notes to your physician and to keep him or her posted on how much bad fat you are eating each day. For the most part, this program is up to you. It's *your* heart—and *your* life. *Cheaters are buried!*

If you keep track of the amount of bad fat you are eating, it will make it easier to limit the bad fat that gets into your body. It's simple.

Let's look at a few popular foods and add up the numbers. Suppose you had a breakfast of 2 sunny-side-up fried eggs, 3 strips of bacon, a piece of toast with butter and a glass of milk or coffee with 1 tablespoon of cream. How much bad fat and cholesterol did you eat?

	Saturated Fat (grams)	Trans Fat (grams)	Cholesterol (mg)
2 eggs	3.2	0.0	425.0
1 tsp. butter	2.4	0.5	10.3
3 strips bacon	3.3	0.0	16.2
1 piece toast	0.4	0.2	0.9
Coffee with 1 tbs. cream, half-and-half	1.1	0.0	5.6

Total: 10.4 + 0.7 = 11.1 grams bad fat and 458 mg cholesterol

That's 10.4 grams of saturated fat and another 0.7 of trans-fatty acids, which adds up to 11.1 grams of bad fat just for breakfast, more than someone on a 10-gram budget should eat in a whole day! Look at the cholesterol—458 grams! Way over budget and the day just started!

Compare this with a breakfast of oatmeal, nonfat milk, orange juice, 2 pieces of toast with a no-fat spray spread, jam and a cup of coffee or other beverage with a fat-free creamer:

	Saturated Fat (grams)	Trans Fat (grams)	Cholesterol (mg)
1 cup oatmeal	trace	0.0	trace
Sugar	0.0	0.0	0.0
Nonfat milk	0.0	0.0	0.0
1 cup orange juice	0.0	0.0	0.0
2 pieces toast	0.8	0.4	1.8
Fat-free spray	0.0	0.0	0.0
2 tbs. jam	0.0	0.0	0.0
1 cup coffee	0.0	0.0	0.0
Fat-free creamer	0.0	0.0	0.0

Totals: **0.8 grams saturated fat, 0.4 grams trans-fatty acid, 1.8 mg cholesterol**

This breakfast adds up to only 1.2 grams of bad fat and 1.8 mg of cholesterol.

What a difference!

You may grimace at the thought of oatmeal instead of sunny-side-up eggs and bacon, but doesn't it sound better than all that fat plugging up your coronary arteries? With an intake of just over a gram of bad fat for breakfast, you can spend more of your bad-fat budget at lunch and dinner—giving you more choices then.

Don't get too cocky about doing so well for breakfast that you blow it all at lunch. Think about some alternative lunch and dinner menus. There's plenty of room for imagination.

You saw the differences in the amount of bad fat in the two breakfasts. Now let's look at a typical fast-food lunch consisting of a hamburger with cheese, French fries and a chocolate shake:

	Saturated Fat (grams)	Trans Fat (grams)	Cholesterol (mg)
Cheeseburger	6.4	--	50.0
French fries	4.3	6.4	14.7
Chocolate shake	3.1	0.2	18.3

Totals: **20.4 grams bad fat and 83 mg cholesterol**

Suppose you eat a safer lunch like a chicken sandwich. A broiled, roasted or microwaved chicken-breast sandwich cooked without skin or extra fat contains only 2 or 3 grams of saturated fat and between 70 and 100 mg of cholesterol. This chicken sandwich on whole-wheat with lettuce and sprouts, a glass of nonfat chocolate milk and an orange totals only a little over 2 grams of bad fat and 80 mg of cholesterol.

Here's another idea that may seem strange at first, but how about a bean sandwich? It's an adaptation of a Mexican burrito that's popular in the southwest. Try it. You'll like it!

> Begin with great northern, navy or pinto beans—cooked vegetarian style without added meat or fat. Combine 1 cup drained beans with two small onions, finely chopped. Mash the beans and the onions together with a fork or in a blender or food processor. If you want to add some spice, stir chopped green chilies (either mild or hot) into the bean mix. Cover two slices of whole-wheat bread (or two lowfat tortillas for burritos) with a layer of romaine lettuce. Spread the bean mix on top. Add salsa or tomato sauce to taste. You could add a layer of alfalfa or bean sprouts. Top with bread or roll up the tortillas to complete two sandwiches or two burritos.

If you eat both sandwiches or burritos, have a glass of fat-free chocolate milk and a banana, how many grams of bad fat will you be eating for lunch? Only 2 grams!

Besides tasting good and being quite filling, this lunch gives you plenty of protein and other nutrients.

These are just a few examples of some of the creative meals you can make. You can have lots of fun coming up with good-tasting food without much bad fat.

We hope you're convinced that you can do it. You can. To make it easier for you, in the next chapter we'll take a look at how prepared foods are labeled and some more tips on keeping track of your bad-fat budget.

By the way, is your bad-fat budget 10 or 20 grams a day?

NOTES

1. Castelli, W.P. and Griffin, G. "A Simple Strategy to Limit Saturated Fat after Cholesterol Screening," *Postgraduate Medicine,* vol. 84, September 1, 1988, pp. 44-56.

2. May 8, 1994 may have been the most important Mother's Day ever because from that time forward food products in the United States were required to be clearly labeled with the amount of saturated fat, total fat, cholesterol, calories, serving size and other nutritional facts.

Comparison of Two Daily Meal Plans

High Bad-Fat Meals

	Saturated Fat (grams)	Trans Fat (grams)	Cholesterol (milligrams)
Breakfast			
1 cup orange juice	0.0	0.0	0.0
3 strips bacon	3.3	0.0	16.2
1 egg	1.6	0.0	212.5
2 slices toast	0.8	0.4	1.8
1 tbs. butter	2.4	0.0	10.3
1 cup beverage	0.0	0.0	0.0
1 tbs. cream, half-and-half	1.1	0.0	5.6
Lunch			
1 cheeseburger	6.4	--	50.0
4 oz. French fries	4.3	6.4	14.7
10 oz. strawberry milkshake	3.1	0.2	18.3
1 piece apple pie	2.6	--	0.0
Supper			
1 cup soup (cream of mushroom)	5.1	--	19.8
6 oz. steak, marbled	13.6	1.8	116.2
Hash brown potatoes	2.5	--	0.0
Broccoli	0.0	0.0	0.0
2 tbs. hollandaise	5.2	--	23.6
2 baking powder biscuits	2.0	trace	0.0
1 tbs. stick margarine	2.4	3.2	0.0
1 avocado	4.5	0.0	0.0
2 fudge-walnut brownies	8.0	--	160.0
Snacks			
1 glazed donut	3.5	3.8	3.6
1 cup creamy yogurt	5.2	0.2	31.1

Totals: **77.6 + 16 = 93.6 grams bad fat and 683.7 mg cholesterol**

Low Bad-Fat Meals

	Saturated Fat (grams)	Trans Fat (grams)	Cholesterol (milligrams)
Breakfast			
1 cup orange juice	0.0	0.0	0.0
1 cup oatmeal w/raisins	trace	0.0	0.0
w/fat-free milk	0.0	0.0	0.0
1 plain bagel	0.2	0.1	0.0
1 tsp. fat-free tablespread spray	0.0	0.0	0.0
1 tbs. strawberry jam	0.0	0.0	0.0
1 cup beverage	0.0	0.0	0.0
2 tsp. lowfat creamer	0.0	– –	0.0
Lunch			
Tossed salad with salsa	0.0	0.0	0.0
Great Northern beans	0.0	0.0	0.0
Barbecue sauce	trace	0.0	0.0
6 oz. broiled skinless chicken breast	2.6	– –	107.4
Mushrooms	0.0	0.0	0.0
1 tbs. olive oil (to sauté mushrooms)	1.8	0.1	0.0
2 slices fat-free bread	0.0	0.0	0.0
1 tsp. soft diet spread	1.8	– –	0.0
12 oz. orange freezee	trace	0.0	0.0
Supper			
1 cup consommé	0.0	0.0	0.0
6 oz. orange roughy	trace	0.0	30.0
1 tbs. canola oil (to sauté fish)	1.0	0.0	0.0
Seafood cocktail sauce	0.0	0.0	0.0
Baked potato with chives	0.0	0.0	0.0
Green peas and lemon pepper	0.0	0.0	0.0
2 slices white bread	0.8	0.4	1.8
Fat-free spread spray	0.0	0.0	0.0
Spinach/tomato salad with vinegar	0.0	0.0	0.0
Angel food cake w/strawberry glaze	0.0	0.0	0.0
Snacks			
1 apple and/or banana	0.0	0.0	0.0
fat-free frozen yogurt	0.2	0.0	3.0

Totals: **8.4 + 0.6 = 9.0 grams bad fat and 142.2 mg cholesterol**

How to Decode Food Labels

IT S SIMPLE!

We shouldn't be eating so much cholesterol. *The National Cholesterol Education Program's* expert panel suggests most people should limit their cholesterol intake to 300mg per day. Those at risk should limit their dietary cholesterol to 200mg a day. It's good that so many people understand that eating too much cholesterol pushes up the amount of cholesterol in someone's blood, especially the bad LDL cholesterol.

When we eat saturated fats or trans-fatty acids, our body makes cholesterol. Most of the elevated cholesterol that floats around in our blood comes from eating bad fat. So yes, it is important to limit the amount of cholesterol we eat. It is good to find snacks that don't contain much cholesterol. The most important thing is to limit the consumption of saturated fat and trans-fatty acids—the bad fat.

The first thing you see about nutrition on a package of potato chips may be big words promising **"NO CHOLESTEROL!"**

So into a shopping cart the bag of chips may go—with a big feeling of relief. The problem is that this "r-e-l-i-e-f" should be spelled "t-r-i-c-k-e-d!"

It's true that there is "NO CHOLESTEROL" in these chips and if the label says these chips were fried in "100% vegetable oil," that's true, too. What the label fails to feature is that these chips contain a lot of *saturated fat.*

If the sales pitch on a package merely says "NO CHOLESTEROL," be suspicious. If a product doesn't contain much fat or much saturated fat, this overriding advantage will very likely be the lead copy on the package instead of the words "NO CHOLESTEROL."

Nutrition Facts	
Serving Size 1 Tbsp (14g)	
Servings Per Container 32	
Amount Per Serving	
Calories 90	Calories from Fat 90
	% Daily Value*
Total Fat 10g	**15%**
Saturated Fat 2g	**10%**
Polyunsaturated Fat 2.5g	
Monounsaturated Fat 2g	
Cholesterol 0mg	**0%**
Sodium 90mg	**4%**
Total Carbohydrate 0g	**0%**
Protein 0g	
Vitamin A	**10%**
Not a significant source of dietary fiber, sugars, vitamin C, calcium and iron.	
*Percent Daily Values are based on a 2,000 calorie diet.	

INGREDIENTS: LIQUID SOYBEAN OIL AND PARTIALLY HYDROGENATED SOYBEAN OIL, WATER, WHEY, SALT, SOY LECITHIN, VEGETABLE MONO AND DIGLYCERIDES, POTASSIUM SORBATE AND CITRIC ACID AS PRESERVATIVES, ARTIFICIAL FLAVOR, COLORED WITH BETA CAROTENE, VITAMIN A (PALMITATE) ADDED.

This typical label is on all food products. This margarine has 2 grams of saturated fat per tablespoon. If the first or second item in the ingredients is "hydrogenated," double the saturated fat to allow for the trans-fatty acids, making 4 grams per tablespoon of saturated fat for this product.

Turn the package over and read the *Nutritional Facts* label to see exactly how much total fat and saturated fat is in each serving and what the serving size is. If hydrogenated fat is listed, figure that there is as much trans-fatty acids in the product as there is saturated fat. You have to do that mental calculation because trans-fatty acids are not listed on the label.

We hope you will read the facts labels and not just the promotional words. The *Nutritional Facts* make it easier than ever to follow the simple system we're explaining.

There are plenty of numbers on these labels—more than you need to follow our plan. The first thing you need to know is what the manufacturer considers a *serving size.*

The serving size may be 6 corn chips . . . 5 crackers . . . 1 bun . . . 1 bagel . . . or 1 slice of bread.

For most table spreads and salad dressings, the serving size is 1 tablespoon. A serving size of one kind of cookies may be 1 cookie, while the serving size listed on another brand is 6!

When you open the box, these cookies don't look like the ones your mother used to make. These are *small* cookies! They may taste pretty good for having *only* 1.5 grams of saturated fat per serving. But those 6 tiny cookies go down in a hurry.

Find out the exact *serving size* of every product you pick up.

After checking the serving size on the *Nutritional Facts* label, you'll also want to know how many calories are in one serving. The answer is helpful if you are trying to keep your weight under control. It will amaze you to find just how many calories are in one chocolate-covered donut or a double cheeseburger.

Then as you look at the *Nutritional Facts* label, be sure there's not way too much cholesterol in a *single serving* of what you are considering eating. A quick glance will also tell you if there's so much total fat in the product that you'll want to use it sparingly . . . if at all.

The second important fact you need to know (after serving size) is how much *saturated fat* is in a serving.

Only 1 gram per serving might not be bad, depending on the serving size and your daily budget. If there's another gram of trans-fatty acids per serving, that makes the bad-fat total come to 2 grams.

Two grams of bad fat in a serving doesn't seem like much—and it may not be, depending on what else you want to eat today.

What if there are 4 grams of bad fat per serving?

That's quite a bit, even if your daily budget is 20. If your budget for a day is only 10 grams of bad fat, 4 grams is a lot to spend on one thing. On the other hand, if you have kept breakfast down to a gram or so of bad fat, you may feel good about having a dinner entrée or even a dessert, that will give you 4 grams of saturated fat.

Speaking of dessert, one brand of frozen yogurt listed only 1 gram of saturated fat, which sounded good. The problem? This rich yogurt had one gram of bad fat *per ounce.* Who eats only an ounce of ice cream or frozen yogurt? Most of the lowfat ice creams list 1/2 cup (4 ounces) as a serving. A more typical serving is about 8 ounces—a total of 8 grams of saturated fat. Check the *Nutritional Facts* label for two things: the serving *size* and how many grams of saturated fat are in *each* serving.

How you spend your 10 or 20 grams of bad fat per day is entirely up to you. Think of spending this budget as you would think of spending a budgeted $10 or $20 on a particular day. If you play a video game for a couple of dollars worth of quarters, that 2 bucks is gone. Another 5 bucks on something else that's gone fast leaves you with less to spend on things you may want even more.

Spending budgeted grams of bad fat goes the same way. It's easy to use up your budget frivolously—munching throughout the day, adding a little bad fat here, some more bad fat there. It's just as easy to munch on grapes, chunks of fresh apple, orange slices or something like celery sticks or carrots—which are fat-free. Doing this saves your budget for things you really want at mealtime.

We hope you will choose to limit the amount of bad fat you eat every day to 20 grams if you have no risk factors or 10 grams a day if you have a cholesterol/HDL ratio over 4, have elevated triglycerides or have had a heart attack, heart surgery or any other risk factors (including having a parent who has had an early heart attack).

As you get used to this new way of eating, it will help to keep track of how much saturated fat you are eating throughout the day until you can do it. You will be surprised at how quickly you will know how much saturated fat you are eating—and if you go over your limit. For now, we suggest keeping a simple "Bad-Fat Tally" every day. At first, you may want to also jot down the milligrams (mg) of cholesterol you are eating so you can learn to keep this under 300mg a day—or under 200mg a day if you are at risk

Keeping these notes will help you make choices of what to eat and how much to eat at each meal and snack time. Keeping this log will also help you see how your budget is working. You may even find that this personal challenge is fun—something like keeping your own score in a golf game and then working on ways to improve it. After omitting things like liver and other organ meats that are high in cholesterol, choosing small portions of extra-lean meat and deciding to eat egg yolks only on special occasions, you probably won't have much trouble keeping within your limit of dietary cholesterol.

How much bad fat have you eaten in the last 24 hours?

Depending on your recall ability, you might be able to stop and figure it out pretty closely right now—maybe even in your head. If you can't, that's OK. That's why writing down what you eat is a good idea.

"How do I know how much saturated fat is in food that doesn't come with a *Nutritional Facts* label?

Good question. We'll give you some easy ones to remember in the next chapter while we talk about how to choose tasty foods without much bad fat.

Tips on Eating Less Fat at Home

This chapter is filled with good news. In just one minute, you are going to know how much saturated fat there is in dozens of different foods! Even if you have trouble remembering numbers, this is easy. The reason why this is so easy is because two big food groups contain essentially NO fat.

Think—fruits.

Think—vegetables.

And that's it. Now you know dozens of foods that contain almost *no* bad fat. With the exception of avocados and olives, fruits and vegetable have *zero* fat.

How many fruits can you think of, including your favorites and others you may not have tried?

Oranges, bananas, mangoes, watermelons, cantaloupes, pears, grapes, honeydews, apples, plums, tangerines, nectarines, apricots, peaches, lemons, limes, grapefruits, tomatoes, rhubarb, cherries, strawberries, raspberries, blueberries, blackberries . . .

You can probably think of even more. As more exotic fruits become available, feel free to try them. All are essentially fat-free.

Imagine you are the head of a large ad agency and in charge of creating a series of radio or television commercials for an *apple*—not the computer—the fruit! With a little thought and imagination, you could create a fantastic commercial for an apple, because the product is so perfect. Think about it—a self-contained, crunchy, delicious, healthful snack! With enough resources, just imagine what you could do to create a commercial for oranges, pears, bananas, strawberries or any other fruit.

Besides the popular Red Delicious apples, there are other tasty varieties such as Golden Delicious, Jonathan, Granny Smith, Rome Beauty, Winesap or Gala. Include them in main dishes or use them in a side dish—their use goes far beyond a simple snack food.

When you think about it, fresh fruits are far more appealing than candy or almost any other fast food or snack. Their natural sweetness and flavor are very satisfying.

Now, how many vegetables can you name?

Carrots, peas, green beans, asparagus, artichokes, squash, cauliflower, broccoli, turnips, spinach, chard, lettuce, celery, beets, onions, chives, cucumbers, cabbage, potatoes . . .

And there are many others. Are there some of these you haven't eaten for a while or thought you didn't like? Did you know that none of them have any bad fat?

Now, add all the grains and legumes you can think of.

Whole-wheat, corn, oats, rice, split peas, black-eyed peas, pinto beans, navy beans, black beans, red beans, soybeans, barley and more.

They don't contain fat either.

You can eat and enjoy all these nutritious basic foods and they won't count against your daily saturated-fat budget limits. Take care in cooking and don't add fats to sauces or toppings. We'll help you figure out how to enjoy these things with just a *little* healthy fat.

In addition to the many vitamins and other nutrients found in fruits, vegetables, grains and legumes, they are a great source of healthy complex carbohydrates and fiber, plus soluble and insoluble fiber.

Dietary fiber is the roughage in plant cell walls that is not broken down or digested by the enzymes in our digestive tracts. Some fiber in wheat, corn, rice or other grains that does not dissolve in water is called *insoluble fiber.* Insoluble fiber helps prevent colon cancer and intestinal problems.

Soluble fiber is found in dried beans, oats, black-eyed peas, soybeans, potatoes, fruits and vegetables. This *soluble fiber* reduces the amount of cholesterol in our bodies—probably acting like little sponges in the intestinal tract absorbing the bile acids,[1] helping them pass from the body. To accomplish this, we must eat more food containing soluble fiber than the occasional bowl of oatmeal or a few beans now and then. They must become part of our regular eating pattern.

Oats

Whole-grain cereals like oats, hominy or grits used to be typical breakfast foods. But, the enticing aroma of bacon and eggs along with hurried-up lifestyles, changed the tradition of eating hot cereals for breakfast.

Oats start out with a tough outer husk that is scoured off. Then the oats are partially cooked with steam and crushed with a roller, which is why they are called *rolled oats.* When finally chopped or cut for faster cooking, they are called *one-minute* or *quick oats.* These are the bran-filled oats we want.

Even though some think oatmeal takes a long time to cook, it doesn't. Cooking oatmeal cereal is quick and easy in the microwave or on the stovetop. Bring water to a boil on the stovetop or in a microwave oven, then add the oats and stir into a crunchy breakfast. Prepared instant oats only require adding hot water and giving them a quick stir. Read the labels because some *instant oats,* especially in individual serving packets, contain saturated fat from coconut, palm or palm-kernel oil. That you don't need!

Try serving oatmeal with nonfat or lowfat milk, a little maple syrup or sugar and cinnamon or grated orange peel. You may want to add raisins, applesauce, sliced apples or other fruit before cooking. For added texture, top with your favorite cold cereal. Create your own combinations, but avoid using whole milk, cream or butter!

Although many cold breakfast cereals are made of oats, to get enough soluble fiber, you'll need more than one bowl for breakfast.

Beans

As mentioned on page 48, soluble fiber reduces the amount of cholesterol in our bodies. Beans are one source of soluble fiber.

In the southern United States, black-eyed peas are a traditional food staple. When cooked, these legumes contain 1 gram of soluble fiber per cup. Cooked soybeans are the fiber champions of beans with 1 cup containing 4 grams of soluble fiber. By comparison, oat bran has 3 grams of soluble fiber per cup.

Red kidney beans often found at salad bars are also rich in soluble fiber, proteins and complex carbohydrates. So are pinto beans, a major source of these nutrients in the foods of Mexico and other Latin American countries.

Split peas, great-northern and navy are mild beans with considerable soluble fiber as well as good flavors. See pages 169–175 for recipes with these excellent legumes.

Although traditional chili is made with beef, a delicious vegetarian chili can be made with pinto beans, onions, tomatoes, chiles and spices. Instead of pinto beans, you can use garbanzos (chick peas) and white kidney beans. Zucchini and carrots are also flavorful additions to vegetarian chili.

What about too many beans? Some people who eat beans or other foods with soluble fiber have uncomfortable and sometimes embarrassing intestinal gas. Gradually increasing serving sizes over a period of time seems to help the body adapt.

If there is still a problem, some people find taking one or two capsules of activated charcoal before eating beans and then an hour later is helpful. There are products available to sprinkle on your food before eating it with the claim that they help to reduce intestinal gas.[2] Other suggestions include changing the bean-soaking water two or three times.

Other Sources of Soluble Fiber

Green peas are also rich in soluble fiber. Eat them raw in salads or as a snack food. Or cook them briefly until they are tender, yet crisp. Corn, zucchini, Brussels sprouts, carrots, beets, cabbage, broccoli, eggplant and onions also are sources of some soluble fiber.

Other fruits and vegetables don't have much soluble fiber but it all adds up. The point is to make a conscious effort to eat soluble fiber every day. One way is to start your day with oat cereal and include beans and good-sized servings of other sources of soluble fiber in your other meals.

Potatoes and French Fries

Almost everyone likes baked potatoes. They are a good source of soluble fiber, especially when the skin is eaten, which we recommend. For those who long for French fries—even though they contain too much bad fat—you can roast or broil potato slivers in a hot oven. Spray lightly with lowfat vegetable-oil cooking spray before cooking. Add a sprinkle of dried herbs for more flavor.

Avocados and Olives

What about avocados and olives which, unlike other vegetables and fruits we know about, contain some saturated fat?

A medium-size avocado contains 5 grams of saturated fat—a lot if you plan to eat the whole avocado. The good news is that avocados also contain quite a bit of good monounsaturated fat. So, avocados eaten in moderation are not all bad. Take your time enjoying small servings instead of large ones.

When you make guacamole, add some finely chopped roasted green chiles, slivered onions and vinegar or lemon juice to the mashed avocado. Then, instead of dipping into the guacamole with tortilla chips or spreading it onto meat (as is traditional), consider adding the guacamole to 4 individual salads consisting of lettuce leaves and sliced tomatoes. That way you will be consuming only about 1 gram of saturated fat per serving as you enjoy that incredible avocado flavor.

As for olives, 4 medium-sized olives contain only a trace of saturated fat. Judging from the beneficial effects that olives and olive oil seem to have on heart disease in the Mediterranean cultures, it's probably a good idea to eat a few olives now and then. You can also use moderate amounts of olive oil in salads and in other ways. There is good evidence that the monounsaturated fat in olives, avocados and nuts (without added oil) may actually increase blood levels of healthful HDL cholesterol.

Coconut is a NO-NO!

Something else that grows on trees is a real problem—coconut. The oil is used extensively in processed foods and especially in baked goods to add flavor and prolong shelf life. Just one tablespoon of coconut oil contains 11.9 grams of saturated fat. Do not use it in cooking. Don't buy bakery goods made with it.

What about white coconut meat? A quarter cup of shredded coconut contains 6 grams of saturated fat. If you want to use it for flavor or texture, be sure each serving contains no more than one tablespoon which equals 1.50 grams of saturated fat.

Gelatin Desserts

Getting back to completely fat-free foods you can enjoy, take a look at the grocery shelves filled with various gelatin desserts which can be served chilled, whipped, mixed with fruit or even blended with ice into a frozen dessert.

These gelatin desserts can also be served with or used as a topping for angel food cake—also fat-free because it's made with egg whites. Of course, angel food cake can be served plain or with fruit or syrup toppings.

Butter, Margarine and Trans-fatty Acids

Speaking of toppings, one of the big problems is tablespreads used on bread and vegetables. Butter has 7 grams of saturated fat per tablespoon, plus about 0.3 gram of trans-fatty acids. Even though you may not use a tablespoon of butter on a piece of toast or on a sandwich, the bad-fat grams add up rapidly. It's easy to melt a tablespoon (or more) of butter on a hot baked potato. That's at least 7.3 grams to consider against your 10- or 20-gram-a-day budget of saturated fat.

Solid-stick and soft margarines also contain worrisome trans-fatty acids in the same amount as the saturated fat. Consider these trans-fatty acids as additional saturated fat.

"What are these trans-fatty acids you've been talking about?" you may be wondering. Trans-fatty acids are one of the undesirable by-products produced during the hydrogenating or hardening process involved in turning oils into solid shortenings and margarine.[3] Although trans-fatty acids are technically unsaturated fat, they are *really bad fats.* Like saturated fat, they raise LDL levels. Some reports show they may *decrease* HDL.

So how much trans-fatty acids are in margarine and what does this all mean? At this time, trans-fatty acids are not listed on any food labels. Why? It is nearly impossible to pin down how much trans-fatty acids there are in margarine because the manufacturers change the composition depending on the availability and prices of components that go into the margarine. As the composition changes, so does the amount of trans-fatty acids.

Some regular margarines with 2 grams of saturated fat per tablespoon typically have up to another 2 grams of trans-fatty acids per tablespoon. The 4 grams of bad fat in the worst kind of margarine is less than 7.3 grams of bad fat in a tablespoon of butter. We consider even 4 grams in a spread is still too much.

There are better choices than solid-stick margarine that starts with 2 grams of saturated fat and 2 grams of trans-fatty acids. We used to think a tablespread with 1 gram of saturated fat per tablespoon was a good choice. The trouble is that there is almost a gram of trans-fatty acid in these 1-gram saturated-fat spreads—including soft margarines.

Manufacturers have improved the taste and texture of spreads over the years without adding much saturated fat. Some are definitely better than others. You can choose the best-tasting one you can find that contains the least amount of bad fat.

For now, start with the tablespreads with little or no saturated fat. Even the ones labeled "Fat-free or 0 gram saturated fat" actually have just a little. Government rules allow rounding off the numbers so anything under 0.5 gram can be listed as 0. Because trans-fatty acids are produced during the hydrogenating or hardening process, a liquid spread with a little saturated fat is likely to have less trans-fatty acids than the soft fat-free tub spreads. Tub spreads have less trans-fatty acids and saturated fat than solid sticks.

In review, solid-stick margarine usually has almost 2 grams of trans-fatty acid plus 1 to 2 grams of saturated fat per tablespoon. Soft margarine usually has almost 1 gram of trans-fatty acids, plus 1 gram of saturated fat per tablespoon. "Fat-free" tablespreads are likely to have less than 0.5 grams of saturated fat and about the same amount of trans-fatty acids.

A helpful clue is to look at the list of ingredients, which are always listed in the order of amount in the product. One very safe ingredient—*water*—usually heads the list in safer spreads. It tells you the spread probably has relatively little trans-fatty acid and saturated fat. Conversely, do not eat margarine or tablespreads that begin the list of ingredients with the words *liquid, partly* or *partially.*

What can you do? There are several good solutions. One is to eat bread and toast dry—without *any* spread or oil. Almost any spread is loaded with calories. You may like honey on your bread or toast, but remember that it is concentrated sugar. Lots of calories! Bread + spread is usually fattening! Instead, why not consider a mashed banana, fresh or frozen strawberries, raspberries or fresh, canned or frozen peaches?

You can also use jam on toast instead of any spread. Another idea is to dip bread or toast in a mild olive oil like Italians and others in the Mediterranean area do. In some Italian restaurants, you'll find a little dish of olive oil on the table. This olive oil may be flavored with balsamic vinegar, garlic or herbs.

At other times, you may want to pick the best-tasting fat-free spread possible—perhaps one of the newer butter-flavored liquid-sprays.

As you choose spreads and other products, be aware that foods containing hydrogenated vegetable oils as in solid margarine or shortening also contain trans-fatty acids in addition to the saturated fat listed on the label.

We suggest completely avoiding solid-stick margarine and carefully keeping track of the amount of trans-fatty acids and saturated fat in everything from potato chips to soft margarines.

Ice Cream and Frozen Yogurt

Just as there have been giant steps in better tasting and healthier table-spreads, it has been exciting so to see progress in the development of lowfat and fat-free ice cream and frozen yogurt. You will be surprised and delighted as you check out the labels on the frozen-dessert products at your supermarket.

Breads, White Flour and Sugar

Most ordinary bread has only a half to one gram of saturated fat *per serving*—usually 1 slice, 1 roll or 1 bun. A half gram or so isn't much bad fat, but a sandwich is typically 2 slices and that can be 1 to 2 grams of saturated fat, not counting whatever is spread onto the bread.

A big problem with bread is *calories*. It's easy to consume calories while eating bread. Eating too much bread, or other things made with white flour or lots of sugar, is a problem for three reasons:

1. Increased calories make it difficult for most people to control weight—some more than others.
2. Consuming calories is a big problem for anyone who has a triglyceride problem. Whenever someone with a triglyceride problem consumes many calories, the triglyceride level in the blood increases almost immediately. So, even if your

overnight fasting triglyceride levels seem controlled, if your triglycerides have ever been over 150, your triglyceride level will rise for a while every time you eat a lot of calories.

3. Eating high-calorie foods makes it difficult for those with diabetes to control their blood-sugar levels.

Is there an answer? For one thing, cut down on foods containing sugar.

What about bread and other things made with refined carbohydrates? Looking at the big picture, a slice of white bread now and then probably isn't a problem. It's very easy to eat lots and lots of white bread without feeling *full.* Try switching from white bread to whole-wheat or multi-grain breads especially if you have problems controlling weight, triglycerides or diabetes.

As you set out to choose your favorite whole-wheat bread, you will find all sorts of variations. Just the color won't tell you if it's really whole-wheat or not. Also, read the label for saturated-fat information.

For an occasional alternative to whole-wheat bread, one of the best-tasting breads you can buy or make is genuine French bread—especially when it's fresh. French bread is also called *baguettes* or *petit pain,* referring to the shape or size of the loaf. Traditional French bread has a simple lineup of ingredients: flour, water, a little salt and a little sugar. There's no oil!

Not every slender crusty loaf labeled "French Bread" is made without oil. Oil is sometimes added for flavor and a softer texture. If you make your own French bread, you'll know it is fat-free. There's an excellent recipe on page 164. Enjoy!

We encourage you to eat plain bagels which are often fat-free. Egg bagels typically have over a half gram of fat. When you eat bagels, think about using a lowfat topping or spread. Fat-free cream cheese is one good choice. Forget about eating popovers and doughnuts. They soak up lots of fat, which you don't need!

Eggs

Even though we may have convinced you to eat oatmeal or another cereal most of the time for breakfast, it's still difficult to forget about eggs. Eggs taste great! Whether poached, boiled, scrambled or in a fancy omelet, they are quick and easy to prepare. One egg yolk contains 212 mg of cholesterol—more than a day's ration of choles-terol for people at high risk. Those two-egg breakfasts or three-egg omelets contain 424 to 636 mg of cholesterol—all at once!

An egg yolk has lots of cholesterol, but an egg white doesn't—no saturated fat either! Even though egg whites are great in angel food cake and in other baked things, it's not very exciting to think about cooking a skillet of plain egg whites. Even so, you can prepare omelets made with egg whites or egg substitutes and they'll taste better than you may think.

Those who love eggs don't have to give them up completely. You've probably seen several egg-substitute products. They come dried, frozen or fresh in the market dairy case. Most of these products are made with egg whites, natural flavors, guar gum and a small amount of corn oil. Essentially, they contain NO FAT or CHOLESTEROL. They work well for most baking. For those who find the substitutes bland, try adding a dash of spice, hot sauce or fresh herbs for a tasty omelet or scrambled-egg dish.

Because these products are constantly changing, always read the fat content on the package and be willing to try new products as they appear.

There's another way to use fresh eggs without overloading on cho-lesterol. To make an omelet, French toast or as a base for other egg dishes for your family, simply use one egg yolk with several egg whites instead of a whole egg or two apiece. Or use a few drops—maybe up to a quarter of one egg yolk—along with one, two or three egg whites. To make an egg-white omelet more interesting, simply add lowfat or fat-free cheese, tomatoes, onions, salsa, mushrooms or herbs.

The key is that you do have choices. It's your life. Spend your bad-fat budget any way you want—or break it. It's all up to you.

Milk and Dairy Products

As wholesome as milk seems to be, drinking it with a full measure of cream adds grams of saturated fat in a hurry. There are 5 grams of sat-urated fat in an 8-ounce glass of whole milk. You can do better by drinking 2% milk with only 3 grams of bad fat per glass, 1% milk (or buttermilk) with only 1.5 grams or nonfat (skim) milk that contains essentially no saturated fat.

Using skim (nonfat, fat-free) milk in cooking is something everyone can do immediately. For example, try instant puddings made with skim milk. You won't notice much, if any, difference when you use skim milk in cooking.

If you've grown up drinking creamy homogenized milk with 4% butterfat, the idea of drinking skim milk may not appeal to you. We can understand this. When you think about those cream-colored plaques forming in your coronary arteries, drinking rich 4% milk may be even more unappealing. Don't do it!

There's more than taste causing the problem of changing from drinking whole milk to drinking skim milk. There's color, thickness or thinness and the name *skim*. It may help to use the words *nonfat* or *fat-free* instead. Whatever you do as you change, be sure you are not drinking whole milk. If you are a milk-drinker, consider reducing the amount you drink, as well as the fat content. You'll find it hard to keep within your daily budget of saturated fat if you are adding many units of 3 and 5 grams at a time.

We are not recommending limiting milk products to fat-free yogurt, cottage cheese or milk and avoiding rich ice cream for very young children. Remember, babies and toddlers need the fat in their milk and formula for the first two or three years.

Heavy Whipping Cream

If you enjoy heavy whipping cream, just one tablespoon has 6 grams of saturated fat and 25 mg of cholesterol; heavy cream has 3 grams of saturated fat and 12 grams of cholesterol per tablespoon. Substitute nonfat milk or one of the many nonfat creamer products for heavy whipping cream or heavy cream.

Fat-free Yogurt

A good way to get the calcium and proteins you need is to eat fat-free yogurt. Choose the flavor you want or start with plain fat-free yogurt and mix it with fresh, frozen or canned fruit and a little sweetening as needed. Mixing yogurt with hot or cold applesauce, sugar and a little cinnamon can be a quick and enjoyable snack or main dessert. Or try mixing or layering yogurt with your favorite flavor of gelatin dessert.

Cottage Cheese

Another popular dairy product is cottage cheese. If you eat a full cup of cottage cheese made from whole milk with 4% butterfat, you will consume 6 grams of saturated fat. If the cottage cheese is made from 2% milk, the bad fat is down to 2.8 grams per one-cup serving. You can enjoy lowfat cottage cheese made from 1% milk and spend only 1.5 grams of your bad-fat budget. Even better is fat-free cottage cheese with only a trace of saturated fat.

Cheese

What can take the place of good old-fashioned cheddar, mozzarella, Swiss and other cheese favorites? At first, the fat-free cheese substitutes had only fair flavor and were leathery or stringy. Little by little the creativity of food product developers has provided some amazingly good fat-free or fat-reduced cheese products. Do your own taste-testing and watch for new products because they continue to improve. Keep reading those labels.

Most cheese has 7 grams of fat per 1-ounce slice and 5 grams of that are saturated fat. When was the last time you ate only one slice of a good cheese?

Cream Cheese

Traditional cream cheese has 6 grams of saturated fat in every ounce. This is really tough news because cream cheese is so good on a cracker, a piece of bread, a celery stick or in all sorts of favorite things, including cheesecake.

Now you can buy fat-free cream cheese that tastes good. While it isn't as creamy as regular cream cheese, it's close. With fat-free cream cheese, we can go back to enjoying cream cheese in myriad ways.

Fat-free cream cheese is just one more example of giant steps of progress by food producers who have developed and created excellent alternatives to foods laden with bad fat. We tip our hats and thank them for making outstanding products such as fat-free cream cheese.

The idea of being successful at keeping on your limited budget of bad fat is to be creative in thinking of combinations you like. Experiment and try new things along with modifying your own favorite foods with new products like this fat-free cream cheese.

Cooking Oils vs. Shortening

Never use *any* solid shortening. The fats in solid shortening are *hydrogenated.* Even when shortening is made from vegetable oil, it contains both trans-fatty acids and saturated fat.

Clue number one about cooking oil: Use *liquid oil.*

Clue number two: All cooking oils, even the good liquid vegetable oils, contain *some* saturated fat. Some more than others. All have unsaturated fat, which we only need a little of.

Olive Oil, Canola Oil and Two Kinds of Unsaturated Fat

There are two kinds of unsaturated fat: *polyunsaturated fat*[4] and *monounsaturated fat.* We tend to favor monounsaturated fat. Why? People (like Mediterraneans) who use a lot of olive oil, one of the main monounsaturated fats, have little coronary-artery disease. The main oils that are mostly monounsaturated fat are olive oil, canola oil and peanut oil. There is evidence that monounsaturated fat may actually help to increase the good HDL cholesterol, which is especially helpful for those with high cholesterol and/or high triglycerides.

Olive oil comes in various grades, with flavor from mild to pronounced. It is best to use olive oil soon after buying it because its taste tends to get stronger as it ages. The 2 grams of saturated fat in a tablespoon of olive oil should not dissuade anyone from using olive oil. It has a history of contributing heart-healthy monounsaturated fat.

Canola oil, known as *rapeseed oil* in Europe and elsewhere in the world, has become one of the most popular cooking oils in North America. Canola oil contains only 1 gram of saturated fat per tablespoon. With its monounsaturated fat, Canola oil may prove to be as good as olive oil, but we don't know for sure yet. Canola oil has not been used in North America long enough for us to learn just how good it is.

We already know the value of olive oil. So, a good balance may be to use both olive oil and canola oil when preparing food at home, realizing we will get small amounts of polyunsaturated safflower, corn or sunflower oils when we eat away from home.

You may want to choose canola oil mostly for the limited frying you do. Use either canola or olive oil in recipes that call for oil and use olive oil in vinaigrette salad dressings and as a dip for bread.

Fish

People who eat seafood regularly instead of fatty meat are less likely to have plugged coronary arteries or heart attacks. Seafood is also a wonderful source of protein. Japanese, Eskimos and others who consume lots of fish and seafood don't typically have heart attacks from fat-plugged coronary arteries.

One of the factors that may help is omega-3 oil. Omega-3 seems to prevent platelet cells from getting sticky, cutting down the tendency for blood clots to form. Just taking capsules of this oil alone does not seem to produce the protection that eating fish does.

It is recommended that we eat fish or other seafood twice a week. Of course you can eat it more often than that, thereby increasing the benefits.

In addition to fish, there are two groups of shellfish. The group that doesn't move during its lifetime includes clams, mussels, oysters and scallops. They lie on the ocean bottom and suck in *phytoplankton*—the vegetables of the sea. They contain very small amounts of cholesterol and saturated fat.

The other group of shellfish, *crustaceans,* are the ones that move—crabs, crayfish, shrimp and lobsters. They are fine to eat, too, even though they contain some cholesterol. Six medium-size shrimp, weighing about 1/4 pound (100 grams), contain about 120 mg of cholesterol, but only 0.3 grams of saturated fat—about the same as a similar amount of skinless chicken breasts.

Fish, clams, mussels, oysters and scallops are obviously the best. If properly prepared, they can be eaten without much limitation. Although low in saturated fat, shrimp, crab, crayfish and lobsters all contain some cholesterol. In other words, "an all-you-can-eat" shrimp dinner is not a good idea. A half-dozen boiled, broiled or grilled shrimp may be just fine.

Don't be trapped into thinking because it's seafood, it's all right no matter how it's prepared. Many people choose the right entrée, but get shrimp covered with breading that soaks up the deep fat it is cooked in or order scampi drowned in butter. Other times, fish are served or topped with butter or cheese sauce. Of course, you would not want to order fish this way, but if there's no choice, just scrape off the sauce, breading or batter and don't eat it.

Rather than dipping crab and lobster into melted butter, enjoy them with seafood cocktail sauce. You can easily make cocktail sauce by mixing a little fresh (non-creamy) horseradish with catsup or chili sauce. Although this tomato-based sauce is customarily served with cold shrimp, crab or lobster, it is delicious with almost any kind of hot seafood.

If salt and pepper are not enough flavoring for fish, grill it over wood or mesquite charcoal or chips to import excellent smoky flavors. Other flavor enhancers for seafood are malt vinegar or juice from a lemon or lime. You can prepare blackened fish without the usual load of fat by using the Cajun Pepper Mix on page 186.

Deep-frying fish or other seafood is a no-no. It's better to bake, grill or poach it. The cod in "fish and chips" is a great choice, but the batter contains fat and also soaks in the oil, picking up even more saturated fat. Batter-coated frozen fish may be fine, but the batter will usually contain considerable amounts of saturated fat. Whether it is fresh or frozen, once you've cooked it, just take off the crusty batter and eat the fish.

If you aren't accustomed to eating fish or seafood, you may want to begin with some milder-tasting varieties such as cod, haddock, orange roughy or halibut. Almost everyone who tries these fish likes them.

Trout is another deliciously mild fish with a little more omega-3 oil than the others. Salmon has even more omega-3 than trout and, when fresh or smoked, is mild and has a deliciously distinctive taste.

Chicken and Turkey

Chances are you'll find white-chicken and turkey-meat entrées among your favorite foods. Hopefully, you've already decided not to eat deep-fried chicken. Even if you grew up loving southern-fried chicken, remember that besides all the fat in chicken skin, the chicken meat soaks in more fat in frying than your arteries can handle.

Broiling boned-and-skinned chicken-breast strips on top of a grill is a good way to prepare an excellent dinner entrée. Cook them plain or seasoned with lemon juice, Cajun seasoning or lemon pepper. A 3-ounce serving of skinless chicken or turkey breast only has 1 gram of saturated fat, while the same size serving of dark meat has 2 grams. For those limiting saturated fat intake, it is a big advantage to eat properly cooked white poultry meat.

Additional water, oil and flavoring are added to frozen turkeys. While it may enhance the flavor a little, the extra oil adds more bad fat. Look for turkeys *without* extra oil poured in or injected. They are hard to find unless you get a fresh turkey, which is probably a better idea anyway.

Whether chicken or turkey, poultry skin contains saturated fat, so don't eat the skin. Because chicken and turkey are thought of as healthful meat products, many people have switched to turkey burger. We suggest you avoid ground turkey because turkey burger (or any ground-turkey product) is made with turkey scraps, including fat, skin and scraps of dark meat with twice as much saturated fat. Anytime you are tempted to buy turkey burger, think twice and read the label four times. Then you may decide to buy extra-lean ground beef that doesn't have any added fat you can see.

Beef

Meat producers have made big strides in raising beef and pork with less saturated fat than it once had. More and more meat from specially fed and cared-for animals is being advertised. So you don't have to do without red meat completely. If you want to be a vegetarian, that's OK. If you like beef or pork occasionally, that's fine too. It's OK to enjoy small servings of red meat without feeling guilty. Small amounts of very lean meat will not plug up your coronary arteries. Unless you are doing lots of heavy work in freezing temperatures, it's a good idea to eat meat sparingly.

Every packing plant in the United States has an inspector from the Department of Agriculture to check how much fat is in the meat. *Prime*—heavily marbled to give meat a juicy flavor—used to be thought of as the best beef. Now we know prime meat is the most dangerous because it contains the most fat—usually over 35% and often as much as 40%.

The meat grade called *choice* ranges from 15% to 30% fat by weight. You can choose to put packages of *choice* meat back in the display case along with those marked *prime*.

The third grade is what used to be *good* and is now called *select,* a much better name for this beef because it only contains 10% fat by weight. Those who don't know how meat is graded and labeled and the relative fat content are likely to choose the more market-appealing names of *prime* or *choice.* Choose SELECT BEEF.

Some producers now supply even leaner beef than is required to qualify for the *select* grade. Cuts of this leaner beef contain only about 7% fat. This is pretty good especially when you eat it sparingly. For now, buy the leanest-possible meat you can find, trim off all the visible fat and then eat small portions.

How about hamburger? It's easy to be confused by the different *lean* and *extra lean* name tags. Look for *select* beef and then choose the leanest of the lean.[5] Incidentally, it is easy to identify because it costs more than any other ground beef.

Broiling is an excellent way to cook hamburger because some fat melts and drips into the fire or drip pan instead of onto a bun or into your chili or casserole. Two simple tricks can get even more fat out of hamburger. When you are broiling lean ground beef over a gas or charcoal grill, start with thin patties. As they cook on each side and after you take them off the grill, squeeze the burgers several times with a spatula, then blot them with a wadded paper towel. You'll be amazed at how much fat comes out! This demonstrates how much fat is present, even in the leanest ground beef. You cannot squeeze and blot out enough fat this way to make using ordinary fatty hamburger a good idea.

There's an even better fat-removal method for preparing lean ground beef for tacos, chili, rice and meat or other hot dishes: Cook it slowly in a large pan on the stove top, squeezing and blotting out or pouring off the grease several times. When the meat is about ready, pour the hot ground beef into a strainer and run a heavy stream of hot tap water over it so more of the melted fat is carried through the strainer and down the drain. This far-from-perfect method decreases the amount of saturated fat in your ground beef.

It's hard to know how much fat is in this "degreased" beef. It depends on how careful you are in choosing very lean meat to start with and how diligent you are in squeezing, blotting and washing out the fat.

Regular hamburger has 5 to 7 grams of saturated fat in a 3-ounce serving. With the best of *select* lean steaks and roasts, you may be looking at only 2.5 to 4 grams of saturated fat in a 3-ounce serving—

quite good as compared to 4 to 11 grams of bad fat in marbled steaks and roasts.

When you are ready to cook a steak or roast, trim off all of the fat you can see before cooking, just as you would before cooking chicken, turkey or pork. This is important because while the meat cooks, a considerable amount of fat melts and is absorbed into the meat.

Taking the Fat Out of Broth

After you go to all the trouble to buy meat without much fat and then to go to these extra steps in preparing it, don't turn around and load your potatoes with fatty gravy! You can make fat-free gravy with bouillon granules or cubes or with defatted chicken broth you can make after boiling chicken breasts or cooking leftover chicken bones and meat (without fat).

Even without the turkey or chicken skin and fat drippings we always used to add to our turkey or chicken soup, there is always some fat in the broth you cook. After cooking the leftover bones and lean meat scraps for 45 minutes to an hour, strain and discard everything except the white meat. Put the broth in the freezer or refrigerator. When it has chilled, you will see a layer of fat on the top. Carefully scoop off this fat and discard it. If elusive bits and pieces of fat are floating around, trap and discard them with a piece of paper towel.

If you are in a hurry, drop ice cubes into lukewarm broth. Some fat will cling to the cubes. Remove the ice cubes and skim off any remaining fat.

Another way to get fat off of broth is with a fat-skimmer. When the fatty broth is chilled, most of the fat rises to the top. The inside opening of the spout is near the bottom of the container, so the broth comes from underneath the fatty layer of clear grease. Of course, the idea is to stop pouring before visible fat begins to enter the spout. These skimmers are available where kitchenware is sold.

The lowfat broth you make is great for gravy or soup. You can make all sorts of wonderful lowfat soups beginning with your lowfat broth. Recipes for beef, chicken and vegetarian lowfat broths are in the recipe section.

Pork and Ham

Sometimes you see ads for pork with the words, "the other white meat," implying it might have the same small amount of saturated fat as chicken and turkey white meat. Pork and white turkey or chicken meat do have about the same amount of cholesterol. Three ounces of lean pork usually contain about 4 grams of saturated fat. As a comparison, chicken and turkey breasts without skin and fat contain only 1 gram of saturated fat per 3-ounce serving.

Some very good lowfat pork products are available, especially lowfat hams. You will probably see various packages of ham that say 97% FAT-FREE. This is pretty good, but 97% FAT-FREE still has 3% fat. It's *not* fat-free.

While you may see ham advertised as completely fat-free, it isn't. Producers can call the product *fat-free* when the amount of fat is less than 0.5 gram per serving. Check the serving size. Just because a particular ham—or any other product—is labeled fat-free, it is not OK to eat very many thin slices because each one contains only half a gram of fat.

When you choose a ham, check the *Nutritional Facts* label on different packages and pick the one with the best numbers and the least visible fat.

Hot Dogs (Wieners)

One regular hot dog typically contains 5 to 11 grams of saturated fat. The good news is that most of the major meat-packing companies have created special lines of lowfat wieners.

If you or your children really like them, you can get lowfat ones with only half a gram of saturated fat per hot dog. Some lowfat hot dogs are labeled *fat-free,* but you know half a gram of saturated fat or a little less allows them to be labeled fat-free. Expect to pay more for these wieners.

Picnics and Cookouts

For cookouts, consider cooking fish steaks or fillets (salmon, orange roughy or tuna) on your backyard grill. This is especially good eating.

Potato Chips

What about potato chips for your picnic, cookout or buffet? They're traditional and some people expect you to serve them. We already mentioned that a package of ordinary potato chips that says "NO CHOLESTEROL" is misleading because the real problem is too much bad fat. There may be 2 to 3 grams of saturated fat in 10 to 16 potato chips—plus some trans-fatty acids and lots of unsaturated fat. Although you are only keeping a budget record of saturated fat, you always need to be careful not to load up on total fat. As much as you may like them, regular potato chips are *not* good for your heart.

You'll see various kinds of chips with a little less fat. When you check the Nutrition Facts chart on the back of the package, you will see that each serving contains 1 gram of saturated fat, plus 4 grams of polyunsaturated fat and 1.5 grams of monounsaturated fat.

As you look further, you may find some fat-free and almost-fat-free potato chips that are baked instead of fried in hot grease. These are pretty good but maybe not as tasty as chips with some fat—even the reduced-fat varieties. Another potato-chip substitute is baked puffed chips made of potato flakes.

Talking about chips, you may want to try *Frozen Banana Munchies.* These different kind of fat-free "chips" are quick and easy to make:

> Squeeze some fresh lemon juice in a bowl and add banana slices, stirring them around so they are well coated. Then line the banana circles on a small non-stick cookie sheet lightly sprayed with fat-free vegetable cooking oil. Place the tray of banana slices in your freezer. When frozen, scoop them into a plastic bag with a spatula. Put the bag of frozen banana munchies back in the freezer and save until you need a snack.

Other Possibilities

You can enjoy eating without killing yourself and your family with too much bad fat. It takes some thought, ingenuity and creativity.

If you are in a hurry, you can find some very good pre-prepared lowfat frozen dinners at your market. Some provide an enjoyable meal without much bad fat. Others are promoted with lowfat claims but contain more fat than you want. So read the labels and taste-test the ones that look like they meet your criteria. Don't dismiss them all if you don't happen to like one.

Try these and other ideas. While they won't all work for you, some will. Then get together with friends and family and have some potluck meals so you can try each other's best fat-free and lowfat entrées, meals and snacks.

We hope you have fun trying these and other quick-and-easy recipes as well as some slightly more challenging ones that you and your family can enjoy. You'll know you are not building up more fat plaques in your coronary arteries.

NOTES

1. Because one way the body gets rid of cholesterol is to convert it to bile acids, cholesterol is decreased when bile acids are passed with the help of soluble fiber.

2. We don't know of any definitive studies to establish the effectiveness of either charcoal or sprinkle-on products in reducing intestinal gas. When charcoal is taken, expect stools to be black. And if you are on cholesterol-reducing or other medications, get approval from your physician before taking charcoal because it absorbs and inactivates some medications.

3. Steinberg D., et al. *Circulation* 85:2338, 1992.

4. Polyunsaturated fats (PUFAs) found in corn oil, safflower oil and sunflower oil are three of the most popular cooking oils because of their particularly good flavor. Cottonseed and soybean oil are also predominantly polyunsaturated fat oils. We don't need much polyunsaturated fat oil—probably a couple of teaspoons a day are sufficient—and we get that in tablespreads and other prepared products.

5. If your butcher shop or market does not have *select* grade beef, ask for it. As with other lowfat and fat-free products, it may not be carried till you ask—sometimes many times. Customer demand is what gets the products you want and need into your market.

How to Eat Less Fat
When You're Eating Out

Eating a limited-fat diet is easy at home, but it is more challenging when you eat out. At first, it was an extra effort to eat out without eating more fat than we wanted to consume.

After a while we found that eating out usually can be quite enjoyable without going off our bad-fat budgets of 10 grams a day.

You may wonder how we can say this when meals are usually prepared by people who don't understand that we really don't want to eat fat-laden foods. It's surprising how quickly people catch on and will go out of their way to prepare lowfat meals we can enjoy. Sometimes they try and don't do very well. Even so, without doing or saying much, these experiences often turn into helpful learning experiences for the diners as well as the hosts.

A Big Plate of Fatty Food—Just for You!

You visit friends who don't know of your aversion to fat and find they've prepared a steak with potatoes and gravy. What's a person to do? Or, you are at a wedding reception where the healthiest thing available is cheesecake. It sometimes seems that those who planned the party had a contest to see who could serve the greatest amount of bad fat.

These are times when the only reasonable answers come from good common sense. The fact you are working from your own *budget* is a big advantage. When you know you will be eating out or going to a party, use very little of your bad-fat budget at breakfast and lunch. When you anticipate being served things like deep-fried chicken livers stuffed with cheese or baked Alaska with whipped cream, eat a good breakfast and lunch with almost no saturated fat. But what are you going to do about the chicken livers and baked Alaska?

Hopefully, you won't be served such fatty foods and most receptions you attend will have some healthy choices. If healthy food is scarce, eat around the grossly fat stuff. Some not-so-fat things are almost always served at a meal like this—bread, salad and veggies. Nibble. You might even find enough to feel you are not being short-changed. If not, you may want to fix yourself something really good when you get home. Joking about your situation is not an option—that's bad manners! Self-deprecating humor is merely disguised criticism of what is being served, so don't do that, either! It's not in the best interest of friendships or acquaintances to preach about your own lowfat eating requirements.

In most situations, just "fake it." If the entrée is southern fried chicken, peel off the skin and take a few little bites of the white chicken meat inside. If it's a big pork chop or spare ribs, trim off the fat and take a few small nibbles of the leanest meat you can find.

Remember, you can spend your bad-fat budget any way you want, so your secret is quantity—eat only small quantities. One of two things will happen—people will notice or they won't. If they don't, great. If they do, that could be even better. They may learn something. You may be surprised that the next time you are asked over to dinner, the people who fed you such a fatty meal will go out of their way to feed you something very good that contains little fat.

Another interesting phenomenon is that after friends know you know something about lowfat eating, when they choose something to eat for themselves that isn't healthful, they will often make excuses and even apologize to you—as if you are their conscience! Don't say a thing. Just watch to see what happens.

Look for "Heart-Healthy" or "Lowfat" on the Menu

When you go out to eat at a restaurant, it is usually easier to stick to your lowfat budget than when you have been invited to someone's home. There's always more variety at restaurants. More and more restaurants are offering lowfat entrées on their menus, sometimes flagged with a little red heart or footnoted as *heart-healthy*. These items often contain very little saturated fat, although sometimes the promise is better than what's delivered.

Some restaurants have no lowfat entrées because whoever is managing the place doesn't understand the need. Don't be afraid to ask how something is prepared—or to make suggestions about how to do it better. In other words, if you don't see anything on the menu that looks heart-healthy, explain what you want and ask them to fix it for you.

When asked, chefs and servers are usually very helpful. Most will make a special effort to please if you explain you are on a lowfat diet. Restaurant people are in business to satisfy you so you will leave a nice tip—and come back. Just ask. Keep it low-key, especially if there are several people at your table. Write out your special order or request on the back of a business card or on notepaper. Such a note with a few simple explanatory comments is an excellent way to get the message straight to the chef.

An especially easy lowfat request for most restaurants is baked or broiled salmon—without any butter or cheese sauces. When any salmon entrée has been on the menu, no one has turned down our requests to broil or bake it plain or with pepper and lemon. Ask the server to bring you some extra lemon or lime wedges or some seafood cocktail sauce. The same applies when ordering other types of fish. Instead of ordering French-fried shrimp or scallops, ask the chef to broil them—maybe even over mesquite if you are in a southwest-style restaurant. Salmon and tuna are particularly good broiled over mesquite or alder wood. Even if the specialty of a seafood house is fried fish and chips, a good chef will usually help you enjoy a good meal without breaking your fat budget.

The same is true with chicken. At home, you trim the fat and skin off the white chicken meat before you cook it, which is best. Many restaurants offer skinless chicken-breast entrées now. If they don't, speak up! Unless you happen to be in a place that specializes only in fried chicken, most places will be accommodating. Some chicken franchises now offer broiled or rotisserie chicken. Most are cooked with the skin on and, even if much of the fat drips off as the chicken is turned, there is still fat left. You don't have to eat the crusty skin. Trim off the skin and don't eat too much of the white meat—especially if fat has soaked in. Some places even have lowfat baked or broiled chicken breasts cooked without the skin.

If there's no choice about chicken or fish that has been dipped in a batter and deep-fried, remember that this crust soaks up lots of oil. Sheer quantity is a problem—even if the menu proclaims that it is

71

fried in "pure vegetable oil or canola." More of this fat than you want penetrates into the meat. So if you are served greasy fried chicken or fish and you have no choice, peel off the crusted batter and skin and eat only a little of the white meat. Don't think you are eating a lowfat dinner. It is much better to choose a place to eat where you can get broiled, poached or grilled fish.

Eating out without overloading on bad fat is easier than most people think. When you have a choice of restaurants, think about choosing a favorite buffet, but not necessarily always. When you go, look at the menu (or buffet) items and think through your choices carefully.

If you are at a restaurant and want to order something that's not on the menu, build on something you think they might be able to easily adapt from other items on their menu.

Be creative. Don't be afraid to ask for your fish to be broiled or your chicken breast to be trimmed of all skin and fat before it is broiled. If you like seafood cocktail sauce, don't be bashful about asking for some for your salad.

If you are eating breakfast in a restaurant, oatmeal is almost always available. Ask for it to be served plain or with syrup, nonfat milk or applesauce. Orange juice and fruit are also usually available. If you want an omelet, order one made with no-cholesterol egg products. Use salsa, picante sauce or catsup to spice it up. You may want to treat yourself to a small slice of very lean ham to go with it.

Salad Bars Can Help

Some of our favorite places to eat out are buffets or restaurants that offer an extended salad bar. That provides a wide variety of good choices without having to negotiate with anyone except ourselves. Eating lowfat meals at a good buffet is a much easier experience than at most fast-food places and ordinary restaurants.

You've probably noticed more and more franchise salad-bar buffets opening up. They are usually much more than salad bars offering hot and cold pastas, peas and beans, plus a wonderful assortment of fruit, vegetables and traditional salad components. Many of these buffets have a lot of fat-filled food, especially at the dessert bar, but you may also find fat-free frozen yogurt. Even if they don't, most buffets include a variety of fruits which can more than make up for skipping high-fat desserts.

Alternative Toppings

What if a restaurant doesn't have a fat-free salad dressing for your salad? While this is possible, it is not nearly as likely now as it was a few years ago. There are usually plenty of other choices.

Try just plain vinegar on sliced tomatoes or on a tossed salad. Even better are salad vinegars with a touch of garlic or other seasonings. Salad vinegars or freshly squeezed lemon or lime juice are great zero-fat solutions to dressing a salad or an elegant serving of hot or cold vegetables. For a change, try salsa, picante sauce or catsup as a topping.

Another excellent fat-free salad topping that most restaurants have on hand is seafood cocktail sauce. If prepared cocktail sauce is not available, it is easily and quickly made by combining catsup with a little fresh (not creamy) horseradish and coarse pepper. This sauce is one of the things most people like about shrimp cocktails. Even without the shrimp, this cocktail sauce tastes good on a lettuce or spinach salad.

You may grow to like one of these alternatives even more than some of your favorite fat-filled bleu-cheese or thousand island dressings. Whether you are at a friend's home, a buffet or at a fancy sit-down restaurant, you need to be ready with alternatives to the typical butter or sour-cream toppings for baked potatoes and cheese sauces for vegetables and other fat-filled things.

What *do* you put on potatoes, rice or cooked vegetables when you're eating out? Restaurants can usually provide lowfat diet spreads, if asked. Other options include chopped broccoli, cottage cheese or finely chopped fresh tomato. Others like plain catsup on their baked potato or small amounts of fat-free or lowfat salad dressing.

Fast-Food Restaurants

Eating at fast-food restaurants is a challenge. As we mentioned before, a big hamburger with cheese, a big order of fries and a milkshake can contain as much as 24 grams of saturated fat. That's way too much bad fat whether at a fast-food place, in a sit-down restaurant or at home.

Your chances to get something to eat at a fast-food restaurant without too much fat are much better now than they were a few years ago.

Some fast-food places now even have salad bars. The very definition of fast-food focuses on a limited menu of things to be served in a hurry. That's why the menus seem to specialize in fat.

At some fast-food chains, you can ask for and get a printed list of all their menu items listing the saturated fat in each one. Also watch out for big globs of mayonnaise and other sauces that add more fat grams!

Fried fish, chicken, pizza, fries and burgers as well as ice cream and shakes are very popular with children and adults. These things taste good. At least they taste good until you've been off a high-fat intake for a while. Then, if you load up on 20 to 40 grams of saturated fat in a meal, you could find all that fat leaves you feeling uncomfortable.

Choosing a fast-food restaurant with healthy options is important—not just for yourself, but for your family. Everyone with children or grandchildren knows how programmed they have become to wanting to eat at *their* favorite place. Advertising is extremely effective, especially with the younger set, and hard to counter.

Overdoses of saturated fat are not just a problem for those of us who have been around for a while. Fat is not good for children either. The more effective we are at helping them make better choices about food, the less plaque will be deposited in their coronary arteries.

Fortunately, many ice-cream shops and fast-food restaurants are offering good-tasting nonfat or lowfat frozen yogurt and frozen-yogurt shakes. It may take some selling and persuading on your part to get the children who are important to you to choose these healthier foods, but the effort could add years to their lives.

Lowfat Eating While Traveling

Eating while traveling provides interesting situations. When you're driving, it's usually possible to find a grocery market not far off the freeway. There are all kinds of fruits, vegetables, no-fat yogurt and lowfat deli items available for you to buy in a hurry to eat on the way.

If you are planning a cruise, most cruise lines offer magnificent dining-room menus and buffets. Have your travel agent phone, FAX or write for information on the lowfat menus that may be offered on the cruise you plan to take. Some cruise lines have listened to their passengers' requests and provide excellent lowfat choices for salads and entrées, often with calorie and fat counts right on the menu. Of course, there will be plenty of fried foods, entrées smothered in cream, butter and cheese sauces, as well as high-fat gourmet desserts. Even so, the menus and buffets almost always include delicious salads, fresh fruits and a wonderful assortment of other lowfat foods.

Some in-flight food service has been cut back to a bag of peanuts or pretzels and a soft drink, so you may want to take along a box lunch of some of your favorite lowfat foods. When you are traveling during the hours airlines serve meals, you may be given à la carte choices—especially at breakfast. Other times, the airlines will give you two choices for their prepared meals—as long as the choices last. All of these usually contain more fat than you'll want. Instead of leaving it to chance when you make airline reservations, ask your travel agent or airline representative if a meal is included on your flight. If so, order a low-fat, low-cholesterol meal when you book your ticket. If you travel much, your travel agent or frequent-flyer records can set up your account so lowfat meals are automatically ordered whenever you book a reservation.

Be sure to place your special meal requests several days before your flight or earlier when possible. It isn't reasonable to expect the airline to get a special meal on board for you if you think about it just before your flight. Each airline has its own rules for how much advance notice is needed to get a special meal on your plane. Although most airlines are helpful about getting you the kind of meal you want, there are times when it doesn't happen.

Once on the airplane, you may be asked to identify yourself so the stewardess will know who gets which special meal. Your name is on that tray. Although what you get won't be totally perfect, it will come much

Here are some airline special meal choices and the codes travel agents use to order them.

CODE	SPECIAL MEAL
AVML	Asian vegetarian
BLML	Bland
CHML	Child
DBML	Diabetic
FPLM	Fruit platter
LFML	Low-fat/Cholesterol
LPML	Low protein
GFML	Glutent-free
HFML	High fiber
HNML	Hindu
KSML	Kosher
LCML	Low calorie
LSML	Low sodium
MOML	Moslem
ORML	Oriental
NLML	No lactose
PRML	Low purine
RVML	Raw vegetable
SFML	Seafood
SPML	Special
VGML	Pure vegetarian
VLML	Vegetarian (Lacto)

closer to your lowfat eating plan than if you had not asked for a special meal. Even with your lowfat main course, expect a pat of butter, an ice-cream bar or a chocolate brownie to end up on your tray. Of course, you don't have to eat them.

Plan Ahead for Banquets and Special Meetings

There are other times when you may feel trapped into eating whatever is being served. You may be able to plan ahead for meals you will be served at events like meetings and banquets. Organizations are often able to provide specially requested meals. Depending upon the kind of event, ask the organizers what menu choices are available for people who need special meals.

If you arrive at a banquet event and the menu seems fixed, quietly ask a head waiter or supervisor if they can provide an alternate—such as a seafood, fruit or vegetable platter. Once a fatty meal is served, you can choose not to eat what is served or you can eat only a small portion. Choosing not to eat everything is hard for some of us who were taught to clean up our plates and not waste a thing. It is even harder when you are hungry and a big juicy steak is put in front of you. Refusing the meal, sending it back or just leaving it untouched may seem unthinkable. The question is: Is it more wasteful to eat something that will coat your coronary arteries with fat—or send it back to the kitchen uneaten?

Most of the time you really don't need to send it back. You can do very well by trimming off all the visible fat, pushing aside any rich sauce and eating a reasonable amount of the juicy steak. Cut very thin slices of the leanest part of the meat and eat tiny bites slowly. That way you'll get some enjoyment from the flavor, which will probably be pretty good. The vegetables, bread and salad will round out the meal. You don't have to eat everything that is served—even if this is what you were taught while you were growing up. When the dessert comes around, just assume that you'll probably refuse it unless it's something without much fat, such as raspberry sorbet.

Be imaginative. Apologies are never necessary. Of course, be appreciative—as you enjoy eating out. It can be fun without too much bad fat. Enjoy!

Should I Be Taking Aspirin, Antioxidants or Folic Acid?

Ask your doctor! Whether or not to take these common non-prescription medications in hopes of helping reduce the risk of a heart attack has been the subject of countless reports, studies and strongly opinionated articles. Before you finish reading an article extolling the benefits of one of these preparations, you'll see another article that concludes it is exactly the wrong thing to do.

The final answers are not available. Until they are, it is important to know what the controversies are about — and what the situation is as this book went to press. Even when apparently definitive evidence comes in, those conclusions may change. Keep asking your physician for guidance on what to do before you start *any* treatment regime or stop a treatment plan your physician has put you on.

Aspirin for Those at Risk

Let's start by talking about who should use aspirin to help decrease heart-attack risk. Those who are at high risk include:
- men over 50
- anyone with a cholesterol/HDL ratio over 4
  - a triglyceride level over 150
  - an LDL level over 130
- anyone with excessive weight
- anyone with high blood pressure
- people who smoke

Taking a low dose of aspirin regularly seems to lower the risk of little blood clots forming on the inside of coronary arteries narrowed by fat plaques.[1] Aspirin does not reduce cholesterol or triglycerides or help to clean out plaques that have formed. Aspirin's anti-clotting properties help keep dangerous blood clots from forming on the plaques in the coronary arteries.

A couple of possible problems must be recognized before deciding to take aspirin for any purpose. Some people are allergic to aspirin— extremely allergic. It isn't very common, but those who are allergic to aspirin can have a serious problem in taking even small amounts. The most common problem is swelling, often of the facial tissues. Swelling can also occur in the air passageway which can be fatal. Other aspirin allergies cause rashes and asthmatic wheezing.

Still another serious problem some have with low doses of aspirin is too much *thinning* of the blood. In other words, the normal benefit of aspirin, keeping the platelet cells from clumping together and clotting, is exaggerated so bleeding occurs. Sometimes this is a nosebleed. This bleeding can also cause easy *bruising,* even from minor bumps. This may be slight or quite severe. Aspirin can cause bleeding in the stomach or intestinal tract, which can be quite serious. In others, bleeding may occur from a tiny blood vessel in the brain, which is a *hemorrhagic stroke.*

Because aspirin can cause these and other problems, it is not something to take without thought. Someone with a bleeding tendency, or with a history of aspirin allergy, should not take it. Period.

What about those who don't have these problems or don't know if they do? As with every decision in medicine, this is a judgment call. Is the risk of taking the medicine greater than not taking it? Why, with all these possible problems, would anyone want to take aspirin to try to cut down on the risk of a heart attack that hasn't even happened?

There is good evidence that shows low doses of aspirin decrease a high-risk person's chance of a heart attack. This may be advisable if someone is not allergic to aspirin and does not have a bleeding tendency. At this point, this is not an *official* indication of the United States Food and Drug Administration (FDA).

Many medications are accepted as standard treatments without having official approval from the FDA. The reason is that if a medication has received FDA approval for treatment of one problem, it can be used for other indications without a new official FDA approval. New approvals cost drug companies tens of millions of dollars.

The best evidence that aspirin works to help prevent heart attacks comes from a 5-year study of 22,000 low-risk U.S physicians who took one aspirin every other day. Their heart attack rate decreased by 47%. That's impressive!

That's the aspirin story. If you fit into a high-risk group for a heart attack, do not have an allergy to aspirin or a bleeding problem, ask your physician if you should be on low-dose aspirin. If so, ask how much you should take and how often. If you do this, be sure to report any evidence of bruising, bleeding of any kind, headaches, swelling, difficulty breathing, wheezing, obvious asthma or ringing in your ears.

One more word about aspirin: Taking aspirin is not a substitute to get your cholesterol and triglycerides down, your blood pressure treated, your weight down or a good exercise program in place (without smoking, of course).

What about Antioxidants?

Antioxidants are compounds that seem to protect the lining of cell membranes from being attacked and *oxidized* by *free radicals*. That's terrific! What are free radicals?

Well, *free radicals* are sort of a garbage result of body metabolism. The chemistry is a process of oxidation—something like rusting metal. Fortunately, these free radicals are usually neutralized by normal body antioxidants. But, when an overload of free radicals occurs. they attack cell membranes and harmful LDL cholesterol is oxidized into a *killer* form of LDL. This killer LDL is even more harmful to the heart than ordinary LDL cholesterol, which is bad enough. Antioxidants seem to help block the damaging chain reactions that do this.

The big question is, do the good effects of blocking the production of killer LDL result from the antioxidants in these vegetables and fruits—or are they due to something else in them? We don't know for sure, but we have good reason to consider antioxidants as "good guys."

The interest in antioxidants in atherosclerosis began with studies of how the fat particles, particularly the LDL cholesterol, entered cells. In the beginning, LDL didn't seem to enter cells very rapidly. Only after LDL was oxidized did it go into these cells to produce a deposit of fat. Then we realized the importance of oxidation.

This is probably all you want to know about free-radicals, but hopefully you can see that antioxidants may help in decreasing the risk of heart attacks.

There is good evidence that eating lots of green leafy vegetables helps protect against heart attacks and maybe even some kinds of cancer. It just so happens that dark-green leafy vegetables like spinach and chard, yellow vegetables like carrots and squash and yellow fruits like cantaloupe and mango are filled with *carotinoids,* which is one kind of antioxidant. Carotinoids are red and yellow pigments with a chemical composition similar to carotene. Carotene is converted to vitamin A in the liver.

Citrus fruits, including oranges, lemons and grapefruit, dark-green vegetables like broccoli and asparagus, as well as potatoes, contain vitamin C (ascorbic acid), another antioxidant. Nuts, whole grains, oils from soybean, sunflower, corn and cottonseed contain vitamin E (alpha tocopherol), yet another antioxidant.

Do Vitamins and Supplements Help and Are They Safe?

If it is proved that antioxidants block the production of killer LDL, then taking supplements of some of these vitamins may be a very good idea. Anyone who is allergic to one of them should not take it, but allergies are unusual. There is always the possibility of another undesirable result from taking large doses of these vitamin supplements, even though they are generally regarded as ordinary and safe.

So, how do we know the answers to these questions: "Do they help?" and "Are they safe?" The answer is to do well designed and carefully controlled studies, some of which are under way. Unfortunately, the studies are not yet complete, so the results are not available.

"What about studies that have already been done?" you ask, remembering reading newspaper reports about various studies that attracted considerable attention in the media.

Vitamin E

Two earlier studies that seemed to show taking supplemental vitamin E protects both men and women from coronary-artery disease used data based on the diet histories of 87,245 female nurses[2] and 39,910 male health professionals.[3] It is important to point out that non-controlled diet-history studies, like these two, are among the weakest kinds of research from a scientific viewpoint. So, though these two studies seem impressive, they are *not* the final answer.

The Cambridge study took a big step in the direction of a definitive answer. In this study, people who had a heart attack were randomly assigned to take vitamin E—or not to take it. Although those in the study who took vitamin E didn't live any longer, the folks who took vitamin E had 77% fewer heart attacks. Think about it—77% fewer heart attacks! That's better than pretty good.

Here's the point: Some people think that something useful must decrease *death rates.* Of course we want to decrease death rates. If we can *reduce heart attacks,* that's a big benefit. Although everyone who has a heart attack doesn't die, everyone who has a heart attack is miserable. They spend a lot of time in intensive care. It's painful and costs lots of money. Besides that, everyone who has a heart attack is out of commission for a while. Many people who have a heart attack lose the ability to do things they like doing. Many end up in surgery. When a skeptic tries to convince you not to do healthy things because a certain study didn't prove a drop in *death rate,* don't be misled into thinking the strategy doesn't have some merit.

How do we get more evidence about the role of antioxidants in helping protect against heart disease?

We need larger, randomized, double-blind trials to protect us from all the potential biases that are so rampant in the diet-history studies. So far, only three carefully designed double-blind research studies have been done to see if taking these products really makes a difference. One of these—the ongoing Physicians' Health study (started in 1984)—included 22,000 physicians who were randomized to take aspirin, beta carotene, both or nothing. This trial showed that young, low-risk physicians (average age 49), who took one aspirin every other day, cut their heart attack rate 47% in five years. The beta-carotene part of the study was stopped because there was no change in health outcomes after 12 years.

Also, a National Cancer Institute study showed a *higher* death rate among smokers (and people who just quit smoking) who had been taking beta carotene. So, even though it seemed for a while that people at risk should be taking beta-carotene supplements, we don't think they should.

We do need to eat plenty of rich yellow vegetables and fruits such as carrots, squash, cantaloupes and mangos to get the antioxidants that are helpful without causing other problems.

No one should expect vitamins to solve all their problems. This is the flaw in many well-intended but misguided programs in which huge doses of vitamins are given. It's never a good idea to listen to those who say, "Take this big dose of vitamins, a magic bullet, which will cure you." This is exactly the wrong way to use vitamins. Treating high-risk people *only* with vitamins is not good medicine.

In other words, antioxidant vitamin supplements may play a helpful role in preventing heart attacks. We repeat: *They may.* Vitamins are not going to help reduce coronary-artery disease in people who keep smoking and eating fat-laden foods.

It is also very difficult to interpret what some so-called studies are reported to prove. When seemingly sensational study conclusions are reduced to a sound bite on the six o'clock news or to a few inches of copy in your daily paper, it is easy to see how people become misled and confused. It's hard enough to know for sure about these study results when you are looking at all the data.

Preventing Coronary Disease

What do we know for sure about preventing coronary-artery disease? The most important things for anyone to do who wants to beat the odds of a heart attack are to carefully limit the bad fat they eat, to exercise, to not smoke and to do whatever else it takes to get cholesterol and triglycerides under control.

This still doesn't answer the question about the value of antioxidants. After a treatment plan is underway, what about the antioxidants?

Eating seven to eight servings of fruit and vegetables a day will supply most of the needed vitamins. The benefits may be from vitamin E and vitamin C or something else. Right now it seems that, in addition to a good solid medical program to lower cholesterol and triglycerides, it may be helpful for people at high risk to take extra vitamin E and vitamin C. There seems to be enough evidence that they may help without much risk.

Anyone who takes these antioxidant vitamins should know they are *not* a substitute for controlling cholesterol and triglycerides with a low-fat diet and medications. In other words, don't expect vitamins to be a "magic bullet."

Ask your doctor if you should be taking antioxidants. If so, how much? While we don't have a final answer as to how much vitamin E is the right dose, if it should be given, a recent study seems to show the optimal amount may be 400 international units a day.

The question is what can you do now, before the answers are in? If someone tells you to eat lots of vegetables and fruits and forget the supplements, that may be right. On the other hand, there are some strong clues that antioxidant supplements may provide some valuable help to those at risk.

What about Folic Acid to Counter Homocysteine?

One more bad substance that can increase the risk of coronary arteries becoming plugged is *homocysteine.* People who don't get enough folate to metabolize harmful homocysteine have three times the risk of a heart attack as those who do.[4]

Evidence from the Framingham Study showed that the higher the level of homocysteine in the body, the greater the risk of blockage in a person's carotid arteries. That's a strong indication that there is also blockage in the coronary arteries.[4,5] Folic acid is a B-complex vitamin found abundantly in dark-green leafy vegetables such as chard, spinach and romaine lettuce, and dry beans, peanuts, wheat germ, whole grains and yeast.

Recent reports indicated that some pregnant women in the United States are not getting sufficient folic acid in what they eat. This insufficiency is resulting in tragic occurrences of neural-tube (spina bifida) and other defects, such as cleft palate, in some babies. The good news is that these defects have sharply decreased as women of childbearing age have been given supplemental folic acid along with their prenatal vitamins. Because the eating habits of men and women in our culture are pretty much the same, the lack of enough dietary folic acid in our culture is almost certainly not limited to women.

Should You Take Vitamins and Other Supplements?

There's no question that it's a good idea to eat dark-green vegetables, dried beans, whole-wheat and the other basic wholesome foods we've been talking about. But what about supplements? It usually makes sense to wait for conclusive evidence before starting to take a medication—even a vitamin or other so-called *natural* supplement.

To date, there are only two well-controlled trials showing benefits for vitamin E at 400 iu (international units) and selenium at 200µg (micrograms). Vitamin E lowers ordinary heart disease and selenium protects against breast, colon and prostate cancers.

In this instance, there is a legitimate argument that the possible benefit of taking these antioxidant supplements may outweigh the risk of taking them. We caution that this line of reasoning is usually unwise even though we all hope that these supplements will be helpful in reducing the odds of a heart attack. There is good reason to believe that folic acid is a helpful part of heart insurance.

So, should you be taking supplemental folic acid, vitamin E and/or vitamin C? Ask your physician. Taking extra vitamin E or vitamin C is *not* a substitute for getting your cholesterol down, your blood pressure down, your exercise down and not smoking. Be sure to eat seven to eight servings of fruit and vegetables every day. Include a plentiful variety of dark-green and yellow vegetables—particularly apples, pears, cantaloupes and mangos and yellow and orange fruits like oranges and other citrus. You can make dried beans, whole-wheat and the other basic wholesome foods we've been talking about a regular part of your eating choices.

NOTES

1. Steering Committee of the Physicians' Health Study Research Group: Preliminary report: findings from the aspirin component of the ongoing Physicians' Health Study. *N Engl J Med*, 1988, 318(4):262-264.

2. Stampfer, M.J., Hennekens, C.H., Manson, J.E., et al: Vitamin E consumption and the risk of coronary artery disease in women. *N Engl J Med*, 1993, 328(20):1444-1449.

3. Rimm, E.B., Stampfer, M.J., Ascherio, A., et al: Vitamin E consumption and the risk of coronary heart disease in men. *N Engl J Med*, 1994, 328(20):1450-1456.

4. Forty percent of the people in Framingham have elevated levels of homocysteine which seems to be associated with a very low intake of folic acid and vitamin B-6. These people also have significant deposits of plaque in their carotid arteries as visualized on ultrasound studies which strongly suggests they also have considerable plaque formation in their coronary arteries.

5. Selhub, J., Jacques, P.F., Boston, A.G., D'Agostino, R.B., Wilson, P.W.F., Belanger, A.J., O'Leary, D.H., Wolf, P.A., Rosenberg, I.H. Association between plasma homocysteine concentrations and extracranial carotid artery stenosis, *N Engl J Med*, 332, 1995, p. 286.

What If I'm Putting on Weight?

"I've been eating very little bad fat these past few years like you've been recommending and I've still gained a lot of weight. Why?" he wanted to know.

Good question!

We live in the first country in the world where people eating a low-fat diet are gaining weight!

Why is this happening? There are three possibilities—all a matter of eating more calories than are being burned off by exercise. Probably two and maybe three of these things are going on.

Number 1: Lack of Exercise

More exercise is needed. How much? As much it takes to burn up the calories. The amount of exercise needed changes from time to time and depends on how many calories are consumed. This is one reason why someone eating a relatively small amount of saturated fat may be gaining weight. Unfortunately, it's an unfair trade-off. Walking 1 mile uses up 100 kilocalories, but most of us cannot walk, run, swim, bike or dance as far (or as easily!) as we can eat.

Number 2: Overdoing Refined Carbohydrates

The second possibility a person eating a small amount of saturated fat may be gaining weight is filling up on carbohydrates, especially sugar and other refined carbohydrates. How could this be? You take in 9 calories for every gram of fat you eat and only 4 calories for every gram of carbohydrates. Thus, gram for gram, you get a lot fewer calories from eating carbohydrates than fat.

COMPLEX CARBOHYDRATES

By complex carbohydrates, we mean fresh fruits, vegetables, legumes and whole grains such as apples, bananas, mangoes, melons, peaches, pears, prunes, raisins, potatoes, yams, rice, corn, oats, beans and wheat.

These contain various healthful carbohydrate chains. Simple sugars and starches, when eaten in excess, add calories and may actually raise your LDL cholesterol and triglyceride levels. That is exactly what you don't want to happen.

It would seem that cutting down on saturated fat would make it easy to trim down on your weight. This can occur—and often does. Gram for gram, fat is more filling. So, when someone goes on a lowfat diet, it is not difficult to quite innocently start eating more and more carbohydrates, even those we consider particularly healthy *complex carbohydrates.*

The big problem is eating foods loaded with sugar and other refined carbohydrates, such as refined white flour. Why? Because it's easier to eat more calories from these refined carbohydrates than it is to eat too many calories from naturally occurring complex carbohydrates. The reason is that sugar and refined carbohydrates are not as filling as complex carbohydrates.

Number 3: Eating More Unsaturated Fat

The third possibility in a case where a person is eating less saturated fat and still gaining weight is they are eating more unsaturated fat than they realize. As far as calories are concerned, fat is fat and calories are calories.

Each gram of unsaturated fat contributes 9 calories, just like saturated fat. Saturated fat is responsible for the fat deposits in the lining of your coronary arteries. The unsaturated fat doesn't do this. The unsaturated fat contributes calories, as do carbohydrates. Unless you use them up in your daily activities and exercise, you *will* put on pounds. What doesn't seem fair is that you can eat lots of calories in seemingly healthful foods such as fat-free bread, potatoes, pasta—and even fruit. As everyone knows, extra weight causes a long list of problems.

Most people should probably be eating around 1800 to 2000 calories a day—or less—just enough to keep you at a healthy weight and activity level. If you are at a healthy weight and activity level, are not gaining weight and do not have diabetes or other problems that make counting calories important, don't worry about counting calories. If there is a reason to be concerned about your weight, you will need to count them.

How many calories you need depends on many factors, including:

• Is your present weight about right for you?
• Is it too much or too little?
• Have you been gaining, losing or staying about the same?

Another factor is whether you do quiet sedentary work or are the hardest-working lumberjack in the world. What about the weather where you are working or expending energy? Is it very cold where you spend most of your time, relatively comfortable or is it extremely hot? People who consistently do heavy work in cold weather require more calories and more fat than sedentary folks do in hot weather.

Are you large or small?

Are you male or female?

These are important questions if you want to know how many calories you should be consuming. There are also other variables, including genetic reasons, some people have a much more difficult time controlling weight than others. The ability or inability to control weight is often one of those things in life that doesn't seem quite fair.

The bottom line here is pretty simple. For whatever reason, if someone is too heavy or is gaining too much weight, the answer comes down to *calories.*

If you follow our plan of limiting the saturated fat you eat to 20 grams or less a day, are careful about not eating too much good unsaturated fat, eat lots of fruits and vegetables and a reasonable amount of grains and legumes and if you stay on a good exercise program, chances are good that you won't put on weight. In fact, if you do all these things carefully, you may be able to trim down a bit if you need to.

So, as you reduce the amount of fats you eat, take advantage of the fact that you get rid of 9 calories with each gram of fat you cut out. As with any healthful change in lifestyle, it is important to be able to reward yourself pleasantly for things you are giving up. We suggest rewarding yourself with lots of really good fruits and veggies. Use good sense. Be sure you get a good variety of these, along with other complex carbohydrates in legumes and grains. At the same time, don't eat too much sugar, baked goods, pasta made with refined flour and other things that will run up your calorie count.

Whole grains such as whole-wheat, oats and brown rice provide more satisfaction than simple refined carbohydrates. This is probably one of the main reasons few people are overweight in societies where these wholesome whole grains are a major part of the diet.

Do I Have to Jog— Or Use One of Those *Exercise* Machines?

"Do I really have to jog?"

No.

In fact, many healthy people never run marathons. They are not big-time runners—and don't even jog.

If you are into running, that's terrific. If you hate the idea of running around the neighborhood, there are lots of other ways to get plenty of exercise. You don't even need to use an exercise machine.

You don't *have* to exercise.

You don't *have* to do anything.

If you want to get and keep control of your cholesterol levels, feel the best and take care of your heart, there is no way to do it without regular, vigorous exercise.

Who knows, you might find it is refreshing to let your feet and legs get you around your neighborhood every morning. You may find that getting back to nature on a running trail gives you time to get away from the rat race and to think. You can do either of these things without running at all. *Walking* can provide all the exercise you need—without ever jogging or running.

If you are already walking, jogging, working out at a health-and-fitness club or doing some other regular aerobic exercise, great! Keep it up! If not, don't be intimidated by the word *exercise*.

After getting a thorough medical checkup, get started on a program of walking, swimming, using a good exercise machine or doing an equivalent amount of vigorous physical work every day. Begin slowly, adding a little each day, rather than suddenly beginning an immediate intensive training program as if you were trying to be an Olympic athlete.

There is a definite correlation between controlling your cholesterol and vigorous aerobic exercise. One of the most difficult parts of trying to get cholesterol numbers in control is to increase HDL. Vigorous exercise helps boost HDL, which is important. As HDL (the healthy cholesterol) goes up, the bad cholesterol (LDL and VLDL) is picked up out of the cells and dumped—so the bad-cholesterol levels go down. In fact, "most experts believe that HDL levels can be increased by at least 10% to 20% with a regular exercise program."[1] Regular exercise is needed to accomplish this.

We are not suggesting that you run marathons or even jog. We hope you will choose a sensible exercise program to do 6 times a week, equivalent to walking vigorously 2 miles a day—unless there is a specific medical reason you cannot do so.

Many people have fun getting exercise while playing, but there is *play* and then there is *play*. Sitting around on a beach doesn't do it. Neither do activities like croquet. We are talking about sports that rev up your body like a fast game of basketball, volleyball or tennis.

Even if you are not into sports, exercise doesn't always have to be something that is done just to be exercising. Many people prefer to accomplish something while they are exercising rather than just running or walking around a track. You may find yourself using the time you are walking, riding an exercise bike, jogging or whatever, as productive *thinking time.* Some folks rig up some kind of reading stand so they can read while they use their exercise bike, treadmill or other workout machine.

Others catch up on the news on television while their bodies are getting in shape. Many people reward themselves for exercising by watching a movie or something else entertaining during their exercise time. You've probably seen others listening to motivational tapes, audio books or music as they walk or run through the park or around the block.

The point is that aerobic exercise does not have to be meaningless work like a rat running on a treadmill. Of course, the benefits of the exercise are not meaningless to the rat's heart. In case you think you are too busy or that doing these things to keep in shape is boring, it doesn't have to be.

If you want to do constructive things like farming, heavy gardening, chopping wood or something else you feel is more productive than walking or running just to be moving your body vigorously, great! You may decide to walk to work or to the market—and save gas, bus fare or subway tokens. The bottom line is don't fail to do some vigorous exercise every day because you can't stand to do something you think is dull. On the other hand, if you want to walk somewhere and just enjoy the beauty of nature, that's your call, too.

How much vigorous exercise do you need? Probably a lot more than you are getting. The exact amount depends on your age, health and other circumstances. Begin your increased activity with guidance from your doctor after a good checkup. Wherever you go everyday to get your mail probably isn't enough—unless you have a very long hall or driveway.

As you think about doing some walking every day, which is one of the best and easiest exercise programs to get into, you may simply want to plan on walking to places you already need to go. Or you may want to ride to a park or mall and then walk through or around it. Lots of people mall-walk every day. Some malls open up earlier than their shops for organized *mall-walking* programs, especially for seniors. Getting together with friends to walk around a mall every day can be a very pleasant social event.

When it's -60F in Minnesota, you'll see lots of folks walking briskly and others a bit slower, around the massive Mall of America. For most people, this is much more healthful than to be outside running or walking when it's cold. It doesn't have to be the Mall of America. Others in Minneapolis and St. Paul walk in the mornings or at lunchtime throughout the intricate skyway systems that connect dozens of downtown buildings. You don't have to go to Minnesota for interesting malls or places to walk. It doesn't have to be really cold for mall-walking to be a good idea. When it's really hot in Phoenix or Houston, Fort Lauderdale or Los Angeles, mall-walking can be a refreshing change of environment which can help make exercise more enjoyable.

There are interesting places to walk wherever you are and ways you can change your habit patterns so you can get the exercise that will help your heart in many ways, including bumping up your HDL.

If you drive to work or the market, you may choose to park farther away, rather than close to where you are going. Sound crazy? Maybe so, but changing from a boring routine might be fun. Spaces in parking lots that are farthest away are more likely to be available. Because others may not want to park so far away, you'll probably see fewer nicks in your car doors!

Another way you may want to build exercise into your daily routine is to use stairs instead of riding elevators. Some people pay a lot of money for a stair-climbing machine. That's OK, especially if you park it in front of your television. If you work or live in a building with more than one level or even in a home with just a single flight of stairs, you already have your exercise machine. You may simply want to take the stairs to where you are going instead of the elevator. Or, if your floor is too high to climb all the way, take the elevator part-way and climb the rest.

Even if there is only a flight or two of stairs in your home or apartment building, you can go up and down that flight as often as is appropriate. Maybe even more important than starting a walking program is to start easy and work up. As you will find, this is because you will really put your body through a workout, especially as you go up many stairs. In proper doses, this may be exactly what you need. Just use good sense and have fun.

What you do for your own exercise program is really up to you. You could do absolutely nothing. Like everything about the program we've been talking about to help you decrease the risks of a heart attack, this is something no one can make you do. We hope you will take seriously the need to get your body moving.

Once you decide to get your body moving, the next thing is to decide to do it regularly—and then to keep it up. Exercise needs to be more than a token effort. If you are a healthy adult, we recommend gradually and wisely increasing your activity enough to push you more than you think you want to be pushed right now. Plan on going up and down lots of stairs, taking some interesting walks, doing some vigorous exercise-bike pedaling or tough physical work.

It doesn't really matter whether you choose walking, biking, swimming, working out on an exercise machine or working—just so you accomplish sufficient vigorous activity almost every day.

Although everywhere you turn, there is a new study telling you how much or how little exercise you must have, we think the most sensible program is to exercise vigorously 6 days a week, for at least 30 minutes a day, unless there is a medical reason you can't. Take a day or maybe two days off—but not much more.

Some research seems to show that exercising 3 or 4 days a week is adequate, but some convincing recent studies show that vigorous exercise 5 days a week is much more effective in raising HDL levels than exercising just 3 days a week. In the Harvard Alumni Study, walking 2 miles a day, 7 days a week, produced the highest protection against getting a heart attack or dying. It is also encouraging to know that keeping up a reasonable walking pace seems to be just as helpful in boosting HDL levels as fast walking.[2]

Then there is the matter of *staying* on a program. We have found, as most people have, that we are much more likely to exercise if we do it every day—at least every weekday—than if we try to remember doing it 3 times a week or every other day. Our suggestion is to decide what you are going to do to get your body moving and then to do it as part of your daily life, 6 days a week.

NOTES

1. Gibbons, L.W., Mitchell, T.L. HDL cholesterol and exercise. *Your Patient & Fitness,* July-August 95, pps. 6-13.
2. Duncan, J.J., Gordon, N.F., Scott, C.B. Women walking for health and fitness, how much is enough? *JAMA* 1991 (226)23:3295-3299.

Other Problems with Controlling Cholesterol

The line-up of genes each of us has might be thought of like the line-up of a baseball team. Each individual player has specific strengths and weaknesses. For the most part, the players are predictable in what they will do over a period of time.

The genes we inherit from our parents have specific strengths and weaknesses. We can often predict problems a person will have with his or her body, depending on the line-up of these genes. Unfortunately, you may get a gene that is going to cause you a lot of problems—such as not having enough LDL receptors to manage this harmful cholesterol. Someone with this genetic pattern has *familial hypercholesterolemia.*

As we've talked about, when we eat too much saturated fat and trans-fatty acids, our bodies make cholesterol. People with normal LDL receptors can handle some of this lousy cholesterol, but may have a problem if they continue to eat large amounts of saturated fat, as most people do in our culture. We are concerned about you whether or not you have familial defects in your genes that prevent your body from controlling cholesterol or triglycerides. That's why we think families should go on our bad-fat budget program together—not just people who are in an especially high-risk group.

A few people do inherit genes from their parents that make controlling cholesterol and triglycerides extremely difficult. Even though they limit the bad fat and cholesterol they eat, exercise regularly and don't smoke, they may not be able to get their cholesterol or triglycerides into a safe range. They may have a lipid disorder (i.e., a cholesterol or triglyceride problem where the total cholesterol, LDL cholesterol or triglyceride is too high for their HDL cholesterol).

What can someone like this do? We can't choose new parents. Even though some breakthroughs are occurring in genetic engineering, for now we are stuck with the genes they gave us. It's mind-boggling to think about the millions of possible combinations of genetic traits that each of us has after chromosomes have paired up from our own parents, each of their parents, and each of their parents and so on. Some inherited traits determine whether we have brown eyes, blue, hazel or some other color. Some traits are dominant, others are recessive. Some traits give us big advantages in strength or other various physical characteristics. Still others give major weaknesses or defects, such as certain kinds of blindness, deafness, diabetes or muscular dystrophy. Others get genes that make it difficult to control cholesterol and triglycerides.

The good news is that if we happened to get genes that cause diabetes, we can do something about it. By regulating what is eaten, exercising and taking insulin and/or medications to help control the high blood sugar, someone with diabetes can usually attain excellent control. So most people with diabetes can live happy lives without the worry of blindness, premature death and other serious problems that uncontrolled diabetes often cause.

What if you picked out some really great parents, who happened to pass on a genetic trait of not enough LDL receptors or a disorder that makes your triglycerides go up like crazy when you eat a little fat? Just as diabetes can be controlled with insulin, a person who can't process fat can be helped with medications. Which medication is chosen depends on the particular problem a person has in handling fatty acids.

Almost everyone with a cholesterol over 300 or triglycerides over 400 has an inherited tendency to over-manufacture these fats or an inability to control their production. Others who don't have levels nearly this high also may have a dangerous familial problem. Low-fat diets alone are not enough to reduce and control harmful cholesterol and triglyceride levels in these people. They almost always need medications.

Even so, every plan to control high cholesterol and triglycerides levels must be built on a solid foundation of an ongoing low-bad-fat diet.

Exercise is also extremely important.

It is absolutely necessary not to smoke.

Close monitoring of elevated total cholesterol, LDL, a high cholesterol/HDL ratio, low HDL levels and/or triglycerides by an interested and informed physician is important.

Medications to Control Cholesterol and Triglycerides

Let's talk about some medications used to control abnormal levels of cholesterol and triglycerides. If you need a medication, you want the best choice and right dosage for you. In general, your doctor should start with the lowest dose of any medicine after a good trial of diet and exercise has failed to bring your numbers to the goal of therapy.

In someone without vascular disease this goal is an LDL choles terol less than 130 (3.4), a total cholesterol/HDL cholesterol ratio of under 4 and a triglyceride of under 150 (1.7). In someone with known clinical vascular disease the goal is LDL cholesterol under 100 (2.6) and a triglyceride under 100 (1.1). The typical heart-attack victim or bypass patient will usually make it to the goal of therapy with just a pill or two of the current medicines.

Your medical and family history, risk factors, what cholesterol- and triglyceride-controlling medications have or have not done for you up till now all need to be considered. So do your past and present levels of HDL, LDL, triglycerides and cholesterol/HDL ratio. And you want someone to monitor you who has experience with the benefits, limitations and side effects of the different medications.

NIACIN

Niacin (nicotinic acid) was one of the first medications used in helping to control high levels of cholesterol. It's still one of the useful players in the lipid-medication line-up, especially when triglycerides are high and/or HDL is very low. Even though niacin is an over-the-counter medication, never consider taking niacin as a "do-it-yourself" project.

Although niacin should probably be used more often than it is (especially as a second drug), we don't think anyone should take it unless a physician supervises its use. Why? Niacin has side effects, as does every medication ever created. Once in a while niacin may raise blood-sugar levels and uric acid. These side effects can be an even bigger problem for those with diabetes, gout, gallbladder or liver disease.

As helpful as niacin often is, almost everyone who takes it has a problem with flushing (which feels like burning skin) and hot flashes when the medication is first started and gradually increased.

It may also cause itching. It usually occurs with the first doses and disappears by the third day. It comes back if you skip a day. It will not hurt you and old niacin-takers are used to this sort of thing. An aspirin, even a baby aspirin, taken a half hour before taking the niacin greatly diminishes these flushes.

There is also the matter of choosing between short-acting and sustained-release niacin. The direct-acting niacin or regular niacin is less toxic to the liver than most of the sustained-release niacin. But the sustained-release niacin causes much less flushing, burning or itching. Doses over 2 grams a day usually lead to liver-enzyme changes.

Niacin was the first drug to lead to a lower death rate and it has been used for over 30 years with an excellent safety record. Rare persons may develop jaundice on niacin. Although this is completely reversible, it tells you they cannot take niacin.

GEMFIBROZIL (Lopid®)

Gemfibrozil became a major player in lipid control after it reduced heart attacks 71% in the Helsinki Heart Study. Gemfibrozil is useful when triglycerides are high and the HDL is low. It is often prescribed for patients with high blood-sugar or high uric-acid levels. Because familial cholesterol or triglyceride disorders (especially types III, IV and V) are often difficult to control, it is quite common for persons with these problems to be given a combination of gemfibrozil and niacin or gemfibrozil and atorvastatin.

Side effects are rather uncommon, but can include minor gastrointestinal symptoms such as gas and/or loose stools, especially if relatively high doses are necessary. A few people have rashes or gallstones (if they cheat on the diet) and even fewer have muscle cramps or inflammation—particularly if used with lovastatin.

Unlike niacin, gemfibrozil does not raise the blood sugar or the uric acid in people with syndrome X. It also blunts the rise of blood sugar and uric acid produced by niacin when it is taken with gemfibrozil.

STATINS: CERIVASTATIN (Baycol®), ATORVASTATIN (Lipitor®), FLUVASTATIN (Lescol®), PRAVASTATIN (Pravachol®), SIMVASTATIN (Zocor®), LOVASTATIN (Mevacor®)

Statins lower LDL cholesterol the best of any drugs we have and are especially useful when there is high LDL with high triglycerides.

These drugs have added a new dimension to our understanding of the benefits of lowering cholesterol. They have been used in large clinical trials. The Scandinavian Simvastatin Survival Study (called 4S) was done in 4444 men and women living in Scandinavia who had just had a heart attack. Half were given simvastatin (Zocor) and the other half were not. Simvastatin lowered the total death rate 30%, the heart-attack death rate 42% and the bypass and angioplasty rate 37% in just five years. And the non-cardiovascular deaths fell 6%. This study effectively put to rest the cholesterol critics' claim that lowering cholesterol did not prolong life and that it caused increases in the non-cardiac deaths from suicide accidents and cancer.

Similar data came from studies using pravastatin in the West of Scotland Study. This study included people free of vascular disease, but who were at high risk because of abnormal cholesterol levels. Results: total death rate fell 22%, coronary heart disease rates fell 31%, the non-cardiovascular deaths fell 11% and like the 4S study the angioplasty and bypass surgery rates fell 37%.

Persons taking statins must have regular liver-function tests because these medications may cause liver-function abnormalities.

With a better diet and exercise along with these medicines, people who have particularly bad genes for cholesterol can now expect to live out better-than-average lives. These drugs also allow us to provide people who have had a heart attack with the realistic expectation of reversing their lesions in the next several years.

CHOLESTYRAMINE (Questran®)
These bile-acid-binding resins were the first cholesterol-controlling medications other than niacin. They are available in tablets and packets of resin granules to be dissolved in juice. The most common side effects constipation, increased gas or nausea. They sometimes cause triglycerides to go up instead of down and can interfere with or enhance the

effects of other drugs. The bile-acid-binding resins are often the best drugs to use when total cholesterol and LDL levels are very high.

COLESTIPOL (Colestid®)

This resin is supplied in tablets or packets to be dissolved in juice or water. With many of the same benefits and disadvantages of cholestyramine, it maybe tolerated better by some patients.

These two resins, cholestyramine and colestipol, are among the safest drugs. They go in one end and come out the other without being absorbed (blocking the absorption of cholesterol by your intestine and lowering your serum cholesterol). They act like a million little sponges in your intestine, absorbing the cholesterol. Of the cholesterol you excrete from your body, 95% comes out of the liver, down the bile duct and into your intestine. Without these drugs a large proportion is reabsorbed and put back into your blood.

Summary

These medications and others that will be developed provide a way to help lower high levels of damaging LDL cholesterol and triglycerides. They can help to increase the good HDL cholesterol, especially in those people with a familial lipid disorder.

However, one should never rely on these or any other medication to be *the* magic answer. These medications should never be used— and we mean *never*—without faithfully limiting the amount of saturated fat and cholesterol that is eaten. A person should never think that once one (or a combination) of these medications is started that he or she can go back to eating more saturated fat—or smoking. It is also important to know that these medications cannot take the place of exercise.

Remember, we're talking about *your* life—or the life of someone close to you. You have a playbook that can help you win.

How Risky Is Smoking?

You probably already know that smoking causes heart disease, lung cancer and emphysema. Smoking is very risky. If you smoke, you've probably quit or tried to quit several times. Quitting isn't easy—that's a known fact!

If you are thinking about cutting down the risks of a heart attack, one very important thing you can do is stop smoking. Smoking is one of the biggest controllable risk factors for coronary-artery disease. Why is that so important to know? Some risk factors we can't change, such as those dictated by our genes. Smoking is 100% controllable. By getting rid of a smoking habit, you can significantly increase your chances of living longer without a heart attack.

It's important to manage controllable risk factors or get rid of them completely, because most of us have risk factors we *can't* control that influence our health. Being male is a risk factor for heart attack, but those of us who are males can't change it. Diabetes and high blood pressure are two conditions you can manage effectively, but can't completely eliminate.

There are two risk factors that people *can* completely change: Being overweight and smoking. Both are difficult to get rid of, but it can be done. How do you lose weight or stop smoking?

The general principle is the same: Making the decision to quit, setting a date and then following through. Some people quit smoking or overeating cold-turkey, on the spot. This is absolutely terrific. Others build up courage and confidence by setting a date on the calendar and then looking ahead to making the change at that time, sometimes tapering down little by little in a controlled way.

Knowing that quitting smoking or losing weight is difficult to do, we encourage you to do so. Get all the help you need. When you quit smoking, the benefits begin immediately. You feel better, your senses of smell and taste are pleasantly enhanced, your lungs work more efficiently and your heart will be healthier in the long run.[2]

So, if you smoke, please quit. As an incentive, think of something you really want and save your "smoking" money for it. It's not just money you'll save by stopping smoking. It will be one of the best presents you can give your heart—and yourself. Go for it!

How to Quit Smoking

You can do it. You really can.

You may be wondering how that is possible, especially if you have been thinking about quitting already and have tried to do something about it so many times before.

First, you must want to quit—*really* want to quit. No one else can make someone who smokes quit. You know that. The important thing is to know that you *can.*

The next thing to do is set a date. So grab your calendar, your planner book or your computer appointment file. Just zero in on a day that looks good to you and enter "I QUIT." Some people find it helps to choose a personally meaningful day on which to quit, such as a birthday, holiday or anniversary. Others join the millions who quit on the American Lung Association's "Great American Smoke-out" day, which occurs every November.

Now you've picked a day on which to quit. What next? There are several routes you can take to reach your quitting-smoking goal. You might want to get help from one of the support groups that help smokers quit every day. Your local hospital or managed-care organization may host a group that gets together every week to help people quit smoking. Or you may want to call the American Heart Association or the American Lung Association—both of which have great programs to help people quit this expensive, damaging habit.

One good thing about joining a quit-smoking program is that there is strength in numbers. It helps to have others there who are facing the same tough problem. You may not need a group. You may be able to do it on your own. If so, that's fine, too.

Even if you're going to do it by yourself, it really helps to let people around you know that you've decided to quit and when. Just telling a spouse, friends and co-workers increases the success rate. As soon as you've set a date, tell everyone around your place your "I quit" day.

One person you might want to share your goal with is your doctor.

It will make his or her day. Knowing one of our patients is going to quit smoking truly makes us happy. It's better than being taken out to lunch! Besides making your doctor happy, you may get some extra help and encouragement.

You've heard about nicotine patches and nicotine gum, and maybe know someone who has used them. You absolutely cannot smoke while you are using them. Nicotine patches don't always work; at least, not the first time. But they can help you wind down from the habit. Although some studies are a little negative about the success rates quitting using nicotine patches, keep in mind that this includes a lot of folks who may have been pushed into using them by someone else and who didn't really start out being motivated themselves.

Recent studies show that a person's chances of stopping smoking with the help of nicotine patches depends on what happens on the first day. You are ten times more likely to fail if you smoke on the first day of trying to stop with the help of a nicotine patch.

We would like to see you "go for it" and look into *all* the ways you might successfully quit smoking. The more things you have going for you, the better. Try to get into a clinic or a class or group sponsored by the American Heart Association or the American Lung Association. Ask your doctor to help you start a nicotine-patch program and get involved in the audiovisual or phone-feedback assistance that these programs provide. We suggest you do all of these or as many as you can.

What if you've tried before but didn't quite make it? Well, almost no one wins all the time. More and more smokers are becoming non-smokers. Since 1965, there has been more than a 32% drop in the number of people in the U.S. who smoke. That's a lot of ex-smokers!

Most people who really want to quit smoking *are successful*—but it may take four or five serious attempts to quit before success is achieved. Each time a person tries to quit and fails, he or she learns a little more about "triggers" (the things that cause them to start smoking again) and how to avoid them the next time. If you've tried before and didn't make it, don't give up. You can do it. Right now is a wonderful time to try again. You certainly have an excellent reason to quit, don't you? After all, we're talking about your heart and your lungs, too.

So, you can quit. And you can do it now.

While you are looking forward to your "I quit" day, be sure not to stock up on cigarettes. When you think about buying more cigarettes, buy a supply of chewing gum in your favorite flavors. When you have tossed that last empty pack of cigarettes and actually "go for the gold," having gum in your pocket or purse or around places you are likely to be (bedroom, kitchen, office, car) will help you.

Then when your "I quit" day comes, do it. Quit!

Use your nicotine patches or nicotine gum. Use your support groups. Look at yourself in the mirror as often as necessary and identify yourself as a nonsmoker. Then, of course, sit in nonsmoking sections of restaurants and other places. When friends light up, find a quick reason to be somewhere else and get there in a hurry.

Well, congratulations, non-smoker!

Think about how good your heart feels and your lungs, brain and nose, too! You're probably smelling and tasting things you haven't smelled or tasted for a while. But what are you going to do when your friends try to get you to light up, you feel stressed out, you want to smoke after a meal, or. . . ?

You can count on all of these things happening. Just plan on how to handle them when they do. Will these encounters be easy? Of course not. But can you do it? Well, it's up to you.

Decide in advance what you're going to do instead of smoking when you are under all kinds of pressure. You can give up or you can stick to your goal and win. You may end up chewing a lot of gum. You may end up making a lot of phone calls to someone who has been through the quitting process successfully. You may even decide to go for long walks or some runs in the clear, fresh air.

So give yourself a present—a more healthful life. From that one gift, you'll find that *not* smoking bestows all kinds of other rewards.

Remember—you are a nonsmoker now.

NOTES

1. It should be emphasized that anyone with high blood pressure, who needs medications to control it, must continue the medication and the entire control program even if he or she feels just fine—because high blood pressure is not something a person can "feel" and know is present.

2. We would strongly recommend getting assistance in getting rid of a smoking habit or in overcoming an overeating problem. Excellent support groups are available for both. For those who would like help in quitting a smoking habit, the American Heart Association and the American Lung Association both provide helpful classes and support groups.

Alcohol and Your Heart

There have been many claims in the press about the miracles that red wine or other forms of alcohol can have in preventing heart attacks. This fulfills our desire to have the magic bullet—or in this case the magic potion—that we take and then we can eat, smoke or do anything we like and still not get a heart attack.

It is time to sober up on the alcohol question. The largest study in the world on alcohol was conducted in the United States by the American Cancer Society. It showed that one drink (one can of beer, one 4-ounce glass of wine or one shot of whiskey taken straight or in a cocktail) lowered the heart-attack rate as well as 2, 3, 4, 5 or 6 drinks. At one drink, the cancer rate and total death rate are lower. At two drinks, the cancer rate is the same as nondrinkers, and both total death and heart-disease death are lower. At three drinks, cancer death is increased. At four drinks, total death and cancer death is increased.

Should we all take one drink a day, *just for medicinal purposes?*

The jury is still out. We know from studies of orphans in Sweden and Iowa that the orphans of alcoholics become alcoholics themselves at four times the rate of nonalcoholics. This evidence suggests that there are potent genetic forces that either predispose you to alcohol abuse or protect you from it. There are people who can't drink even one alcoholic beverage without becoming addicted to alcohol. There are also marked racial differences. People from Asia, who metabolize alcohol differently, are generally unable to tolerate alcohol because it causes them to flush in an uncomfortable way.

With 19 million alcoholics in the United states alone, the gene for alcoholism is not rare! In any case, the benefit is not that great and it is not a substitute for learning about your cholesterol and triglyceride numbers and doing the exercise and diet things that would keep your numbers in the safe area!

Most of the groups in the U. S. who strictly abstain from alcohol all run much lower heart attack rates than the rest of the country.

The *Smart* Way to Play the Odds!

To some, success is investing wisely and making good returns in the stock market. Many do.

Others take terrible chances and lose lots of money. Some lose everything they have worked hard to earn. Anyone who has had anything to do with investing knows how important it is to weigh the risks of winning versus losing. Yet many people ignore the odds and take huge risks with their money.

The same is true about their lives.

It makes sense to figure out how to cut our risks using the best indicators we can find. Amidst all the confusion and differences of opinion, even among those who feel they are experts, what indicators can we use to cut the odds of having a heart attack?

To some, success is getting their *LDL* under 130.

To others, it is getting their *total cholesterol/HDL* ratio under 4.

We hope you will decide to do both—get your ratio under 4 and your LDL at least under 130. We also hope you will get your triglycerides under 150. But if you have had heart disease or heart surgery, we believe you should get your LDL down to 100 and your triglyceride level at 100 or less.

We also hope your doctor and healthcare staff have been helping you monitor these levels. If not, don't be afraid to be a little pushy. If you don't speak up these days, it's easy to be overlooked or missed while guidelines are followed that may or may not be in your best interest. Don't take "No" for an answer just because your HMO doesn't currently seem to offer what you know you need.

Cutting down on excessive bad fat obviously makes sense. How much you cut down depends on several variables, including your own motivation. We have observed that scaring people about health consequences is not the most powerful motivator in the world. It should be a good motivator, but it isn't always. Why?

All too often, people rationalize their behavior and activities. They think, "People should wear seat belts, stop smoking, not do drugs, get pap smears—but I don't have to worry because it won't happen to me!" People sometimes believe they are invincible, that things will happen to everyone else, but not to them.

The fat-plaque story we've been telling you is real. *It can happen to you.* A big step toward improving your odds is to cut down significantly on the amount of bad fat you eat.

"Well, I'm almost convinced, but how do I do it?"

There's no easy way to make a cholesterol or triglyceride problem go away. There is no "cure."

It takes effort.

It takes motivation.

It means cutting way down on the bad fat you eat. It takes being smart enough to follow through. You can do it and we think you will—because the alternatives are terrible.

Even if your cholesterol levels are not high enough for you to be specifically told to cut down on the bad fat you eat, you should. This is a family project for everyone except infants and toddlers. You will want to protect yourself like people around the world who don't plug up their coronary arteries.

Recheck Your Cholesterol and Triglyceride Numbers

If your cholesterol numbers have been out of whack, how soon should you get them rechecked after you get started on your healthy-heart program, including a big cut back on saturated fat?

Of course you want to know how you are doing. Following this plan will make a difference. It takes time. A person's cholesterol level usually stays more or less constant for a while, no matter what is eaten or what medications are taken. It takes several weeks before any significant change can be detected in cholesterol levels after changes are made in eating habits. This is why total blood cholesterol levels can be checked without any fasting.

After beginning a new program of eating, we recommend you wait a couple of months before rechecking your blood cholesterol levels. Then, if progress hasn't occurred, more changes may be needed.

On the other hand, triglyceride levels go up and down almost immediately, depending on what you do or do not eat. This means that getting a meaningful triglyceride level requires fasting for 12 to 14 hours before getting blood drawn for a test. Even then, if someone who runs high triglycerides eats a lot of fat, it may take a few weeks for the fasting triglyceride level to come down to an acceptable level. That means that very soon after eating something fatty, high levels of bad triglycerides begin circulating in the blood and may start depositing damaging plaque material in your coronary arteries.

Cutting way down on the bad fat you consume should help and it will probably make a big difference. Some people will still have a problem, even after carefully limiting the saturated fat and trans-fatty acids they consume. When the total cholesterol is high, there is too much LDL, or not enough HDL and/or the triglycerides are elevated, it is *always* essential to cut down on saturated fat. This is true whether or not medications are needed to get these levels under control.

However, if exercise and limiting bad fat doesn't control an elevated LDL or triglyceride level or if the cholesterol/HDL ratio can't be brought down to 4, *adding medications* almost always can. Even so, no one should rely on medications *without* exercise and limiting bad fat.

People with high cholesterol or triglycerides or low HDL causing the ratio to be high, often have an inherited tendency to over-manufacture cholesterol. People with one of these genetic problems can't handle even small loads of saturated fat. When they eat this bad fat, their bodies not only make cholesterol, but very large amounts of it. Fortunately, excellent medications can help control cholesterol and triglycerides for these people. First they need to know they have a problem. Besides their medications, they must be on a 10-gram bad-fat budget as well as a vigorous exercise program.

As you can see, this *is* a big deal.

If medication is needed, the right choice of medication and dosage are very important, as is proper monitoring and follow-up. Controlling cholesterol and triglyceride problems with medications is *not* a "do-it-yourself" project. If medications are needed, you need the help and guidance of an expert. Don't depend on articles about the latest health fads, sensational pamphlets or a friendly person down the street promising a miracle cure. There is *no miracle cure* for genetic cholesterol or triglyceride disorders.

A *cure* is something that makes a disease process go away. For example, a person properly diagnosed as having appendicitis is *cured* when the inflamed appendix is surgically removed. The problem does not come back again.

On the other hand, at this time, we can't *cure* a person with diabetes. It can usually be controlled with a proper diet along with medications which frequently include insulin. Until it is possible to help a person's pancreas produce the needed insulin, with a transplant or possibly some genetic engineering, the person's diabetes is *controlled,* not *cured.*

Similar to controlling diabetes, we can almost always *control* a person's genetic problem with cholesterol or triglycerides. At this time, there is no way to *cure* it. No one can make a problem with cholesterol and triglycerides go away without continuing a vigorous control program. So, if someone tells you about a great *cure* for severe cholesterol or triglyceride problems, forget it.

If you want to beat the odds of an early heart attack, we want to help you do so—pleasantly. We want to help you find a lifestyle you can enjoy and continue to follow for life.

Being a non-smoker is an extremely important part of not having a heart attack. Not smoking also improves your odds against getting emphysema or lung cancer. So your choice as to what you do is a big one—but it's all yours.

You know now that the most important basic factor in controlling cholesterol and triglycerides is to avoid eating too much bad fat. Just controlling the amount of cholesterol you eat is not enough. You must also control how much bad fat you eat.

Limiting saturated fat, trans-fatty acids and cholesterol is not something to fiddle around with for a few days now and then. *Now and then* isn't enough. Fat plaques will just keep building up. Sooner or later they will probably cause decreased blood flow to your heart, which means *ischemia* and a heart attack. This is not what you want to happen to you or to those close to you.

We are all going to die, but why do things that will create crummy odds for a premature death? We can help you turn the odds around so they are in your favor. If this is what you want, you can *do it!*

Cut your bad fat intake to your own budget—20 grams a day if you have no risks at all and 10 grams a day if you do. Keep your calories under 2000 per day. Adapt your favorite meals so they fit into your budget. Invent others. Trade tips with your family and friends. Check out the recipes starting on page 111. You'll find some that are sure to become favorites. As you review some of the tips we've given you and study these recipes, you'll find clues to help you create your own meals with very little fat. Pretty soon you'll even be figuring out alternatives to the fat-laden food most people in our culture eat. When you start doing creative lowfat cooking, you'll really be into it.

The simple plan is based on eating a variety of good tasting foods focusing on fruits, vegetables, grains, legumes and seafood with limited amounts of lowfat poultry, meat and milk products.

By doing the right things, you can avoid dumping more bad fat into your coronary arteries. You may see a difference in cholesterol numbers in a couple of months—providing you follow through. If you are one of those people with a genetic problem related to handling cholesterol and triglycerides, you will probably need some medications to help.

This is not a 2-week program, not a 1-month program, not an 8-week *cure.* Or any other kind of *cure.* There's no such thing, regardless of what a popular book may have promised. Check your total cholesterol, HDL cholesterol and triglycerides every four months.

This problem lasts a lifetime. This plan is for a whole new life so you can have a good chance of beating the odds of a heart attack and living a longer, healthier life.

Well, that's it.

You can go a long way toward decreasing the odds of a heart attack.

Now, *do* it!

Lowfat, Low-Cholesterol Recipes You'll Enjoy

RECIPE DEVELOPMENT BY
HELEN FISHER, PUBLISHER, FISHER BOOKS

ACKNOWLEDGMENTS

Thanks to Susan Deeming, Ph.D., R.D. for the use of her recipes: Jamaican Bean Pot, Brunswick Stew, Spanish Rice & Bean Pie, Lentil-Tomato Soup, and Oriental Pocket Sandwiches.

Nutritional Analysis

Nutritional analysis was calculated using The Food Processor AE for Windows software program, version 6.0, copyright 1987-1995 by ESHA Research. It has a database of more than 10,000 foods and provides analysis for 113 nutrients and 21 nutrient factors, including food exchanges. It uses data from the USDA and other scientific sources. Analysis given in this book does not include optional ingredients or variations. Where an ingredient amount is a range, the higher number is used. Where there is a range of servings, the lower number is used.

APPETIZERS

*ENJOY APPETIZERS AS A RELAXED WAY
TO INTRODUCE THE MEAL TO COME.*

Start with something light and not too filling. Serve a dip with fresh vegetables cut in convenient sizes to replace a heavier fried food.

Enjoy our Bean Dip with jícama or carrot sticks, or Bean Tostadas as a prelude to a Mexican dinner. If you are in the mood for Chinese food, begin with Turkey Bundles. Serve your appetizer with your favorite beverage.

Whatever you choose, relax with family or friends with a complementary appetizer before dinner.

Chili–Onion Dip

2/3 cup fat-free cottage cheese
4 tablespoons skim milk
2 tablespoons Worcestershire
   sauce
1 teaspoon paprika
3 onion bouillon cubes or
   3 teaspoons instant onion
   bouillon mix

1 tablespoon dehydrated
   onion flakes
1 (4–oz.) can chopped mild
   green chile peppers
Assorted fresh vegetables

Mix all ingredients except vegetables in blender or food processor until smooth. Serve with crisp celery, radishes, cauliflower, etc. This dip makes a delicious topping on fish or baked potatoes. Refrigerate in container with a tight fitting lid. Makes 1 cup.

Each 1/4–Cup Serving Contains:							
Calories	57.0	Fiber	0.8g	Trans-fatty acids	0g
Protein	6.2g	Total Fat	0.3g	Cholesterol	3.7mg
Carbohydrates	7.7g	Saturated Fat	0.1g	Sodium	706.2mg

Bean Dip

1/2 cup fat-free plain yogurt
1/2 cup Fresh Salsa, page 116
1/2 teaspoon garlic powder
1/2 teaspoon chili powder
1 cup drained, cooked, pinto,
   kidney or black beans

Toasted no-lard tortillas or
   pita bread
Assorted fresh vegetables

In a small serving bowl, combine yogurt, Fresh Salsa, garlic and chili powders. Mash beans slightly; stir into yogurt mixture. Serve with tortillas, pita bread and/or raw vegetables. Makes about 2 cups.

Each 1/4–Cup Serving Contains:							
Calories	48.4	Fiber	1.5g	Trans-fatty acids	0g
Protein	3.1g	Total Fat	0.4g	Cholesterol	0.3mg
Carbohydrates	8.6g	Saturated Fat	0.1g	Sodium	39.6mg

Vegetable Dip

1 cup fat-free plain yogurt
1 tablespoon grated onion
1 tablespoon chopped parsley
1 teaspoon dried dill weed

1 teaspoon Bon Appetit®
1 tablespoon capers
Assorted fresh vegetables

In a small bowl, combine all ingredients except vegetables and chill.
Serve with your favorite fresh vegetables. Makes about 1 cup.

Each 1/4-Cup Serving Contains:							
Calories	36.1	Fiber	0.1g	Trans-fatty acids	0g
Protein	3.6g	Total Fat	0.1g	Cholesterol	1.1mg
Carbohydrates	5.1g	Saturated Fat	0.1g	Sodium	126.7mg

Turkey Bundles

1/2 cup (3 oz.) shredded, skinned, cooked turkey breast
1/4 cup finely chopped apple
2 tablespoons chopped celery
1 tablespoon chopped
green onion
1 tablespoon chopped green
bell pepper

3 tablespoons chopped
crystallized ginger
1 tablespoon soy sauce
1 tablespoon rice or cider
vinegar
1/2 teaspoon sugar
8 lettuce or spinach leaves

In a small bowl, combine turkey, apple, celery, onion, pepper and
ginger. Stir together soy sauce, vinegar and sugar. Pour over turkey
mixture; mix thoroughly. For each bundle, place 2 to 3 teaspoons of
mixture on lower edge of lettuce or spinach leaf. Roll over, tucking
ends in, envelope-style. Place seam side down on small serving tray.
Serve at once, or cover and refrigerate until serving time. Makes 8
bundles. *Variation:* For individual salads, double amounts above.
Shred lettuce or spinach leaves and top with turkey mixture.

Each Serving Contains:							
Calories	26.7	Fiber	0.2g	Trans-fatty acids	0g
Protein	2.6g	Total Fat	0.7g	Cholesterol	5.6mg
Carbohydrates	2.7g	Saturated Fat	0.2g	Sodium	171.2mg

Bean Tostadas

12 appetizer-size corn tortillas
1-1/2 cups cooked pinto or
    black beans, drained
1/2 teaspoon chili powder
1/4 cup chopped green onion
Salt and pepper

3 small tomatoes, chopped
1 tablespoon chopped cilantro
    (Chinese parsley) or parsley
3 tablespoons grated Parmesan
    cheese
6 to 8 radishes, sliced

Preheat oven to 350F (175C). Spread tortillas in 1 layer on a baking sheet. Toast in oven 5 to 7 minutes. Remove; set aside. In a saucepan, combine beans, chili powder, onion, salt and pepper to taste. Stir and mash beans as they heat. Remove from heat. Place about 1 tablespoon bean mixture on each tortilla. Top with tomatoes, cilantro, Parmesan cheese and radishes. Serve at once. Makes 12 servings.

Each Serving Contains:					
Calories	76.0	Fiber	2.9g	Trans-fatty acids	0g
Protein	3.5g	Total Fat	1.1g	Cholesterol	1.2mg
Carbohydrates	13.9g	Saturated Fat	0.4g	Sodium	80.0mg

Fresh Salsa

1 cup chopped tomatoes
1/3 cup chopped fresh roasted
    or canned chiles
3 green onions, chopped
1/2 teaspoon dried oregano
    leaves

1 tablespoon chopped cilantro
    (Chinese parsley)
Salt and pepper
Toasted corn-tortilla or
    pita wedges

In a small bowl, combine all ingredients except tortilla or pita wedges. Cover and chill. Serve with tortilla or pita wedges. Makes about 1-1/2 cups.

Each Serving Contains:					
Calories	35.6	Fiber	1.0g	Trans-fatty acids	0g
Protein	1.0g	Total Fat	1.0g	Cholesterol	0.2mg
Carbohydrates	6.5g	Saturated Fat	0.2g	Sodium	102.1mg

Crab-Stuffed Mushrooms

24 large fresh mushrooms
1 (6-oz.) can crabmeat or 6 oz.
   fresh cooked crabmeat
2 green onions, chopped
1 celery stalk, finely chopped
1 teaspoon horseradish

2 teaspoons fat-free cream
   cheese
1/2 teaspoon paprika
3 tablespoons chopped red bell
   pepper or pimiento
Salt and pepper

Remove stems from mushrooms; wipe caps clean with a damp cloth or paper towel. In a small bowl, combine remaining ingredients. Season to taste with salt and pepper. Fill mushroom caps with mixture. Serve. To serve hot, place on baking sheet and bake in 350F (175C) oven about 12 minutes. Serve at once. Makes 24.

Each Serving of 3 Contains:

Calories	42.6	Fiber	0.9g	Trans-fatty acids	0g
Protein	6.2g	Total Fat	0.7g	Cholesterol	16.5mg
Carbohydrates	3.6g	Saturated Fat	0.2g	Sodium	124.5mg

Jícama Sticks

1 jícama, about 1/2 lb., or
   2 cucumbers
3 tablespoons orange-juice
   concentrate, undiluted
2 teaspoons grated orange peel,
   if desired

1/2 teaspoon chili powder
1/4 teaspoon garlic powder
Salt and pepper

Peel jícama; cut into 1/2-inch sticks. If using cucumbers, peel, cut and remove seeds. Combine orange-juice concentrate, orange peel, if desired, chili and garlic powders. Stir to combine. Season with salt and pepper to taste. Pour over jícama or cucumbers; toss to coat. Chill 1 to 2 hours before serving.

Each Serving of 3 Contains:

Calories	20.9	Fiber	0.9g	Trans-fatty acids	0g
Protein	0.4g	Total Fat	0.0g	Cholesterol	0mg
Carbohydrates	5.0g	Saturated Fat	0.0g	Sodium	34.6mg

Stuffed Cherry Tomatoes

24 cherry tomatoes
1 (6-oz.) can cocktail shrimp,
    drained, or 6 oz. fresh
    cooked shrimp
1/4 cup cooked rice or orzo
    (riso) pasta

2 teaspoons curry powder
1/4 teaspoon dry mustard
1/4 cup cooked petite peas
2 teaspoons lemon juice
Salt and pepper

Slice tops from tomatoes. With a melon baller or sharp small spoon, scoop out pulp and set aside. Chop tomato pulp and shrimp. Combine with rice or orzo, curry powder, mustard, peas and lemon juice. Season with salt and pepper to taste. Fill tomato shells with rice mixture. Cover and chill before serving. Makes 24.

Each Serving of 3 Contains:					
Calories	46.8	Fiber	1.0g	Trans-fatty acids	0g
Protein	5.4g	Total Fat	0.5g	Cholesterol	41.5mg
Carbohydrates	5.4g	Saturated Fat	0.1g	Sodium	86.2mg

Turkey-Stuffed Mushrooms

1/4 lb. skinned turkey breast,
    ground
1 tomato, seeded, chopped
1 teaspoon garlic powder
2/3 cup fresh French
    breadcrumbs

2 tablespoons parsley
1 teaspoon imitation bacon bits
2 egg whites
Salt and pepper
18 large fresh mushrooms

Preheat oven to 375F (190C). Spray a 13 x 9-in. baking sheet with vegetable cooking spray. Set aside. Spray a skillet with vegetable cooking spray. Cook turkey until no pink color remains; stir with fork to crumble. Remove from heat. Add tomato, garlic powder, breadcrumbs, parsley, bacon bits and egg whites. Thoroughly combine. Add salt and pepper to taste. Brush mushrooms with a dry cloth; remove stems. Place about 1 tablespoon filling in each mushroom. Place in prepared pan. Bake uncovered about 20 minutes. Serve hot. Makes 18.

Each Serving of 3 Contains:					
Calories	71.9	Fiber	1.1g	Trans-fatty acids	0g
Protein	6.5g	Total Fat	2.6g	Cholesterol	15.7mg
Carbohydrates	6.7g	Saturated Fat	0.7g	Sodium	123.1mg

SOUPS

HOMEMADE SOUP BRINGS BACK MEMORIES
OF HOME AND GOOD, SIMPLE MEALS.

We have a variety from which to choose, ranging from a hearty Minestrone or Split-Pea Soup to a very light, yet flavorful Egg-Drop Soup.

For warm-weather enjoyment, we offer Gazpacho, a cold soup. Cream soups take little time to prepare and can help turn a small portion of leftovers into a satisfying dish.

Basic stock recipes are included for use in preparing your own Beef, Chicken and Vegetarian Broths. Make them when time is available and freeze in small containers for future use. Adjust the vegetables and seasoning to your family's preferences. We want these recipes to serve as a starting point for your culinary creativity.

Leek & Potato Soup

2 leeks, chopped, include
    4 inches of green or 1
    large onion, chopped
1 quart Chicken Broth,
    page 129, or Vegetarian
    Broth, page 123

2 cups chopped raw potatoes
Fat-free plain yogurt
Parsley
Salt and pepper

In a 4-quart pot, combine leeks or onion, broth and potatoes. Bring to a boil; reduce heat, partially cover and simmer for 55 minutes. In a blender or food processor, purée potato mixture. Serve with a topping of fat-free yogurt. Garnish with sprigs of parsley. Season with salt and pepper to taste. Serve hot or cold. Makes 6 servings.

Each 1-Cup Serving Contains:					
Calories	114.7	Fiber	2.2g	Trans-fatty acids	0g
Protein	6.0g	Total Fat	1.2g	Cholesterol	0.3mg
Carbohydrates	20.3g	Saturated Fat	0.3g	Sodium	586.1mg

Split-Pea Soup

2 cups dried split peas
3 quarts water
6 bouillon cubes
1 garlic clove
1 large onion, chopped
4 carrots, sliced

4 celery stalks, sliced
2 bay leaves
1/2 teaspoon dried-leaf thyme
Salt and coarse pepper
Imitation bacon bits, if desired

Rinse peas and place in a 4-quart pot. Add water, bouillon cubes, garlic, onion, carrots, celery, bay leaves and thyme. Bring to a boil; reduce heat. Cover and simmer 45 to 50 minutes until peas and vegetables are tender. If desired, remove bay leaves and purée mixture in a blender or food processor. Season with salt and pepper to taste. Garnish with bacon bits, if desired. Makes 8 servings.

Each 1-Cup Serving Contains:					
Calories	201.9	Fiber	5.6g	Trans-fatty acids	0g
Protein	13.4g	Total Fat	0.9g	Cholesterol	0.5mg
Carbohydrates	36.8g	Saturated Fat	0.2g	Sodium	946.1mg

Gazpacho

3 cups tomato juice
1 beef bouillon cube or
   1 teaspoon granules
3 tablespoons wine vinegar
1 teaspoon Worcestershire
   sauce
4 to 6 drops Tabasco sauce
1 teaspoon olive oil
1 large tomato, chopped

1 cucumber, chopped
1 small onion, chopped
2 celery stalks, chopped
1/2 green bell pepper, chopped
1 tablespoon chopped cilantro
   (Chinese parsley)
1 cup croutons

In a small saucepan, heat tomato juice to boiling; add bouillon and stir until dissolved. Remove from heat; add vinegar, Worcestershire sauce, Tabasco and oil. Cool. Pour into a large bowl or container with a cover. Add tomato, cucumber, onion, celery, green pepper and cilantro. Cover and chill several hours. Serve cold. Top with croutons. Additional chopped vegetables may be added if desired. Makes 6 servings.

Each 1-Cup Serving Contains:					
Calories	73.0	Fiber	1.9g	Trans-fatty acids	0g
Protein	2.5g	Total Fat	1.4g	Cholesterol	0mg
Carbohydrates	14.8g	Saturated Fat	0.3g	Sodium	645.1mg

French Onion Soup

2 tablespoons olive oil
6 or 7 cups sliced onions
1 teaspoon sugar

2 quarts Beef Broth, page 130
1/2 cup white wine, if desired
6 slices French bread, toasted

Heat oil in a 4-quart pot; sauté onions in oil. Cover and cook over medium-low heat until tender. Add sugar and stir about 10 minutes until golden brown. Add stock. Cover and simmer until onions are soft, about 15 to 20 minutes. Add wine if desired. To serve, ladle soup into bowls; top each with a slice of toasted French bread. Makes 8 servings.

Each 1-Cup Serving Contains:					
Calories	158.8	Fiber	2.4g	Trans-fatty acids	0g
Protein	6.2g	Total Fat	4.9g	Cholesterol	0mg
Carbohydrates	22.9g	Saturated Fat	0.9g	Sodium	945.3mg

Carrot & Onion Soup

1-1/2 cups shredded carrots
1/2 cup chopped onions
1 quart fat-free broth
1/4 cup tomato paste or sauce
1 tablespoon uncooked rice

1/2 package imitation butter
   granules
1 cup frozen peas
Chives or parsley, chopped

Place all ingredients except peas and chives in a 4-quart pot and bring to a boil. Simmer uncovered about 35 minutes. Add peas. Garnish with chives or parsley. Makes 6 servings.

Each 1-Cup Serving Contains:						
Calories	60.0	Fiber	2.6g	Trans-fatty acids	0g
Protein	2.7g	Total Fat	0.3g	Cholesterol	0mg
Carbohydrates	12.4g	Saturated Fat	0.1g	Sodium	171.3mg

Egg-Drop Soup

6 cups Chicken Broth, page 129
2 slices fresh ginger root, peeled
2 teaspoons cornstarch
1 tablespoon water
1 teaspoon soy sauce
2 green onions, chopped

1/3 cup frozen peas
1 teaspoon rice wine or
   sherry, if desired
1/8 cup egg substitute
1 egg white

Pour chicken broth into a medium saucepan, add ginger root and bring to a boil. Reduce heat and simmer 5 minutes. In a small bowl, blend cornstarch, water and soy sauce. Stir into broth; add green onions and peas. Continue cooking 3 to 4 minutes. Add wine. Remove ginger root and discard. In a small bowl, beat egg substitute and egg white. Pour in a stream into hot broth; stir lightly, forming threads. Serve at once. Makes 8 servings.

Each 1-Cup Serving Contains:						
Calories	43.7	Fiber	0.4g	Trans-fatty acids	0g
Protein	5.1g	Total Fat	1.2g	Cholesterol	0mg
Carbohydrates	2.6g	Saturated Fat	0.3g	Sodium	658.0mg

Vegetarian Broth

2 onions, quartered
2 parsnips or turnips
3 or 4 medium carrots
4 inches celery tops, including
 leaves

2 bay leaves
2 quarts water
2 cups chopped, mixed fresh
 vegetables
4 to 5 sprigs fresh parsley

In a 4-quart pot, combine all ingredients. Simmer, covered until vegetables are tender. Strain mixture through cheesecloth into a container. Discard vegetables and herbs. Use broth at once or refrigerate, tightly covered. Broth may be frozen for later use. Makes about 6 cups.

Each 1-Cup Serving Contains:							
Calories	719.0	Fiber	52.5g	Trans-fatty acids	0g
Protein	23.6g	Total Fat	2.6g	Cholesterol	0mg
Carbohydrates	165.5g	Saturated Fat	0.5g	Sodium	386.2mg

Minestrone Soup

2 cups tomato juice
1 garlic clove
1 onion, chopped
1 zucchini, chopped
2 celery stalks, chopped
2 carrots, sliced
2 tablespoons chopped parsley
1 (10-1/2-oz.) can beef bouillon
4 cups water
1 teaspoon dried-leaf oregano

1 teaspoon basil
1/2 cup shredded cabbage
1 cup chopped tomatoes
1/2 cup kidney beans, cooked,
 drained
1/2 cup garbanzo beans,
 cooked, drained
1 cup cooked pasta
Salt and pepper

In a 4-quart pot, combine tomato juice, garlic, onion, zucchini, celery, carrots, parsley, beef bouillon and water. Bring to a boil; reduce heat, partially cover and simmer until vegetables are tender. Add oregano, basil, cabbage, tomatoes, kidney beans and garbanzo beans. Continue cooking about 10 minutes. Add pasta, cook until heated. Serve hot. Makes 10 servings.

Each 1-Cup Serving Contains:							
Calories	73.3	Fiber	2.6g	Trans-fatty acids	0g
Protein	4.0g	Total Fat	0.7g	Cholesterol	0mg
Carbohydrates	14.3g	Saturated Fat	0.1g	Sodium	440.0mg

Puerto Rican Black-Bean Soup

2 cups dried black beans
Water
2 quarts Chicken Broth, page
    129, or Vegetarian Broth,
    page 123 or water
2 onions, chopped
2 bay leaves

1 carrot, sliced
2 green bell peppers, chopped
2 celery stalks, chopped
Salt and pepper
Vinegar
2 cups cooked rice
4 chopped green onions

Rinse beans. In a large pot, combine beans and 2 quarts water. Boil 2 minutes. Remove from heat; cover. Set aside 1 to 1-1/2 hours. Drain and discard water. Add Chicken Broth, Vegetarian Stock or water, onions and bay leaves. Bring to a boil; reduce heat and simmer about 1 hour. Add carrot, bell peppers and celery; simmer about 45 minutes, until beans are tender. Season to taste with salt and pepper. To serve, ladle soup into bowls. Season with vinegar to taste, about 1 teaspoon per bowl. Add cooked rice and chopped green onions. Makes 2 quarts, about 8 servings.

Each 1-Cup Serving Contains:					
Calories	196.5	Fiber	6.0g	Trans-fatty acids	0g
Protein	11.5g	Total Fat	1.9g	Cholesterol	0mg
Carbohydrates	33.3g	Saturated Fat	0.5g	Sodium	826.1mg

Spiced Tomato Soup

4 cups tomato juice
1 cup beef bouillon
2 tablespoons lemon juice
2 teaspoons Worcestershire
    sauce

1/4 teaspoon celery salt
1/8 teaspoon ground cinnamon
1/8 teaspoon ground cloves

In a medium saucepan, combine all ingredients. Bring to a boil; reduce heat and simmer about 5 minutes. Makes 4 to 5 servings.

Each 1-Cup Serving Contains:					
Calories	50.1	Fiber	1.1g	Trans-fatty acids	0g
Protein	2.6g	Total Fat	0.3g	Cholesterol	0mg
Carbohydrates	11.6g	Saturated Fat	0.1g	Sodium	1171.2mg

Great Northern Bean Soup

3 cups great northern beans
2 quarts water
1 onion, chopped
1 carrot, finely chopped
2 leeks, chopped
1 bay leaf
2 garlic cloves

1/2 cup chopped celery tops
 (including leaves)
6 beef bouillon cubes or
 6 teaspoons granules
1 pkg. imitation butter granules,
 if desired
Salt and pepper

Rinse beans; place in 4-quart pot. Add water, covering beans 3 to 4 inches. Bring to a boil. Boil 2 minutes. Cover and remove from heat. Let stand 1 to 2 hours. Drain beans, discarding soaking water. Return beans to pot. Cover with 2 quarts water; add onion, carrot, leeks, bay leaf, garlic, celery tops and bouillon. Bring to a boil, reduce heat and cover. Simmer until beans are tender, 1-1/2 to 2 hours. Add butter granules, if desired. Simmer about 15 minutes. Season to taste with salt and pepper. Remove bay leaf. Makes 12 servings.

Each 1-Cup Serving Contains:

Calories	93.6	Fiber	4.1g	Trans-fatty acids	0g
Protein	5.8g	Total Fat	0.3g	Cholesterol	0mg
Carbohydrates	17.7g	Saturated Fat	0.1g	Sodium	472.9mg

Navy-Bean Soup

2 cups dried navy beans
2 quarts water
1 small onion, chopped

1 bay leaf
1 garlic clove
Salt and pepper

Rinse navy beans; place in a 4-quart pot. Add water, covering beans 3 to 4 inches. Bring to a boil. Boil 2 minutes. Cover and remove from heat. Let stand 1 to 2 hours. Drain beans, discard soaking water. Return beans to pot. Cover with 2 quarts water; add onion, bay leaf and garlic. Bring to a boil, reduce heat and cover. Simmer until beans are tender, about 1-1/2 to 2 hours. Season to taste with salt and pepper. Remove bay leaf. Makes 8 servings.

Each 1-Cup Serving Contains:

Calories	74.5	Fiber	4.5g	Trans-fatty acids	0g
Protein	4.5g	Total Fat	0.3g	Cholesterol	0mg
Carbohydrates	14.0g	Saturated Fat	0.1g	Sodium	41.2mg

Cauliflower-Curry Soup

1 medium cauliflower, chopped
1/2 onion, chopped
3 green onions, chopped
1 garlic clove
2 celery stalks, chopped
1/2 cup peas
3 cups Chicken Broth, page 129

2 teaspoons curry powder
1/4 teaspoon dried-leaf thyme
1/4 teaspoon dried-leaf basil
1/4 teaspoon dried-leaf savory
1/4 teaspoon ground nutmeg
Salt and pepper

Place cauliflower in a medium saucepan; cover with water and cook until tender. Remove from heat and drain. Set aside. Spray a 2-quart saucepan with vegetable cooking spray. Sauté onions and garlic. Add celery, peas and broth. Bring to a boil; cover and simmer 15 minutes or until vegetables are tender. Add cauliflower, curry powder, thyme, basil, savory and nutmeg. If desired, pour 2 cups vegetable mixture into a blender or food processor. Blend until smooth; repeat with remaining mixture. Season with salt and pepper to taste. Makes 6 servings.

Each 1-Cup Serving Contains:							
Calories	54.3	Fiber	2.5g	Trans-fatty acids	0g
Protein	4.7g	Total Fat	1.0g	Cholesterol	0mg
Carbohydrates	7.5g	Saturated Fat	0.3g	Sodium	476.1mg

Mixed-Bean Soup

1-lb. mixture of 3 to 15 kinds
   of dried beans
2 quarts water
1 cup shredded, smoked
   turkey breast
1/2 large onion, chopped
2 carrots, sliced
1 (14-1/2-oz.) can tomatoes

Garlic powder
1 teaspoon dry mustard
1 teaspoon dried-leaf marjoram
1 cup cooked pasta
Salt and lemon pepper
1 to 2 tablespoons lemon juice,
   if desired

Rinse beans; place in a 4-quart pot. Add water covering beans 3 to 4 inches. Bring to a boil. Boil 2 minutes. Cover and remove from heat. Let stand 1 to 2 hours. Drain beans, discarding soaking water. Return beans to pot. Cover with 2 quarts water; add smoked turkey and onion. Cook about 45 minutes. Add carrots and tomatoes. Simmer until vegetables are tender. Stir in garlic powder, mustard, marjoram and cooked pasta. Season with salt and lemon pepper to taste. If desired, add lemon juice. Makes 10 servings.

Each 1-Cup Serving Contains:					
Calories	132.6	Fiber	5.2g	Trans-fatty acids	0g
Protein	8.3g	Total Fat	1.4g	Cholesterol	4.4mg
Carbohydrates	22.6g	Saturated Fat	0.1g	Sodium	214.8mg

Curry-Corn Chowder

2 tablespoons canola oil
1/2 onion, chopped
3 tablespoons chopped celery
2 tablespoons chopped
   red bell pepper
1 (12-oz.) can evaporated
   skimmed milk
1/4 cup water

1 (17-oz.) can creamed corn
1/2 cup raisins
1 teaspoon curry powder
1 medium apple, cored,
   chopped
Lemon pepper
Curry powder

In a 2-quart pan, heat oil and sauté onion. Add celery, red bell pepper, evaporated milk, water, corn, raisins and curry powder. Bring to a boil; reduce heat and simmer about 10 minutes, stirring occasionally. Add chopped apple and cook 5 minutes longer. Season to taste with lemon pepper and additional curry powder. Makes 6 cups.

Each 1-Cup Serving Contains:						
Calories	297.8	Fiber	3.5g	Trans-fatty acids	0.1g
Protein	9.6g	Total Fat	7.8g	Cholesterol	3.1mg
Carbohydrates	53.3g	Saturated Fat	1.2g	Sodium	449.7mg

Cream-of-Celery Soup

4 celery stalks, sliced
1 cup water
1/4 cup chopped onion
1/4 teaspoon dry mustard

1 cup White Sauce, page 154
3 tablespoons white wine,
   if desired
Salt and pepper

Combine celery, water and onion in a saucepan. Cook uncovered until celery and onion are tender. Add remaining ingredients. Stir until heated. Season to taste with salt and pepper. Makes 4 servings.

Variation: Omit celery and substitute 1 cup cooked vegetables, season as desired.

Each 1-Cup Serving Contains:						
Calories	77.9	Fiber	8.6g	Trans-fatty acids	0g
Protein	3.0g	Total Fat	3.7g	Cholesterol	1.1mg
Carbohydrates	0.9g	Saturated Fat	0.3g	Sodium	201.9mg

Chicken Broth

2-1/2 to 3 lb. skinned chicken
    pieces
6 cups water
1 large onion, sliced
2 carrots
1 parsnip, if desired

1 celery stalk with leaves
2 bay leaves
4 to 5 whole black peppercorns
4 to 5 parsley sprigs
1/2 teaspoon dried sage leaves
Salt and pepper

Place chicken and water in a large pot. Add remaining ingredients. Bring to a boil. Reduce heat, partially cover and simmer about 2 hours. Remove vegetables and chicken. Refrigerate chicken for future use. Strain broth into another container; refrigerate for several hours. Remove and discard any fat from surface of broth. Adjust seasoning to taste before using. Makes 4 cups broth.

Amount of saturated fat varies considerably depending on how well the fat is trimmed away and how much fat is removed from the surface of the broth.

Each 1-Cup Serving Contains:						
Calories	397.4	Fiber	1.8g	Trans-fatty acids	0g
Protein	69.5g	Total Fat	8.1g	Cholesterol	188.0mg
Carbohydrates	7.5g	Saturated Fat	2.3g	Sodium	264.1mg

Orange-Tomato Bisque

1 (10-1/2-oz.) can condensed
    tomato soup
1 (14-1/2-oz.) can stewed
    tomatoes, chopped
1/3 cup orange-juice
    concentrate (undiluted)

2 teaspoons sugar, if desired
2 teaspoons dried-leaf tarragon
2 teaspoons basil leaves
1/2 teaspoon parsley leaves
2/3 cup skim milk
1 teaspoon orange extract

In a medium saucepan, combine all ingredients; stir to blend. Simmer about 10 minutes. Serve hot or chilled. Makes 4 servings.

Each 1-Cup Serving Contains:						
Calories	107.5	Fiber	2.1g	Trans-fatty acids	0g
Protein	3.9g	Total Fat	1.5g	Cholesterol	0.7mg
Carbohydrates	22.3g	Saturated Fat	0.3g	Sodium	802.2mg

Beef Broth

3 to 4 lb. meaty beef shank or
    soup bones
6 cups water
1 large onion, chopped
2 bay leaves

3 celery stalks with leaves
1 carrot
4 to 5 black peppercorns
3 to 4 parsley sprigs
Salt and pepper

Preheat oven to 350F (175C). Place soup bones in a shallow baking dish. Bake uncovered about 30 minutes, until browned. Place browned bones and water in a large pot. Bring to a boil. Reduce heat; simmer about 2 hours. Remove any foam that may form on the surface. Add remaining ingredients; simmer about 2 hours longer. Remove meat, bones and vegetables. Reserve meat for another use. Strain broth into another container; refrigerate several hours. Remove and discard any fat from surface of broth. Adjust seasoning to taste before using. Makes 4 cups broth.

Amount of saturated fat varies considerably depending on how well the fat is trimmed away and how much fat is removed from the surface of the broth.

Each 1-Cup Serving Contains:							
Calories	354.6	Fiber	1.6g	Trans-fatty acids	0g
Protein	39.6g	Total Fat	18.1g	Cholesterol	131.8mg
Carbohydrates	6.3g	Saturated Fat	7.0g	Sodium	199.7mg

Lentil-Tomato Soup

1-1/2 cups dried lentils
5 cups water
1/2 cup chopped onion
1 garlic clove, minced
1 tablespoon olive or canola oil
2 teaspoons salt
1/8 teaspoon pepper
2 teaspoons sugar

1/4 teaspoon dried-leaf oregano
1/4 teaspoon dried-leaf basil
1 tablespoon chopped
   fresh parsley
1 (16-oz.) can tomatoes, diced
3 tablespoons tomato paste
Parsley sprigs

Sort through lentils, discarding foreign material. Rinse under running water. In a large saucepan, combine lentils and 5 cups water. In a small skillet, sauté onions and garlic in oil until onion is tender but not browned. Add to lentils. Stir in salt, pepper, sugar, oregano, basil and parsley. Bring to a boil; reduce heat. Cover and simmer until lentils are tender, about 45 minutes. Add tomatoes, including juice, and tomato paste. Stir well. Simmer 15 minutes longer. Ladle into bowls. Garnish each bowl with a fresh parsley sprig. Makes 4 servings.

Each 1-Cup Serving Contains:					
Calories	324.2	Fiber	11.4g	Trans-fatty acids	0g
Protein	22.1g	Total Fat	4.5g	Cholesterol	0mg
Carbohydrates	52.6g	Saturated Fat	0.6g	Sodium	1365.7mg

Vegetarian Chili

3/4 cup dry pinto beans
1/3 cup whole wheat berries
2-3 cups water
1 large onion, chopped
1 garlic clove, minced
1/4 teaspoon cayenne pepper
2 carrots, chopped
2 stalks celery, chopped
1/2 green bell pepper, chopped
1/2 red bell pepper, chopped

2 canned mild green chiles,
   chopped
1 teaspoon salt
1/2 teaspoon black pepper
1 tablespoon Worcestershire®
   sauce
1/4 teaspoon Tabasco® sauce
1/4 cup cider vinegar
1/4 cup tomato paste
4 oz. fresh mushrooms, sliced

Soak beans and wheat berries in water at least 8 hours or overnight.

Drain beans and wheat berries. Place 3 cups hot water in a large pot or Dutch oven; add beans, wheat berries, onions and garlic. Bring to a boil; reduce heat and simmer about 1-1/2 hours.

Add remaining ingredients except mushrooms; continue cooking for 30 minutes. If necessary, add water to keep vegetables covered.

Add mushrooms and cook 10 minutes longer or to desired consistency.

Makes 6 servings.

Each 1-Cup Serving Contains:						
Calories	138.0	Fiber	8.1g	Trans-fatty acids	0g
Protein	7.0g	Total Fat	0.7g	Cholesterol	0mg
Carbohydrates	28.7g	Saturated Fat	0.1g	Sodium	738.1mg

SALADS

SALADS ARE ALMOST LIMITLESS
TURN YOUR IMAGINATION LOOSE.

Choose Fruit-Filled Pineapple for a satisfying light luncheon dish. Enjoy Mideast flavors in Couscous Salad, which can be either a meal in itself or a side dish. This recipe is an excellent way to add more grain and fiber to your diet. Marinated Medley is a fine accompaniment for either broiled chicken or fish.

Remember these tips:

- ❧ Salad greens should be rinsed, patted dry with paper towels and chilled before serving.

- ❧ Salad dressing clings to a dry surface better than one that is still wet.

- ❧ For added interest, cut ingredients into bite-size pieces of various shapes.

- ❧ A chilled plate helps keep chilled ingredients crisp.

- ❧ Garnishing is that extra touch appreciated by all.

Fruit-Filled Pineapple

Juice of 1 lemon
1 tablespoon maraschino-
   cherry syrup
1 fresh pineapple
1/2 cup fresh or frozen
   strawberries

3 kiwis
3 oranges
1 apple
1/4 cup marshmallow creme
1/4 cup fat-free plain yogurt

In a small bowl, blend lemon juice and maraschino-cherry syrup. Cut pineapple in half. With a sharp knife, cut in 1/2 inch around edge of pineapple, leaving shell intact. Remove core and discard; cut remaining pineapple into bite-size pieces. In a large bowl, combine with fruit and lemon syrup. Refrigerate at least 1 hour. Fill pineapple shells with chilled fruit. Mix marshmallow creme and yogurt. Pour over fruit. Makes 4 servings.

Each Serving Contains:						
Calories	262.3	Fiber	5.4g	Trans-fatty acids	0g
Protein	3.4g	Total Fat	1.2g	Cholesterol	0.3mg
Carbohydrates	62.2g	Saturated Fat	0.1g	Sodium	25.3mg

Fresh Fruit Cocktail

1 cup sliced strawberries
1 cup melon pieces
2 peaches, sliced
1/2 cup blueberries
1 banana

1/2 cup cran-raspberry juice
1/4 cup club soda, lemon-lime
   soda or sparkling white
   grape juice

Mix all fruits except banana in a bowl. Cover and refrigerate 1 hour. When ready to serve, cut up banana and mix with fruit in bowl. Serve in individual bowls. Mix cran-raspberry juice and soda or sparkling grape juice. Pour juice mixture over each serving. Makes 6 servings.

Each Serving Contains:						
Calories	68.5	Fiber	1.9g	Trans-fatty acids	0g
Protein	0.9g	Total Fat	0.3g	Cholesterol	0mg
Carbohydrates	17.2g	Saturated Fat	0.1g	Sodium	6.1mg

Fruit-Salad Combo

Apples	Guavas	Peaches	2 tablespoons
Apricots	Kiwis	Pears	honey
Bananas	Mangoes	Pineapples	1/2 cup fat-
Grapefruit	Melons	Raspberries	free plain
Grapes	Oranges	Strawberries	yogurt

Make a delicious fruit salad by using a combination of various fruits which may include some of those listed above. Cut fruit into interesting slices, pieces or sections. Allow 2 cups per person. Arrange using a variety of colors. When possible include strawberries, blueberries or kiwis as accent colors. If bananas are prepared before serving, sprinkle with lemon juice to avoid darkening. Stir honey into yogurt. Spoon over salad. Makes 1/2 cup or 2 to 3 servings.

Variation: Powdered orange or raspberry drink concentrate may be blended with fat-free plain yogurt to make a tasty dressing which may be mixed with the fruits or as a topping. Sweeten with honey, sugar or sweetener as desired.

Cucumber Sticks

6 tablespoons fat-free
    plain yogurt
2 to 3 tablespoons minced
    green onion
2 teaspoons basil, mint or
    dried-leaf tarragon

1 tablespoon lemon juice
3 cucumbers or zucchini, cut in
    2-inch matchstick lengths
1 teaspoon paprika
Salt and pepper

In a small bowl, stir fat-free yogurt, green onions, basil, mint or tarragon and lemon juice until well blended. Combine with cucumber or zucchini sticks. Chill before serving. Sprinkle with paprika. Season to taste with salt and pepper. Makes 6 servings.

Each Serving Contains:					
Calories	32.1	Fiber	1.3g	Trans-fatty acids	0g
Protein	2.1g	Total Fat	0.3g	Cholesterol	0.3mg
Carbohydrates	6.3g	Saturated Fat	0.1g	Sodium	60.0mg

Spinach Salad

1 bunch fresh spinach
1/4 red onion, sliced
1/4 pound fresh mushrooms,
   sliced
1 (6-oz.) can sliced water
   chestnuts, drained
2 to 3 radishes, sliced
1 cup frozen peas or pea pods,
   thawed

1 tablespoon Grape Nuts®
   cereal
Lemon or lime wedges
Poppy Seed Dressing,
   page 146, if desired
Salt and pepper

Wash spinach, remove stems; pat leaves dry with paper towels. Line 4 to 6 plates with spinach leaves. Add a layer of onion rings. Combine mushrooms, water chestnuts, radishes and green peas. Spoon mushroom mixture on top of spinach and onion rings. Sprinkle with cereal. Squeeze lemon or lime on each salad before serving. Or serve with Poppy Seed Dressing. Season with salt and pepper to taste. Makes 4 to 6 servings.

Each Serving Contains:								
Calories	77.9	Fiber	6.0g	Trans-fatty acids	0g
Protein	4.8g	Total Fat	15.5g	Cholesterol	0mg
Carbohydrates	15.5g	Saturated Fat	0.1g	Sodium	170.8mg

With Poppy-Seed Dressing:								
Calories	104.9	Fiber	6.1g	Trans-fatty acids	0g
Protein	5.0g	Total Fat	16.7g	Cholesterol	0mg
Carbohydrates	20.0g	Saturated Fat	0.2g	Sodium	198.1mg

Seafood Salad

1/2 cup fat-free plain yogurt
1/4 cup chili sauce or Fresh
   Salsa, page 116
1 celery stalk, chopped
1 tablespoon lemon juice
1 teaspoon prepared
   horseradish
1 (12-oz.) pkg. frozen cooked
   shrimp, imitation crab,
   water-packed tuna or
   pink salmon

Lettuce or spinach leaves
1 (15-oz.) can asparagus
   spears, drained
2 medium tomatoes, chopped
Salt and lemon pepper

In a small bowl, blend fat-free yogurt with chili sauce or salsa. Add celery, lemon juice, horseradish and seafood. Line plates with lettuce or spinach leaves. Spoon seafood mixture on top. Garnish with asparagus spears and chopped tomatoes. Season to taste with salt and lemon pepper. Makes 4 servings.

Each Serving Contains.						
Calories	150.2	Fiber	3.2g	Trans-fatty acids	0g
Protein	23.1g	Total Fat	2.2g	Cholesterol	166.4mg
Carbohydrates	11.0g	Saturated Fat	0.5g	Sodium	737.7mg

137

Artichoke & Asparagus Salad

I lb. fresh asparagus, cooked, or 1 (15-oz.) can
4 fresh artichoke hearts, cooked, or 1 (14-oz.) can plain artichoke hearts or 1 (9-oz.) pkg. frozen artichoke hearts
Lettuce leaves
1 large tomato, chopped or sliced
2 green onions, sliced or 1/2 red onion, sliced in rings
1/2 cup mushrooms, sliced
1/2 red or yellow bell pepper, sliced
4 tablespoons lemon juice or Italian Dressing, page 151
Salt and pepper
1 tablespoon sesame seeds, toasted

Cut asparagus and artichoke hearts into bite-size pieces. Chill 1 hour. Line plates with lettuce leaves. In a bowl, combine tomato, onions, mushrooms and bell pepper. Sprinkle with lemon juice or Italian Dressing; toss to coat. Season to taste with salt and pepper. Place on lettuce and top with toasted sesame seeds. Makes 4 servings.

Each Serving Contains:					
Calories	107.7	Fiber	10.0g	Trans-fatty acids	0g
Protein	6.8g	Total Fat	1.9g	Cholesterol	0mg
Carbohydrates	21.1g	Saturated Fat	0.3g	Sodium	142.0mg

With Italian Dressing:					
Calories	188.9	Fiber	10.0g	Trans-fatty acids	0g
Protein	6.8g	Total Fat	9.3g	Cholesterol	0mg
Carbohydrates	21.5g	Saturated Fat	1.5g	Sodium	158.8mg

With Lemon Juice:					
Calories	111.5	Fiber	10.0g	Trans-fatty acids	0g
Protein	6.9g	Total Fat	1.9g	Cholesterol	0mg
Carbohydrates	22.4g	Saturated Fat	0.3g	Sodium	142.2mg

Russian Potato Salad

Lettuce or spinach leaves
1 (16-oz.) can cubed beets,
    drained
2 small potatoes, cooked,
    peeled, cubed
2 carrots, sliced, cooked
2 tomatoes, chopped
1 green onion, finely chopped

1/4 cup cut green beans, cooked
1 teaspoon lemon or lime, juice
2 tablespoons fat-free
    plain yogurt
1/2 tablespoon beet
    horseradish, if desired
Dill weed

Line salad bowl with lettuce or spinach leaves. In a large bowl, combine beets, potatoes, carrots, tomatoes, onion and green beans. In a cup, blend lemon or lime juice with yogurt and horseradish, if desired. Pour over vegetable mixture and carefully mix. Chill until ready to serve. Sprinkle top with dill weed. Makes 6 to 8 servings.

Each Serving Contains:						
Calories	61.3	Fiber	3.1g	Trans-fatty acids	0g
Protein	2.3g	Total Fat	0.4g	Cholesterol	0.1mg
Carbohydrates	13.7g	Saturated Fat	0.1g	Sodium	230.6mg

Black-Bean Salad

2 tablespoons wine vinegar
2 tablespoons olive oil
1 tablespoon chopped cilantro
    (Chinese parsley) or parsley
1 cup black beans, cooked,
    drained

3 green onions, chopped
1/2 green bell pepper, chopped
2 celery stalks, chopped
1/4 cup sliced green olives
3 tablespoons pimientos,
    chopped

In a salad bowl, mix together vinegar, oil and cilantro or parsley. Add remaining ingredients. Stir to combine. Chill before serving. Makes 4 servings.

Each Serving Contains:						
Calories	137.0	Fiber	3.4g	Trans-fatty acids	0.1g
Protein	4.3g	Total Fat	7.5g	Cholesterol	0mg
Carbohydrates	14.2g	Saturated Fat	1.0g	Sodium	115.2mg

Marinated Medley

2 cups sliced yellow crookneck
   squash
1 cup fresh or frozen peas
1 leek or 1/2 onion, chopped

1/2 red bell pepper, chopped
6 tablespoons Italian Dressing,
   page 151

In a saucepan, cover squash with water and cook until tender-crisp, about 5 minutes. Add peas; cover and remove from heat. Thoroughly rinse leek, if using; trim off green end. Cut lengthwise in half, then into 1-inch pieces. Cook chopped leek or onion in a saucepan with water to cover, about 5 to 7 minutes. Drain squash, peas and leek or onion. Place in a salad bowl, add red bell pepper and Italian Dressing. Stir to coat all pieces. Cover and chill at least 1 hour before serving. Makes 6 servings.

Each Serving Contains:							
Calories	122.8	Fiber	2.4g	Trans-fatty acids	0.1g
Protein	2.1g	Total Fat	9.3g	Cholesterol	0mg
Carbohydrates	8.8g	Saturated Fat	1.3g	Sodium	48.8mg

Glen's Chilled Salad

2 cups bite-size pieces
   cauliflower
1 cup bite-size pieces broccoli
1 (8-oz.) can sliced water
   chestnuts, drained
1 cup cherry tomatoes, halved

1/2 large red onion, sliced
   in rings
1/2 cup drained olives
1/2 cup Italian Dressing,
   page 151

Combine all ingredients in a large bowl. Stir several times to coat mixture.

Cover with plastic wrap and refrigerate at least 8 hours or overnight. Mix once or twice while marinating and again before serving. Makes 6 servings.

Each Serving Contains:							
Calories	141.8	Fiber	4.0g	Trans-fatty acids	50mg
Protein	2.2g	Total Fat	10.5g	Cholesterol	0mg
Carbohydrates	12.2g	Saturated Fat	1.5g	Sodium	226.6mg

Couscous Salad

2 teaspoons frozen orange-
    juice concentrate
1-1/2 cups water
4 teaspoons sugar
1 tablespoon diet soft
    margarine
1 cup couscous
1/2 cup peas, cooked
1 large tomato, chopped

1/2 cup mushrooms, sliced
1/2 cup currants or raisins
1 teaspoon chopped mint,
    if desired
1/4 teaspoon ground nutmeg
3 tablespoons lemon juice
3 tablespoons canola oil
1 (11-oz.) can mandarin
    oranges, drained

In a saucepan, combine orange-juice concentrate, water, sugar and margarine. Bring to a boil. Stir in couscous; cover and remove from heat. Let stand 5 to 10 minutes. Turn into a salad bowl; fluff with a fork. Add peas, tomato, mushrooms and currants or raisins. Gently stir with a fork. In a cup combine mint, if desired, nutmeg, lemon juice and oil. Pour over couscous mixture and gently mix with a fork. Garnish with mandarin-orange segments. Serve either warm or chilled. Makes 6 servings.

Each Serving Contains:					
Calories	193.0	Fiber	2.8g	Trans-fatty acids	0.2g
Protein	3.4g	Total Fat	8.0g	Cholesterol	0mg
Carbohydrates	29.4g	Saturated Fat	1.1g	Sodium	19.2mg

Cole Slaw

3 tablespoons vinegar
3 tablespoons orange juice
1/2 teaspoon pepper
3 tablespoons sugar

1 teaspoon caraway seeds
4 cups shredded red cabbage
1 apple, cored, sliced
1/2 cup raisins

In a cup, combine vinegar, orange juice, pepper, sugar and caraway seeds. In a salad bowl, mix cabbage, apple and raisins. Pour vinegar mixture over and toss to coat. Makes 6 servings.

Each Serving Contains:					
Calories	92.4	Fiber	2.4g	Trans-fatty acids	0g
Protein	1.2g	Total Fat	0.3g	Cholesterol	0mg
Carbohydrates	23.6g	Saturated Fat	0g	Sodium	6.9mg

Orange-Cucumber Salad

2 navel oranges or 2 (11-oz.)
    cans mandarin oranges,
    drained
1 cup sliced red onion
1 cucumber, thinly sliced
2 tomatoes, sliced
1 tablespoon chopped fresh
    mint, cilantro (Chinese
    parsley) or parsley

1/4 cup vinegar
2 tablespoons sugar
1/4 cup canola oil
1/4 cup water

With a sharp knife, remove peel and white membrane from fresh oranges. Cut oranges into thin slices. Place orange slices or segments, onion, cucumber and tomatoes in a large glass salad bowl. In a small container, stir mint, cilantro or parsley with vinegar, sugar, oil and water. Pour over orange and vegetable mixture. Cover and refrigerate 4 hours or longer. Makes 6 to 8 servings.

Each Serving Contains:							
Calories	143.9	Fiber	2.0g	Trans-fatty acids	0.1g
Protein	1.5g	Total Fat	9.3g	Cholesterol	0mg
Carbohydrates	15.8g	Saturated Fat	1.3g	Sodium	6.4mg

Shrimp Salad

Lettuce or spinach leaves
1 papaya, peeled, sliced
1 (12-oz.) pkg. cooked shrimp
2 celery stalks, sliced

1 green onion, finely chopped
1 cup seedless green grapes
2 limes or lemons

Line plates with lettuce or spinach leaves. Place 1/4 of papaya slices on each plate. Add a mound of shrimp, top with celery and green onion. Place grapes on the side. Cut limes or lemons into wedges; place on plates. Squeeze lime or lemon juice over salad. Makes 4 servings.

Each 3-oz. Serving Contains:							
Calories	160.4	Fiber	3.3g	Trans-fatty acids	0g
Protein	19.3g	Total Fat	1.4g	Cholesterol	165.8mg
Carbohydrates	19.8g	Saturated Fat	0.4g	Sodium	213.7mg

Hawaiian Rice Salad

2 cups cooked rice
1 cup seedless green grapes
1 peach, peeled, sliced
1/2 papaya, peeled, chopped
1 (11-oz.) can mandarin
    oranges, drained
1/2 cup Poppy-Seed Dressing,
    page 146, or Fruit Dressing,
    page 151

1 (20-oz.) can pineapple slices,
    drained
1/2 cup cherries
1 tablespoon chopped
    crystallized ginger

In a large salad bowl, combine rice, grapes, peach, papaya, oranges and dressing. Cover and refrigerate at least 2 hours. To serve, place 1 pineapple slice on each plate; top with a mound of rice-fruit mixture. Garnish with cherries and crystallized ginger. Makes 6 to 8 servings.

Each Serving Contains:

Calories	252.1	Fiber	2.5g	Trans-fatty acids	0g
Protein	3.4g	Total Fat	2.2g	Cholesterol	0mg
Carbohydrates	57.9g	Saturated Fat	0.3g	Sodium	48.9mg

Summer Potato Salad

1 cup (1/2 lb.) fresh
    mushrooms, sliced
3 cups sliced, peeled, cooked
    potatoes
2 small zucchini, sliced
1/2 cup chopped celery
4 green onions, chopped

1/2 red or green bell pepper,
    chopped
1 fennel bulb, sliced, if desired
2 tablespoons capers
1/3 cup Italian Dressing,
    page 151

In a large salad bowl, combine all ingredients. Cover and refrigerate at least 4 hours before serving. Makes 6 servings.

Each 1-Cup Serving Contains:

Calories	163.0	Fiber	3.0g	Trans-fatty acids	0.1g
Protein	3.2g	Total Fat	8.4g	Cholesterol	0mg
Carbohydrates	20.7g	Saturated Fat	1.2g	Sodium	136.2mg

Potato Salad

3 cups sliced, peeled, cooked potatoes
1/2 cup chopped dill, sweet or bread-and-butter pickles
2 teaspoons dried parsley leaves
1/4 cup chopped green onions
1 tablespoon prepared mustard
1/3 cup fat-free mayonnaise
1/4 cup fat-free plain yogurt
2 or 3 radishes, sliced
1/4 cup chopped green bell pepper
Salt and pepper

Place potatoes in a large bowl. Add remaining ingredients; stir to combine. Serve either warm or cold. Makes 4 servings.

Each Serving Contains:							
Calories	169.9	Fiber	2.8g	Trans-fatty acids	0g
Protein	3.7g	Total Fat	4.4g	Cholesterol	5.3mg
Carbohydrates	30.2g	Saturated Fat	0.8g	Sodium	486.6mg

Pasta Salad

2 cups cooked ziti or spiral pasta
1 cup chopped broccoli, cooked
1 cucumber or 2 zucchini, sliced
1 small red bell pepper, chopped
1 medium carrot, peeled, sliced
1 fennel bulb, trimmed, sliced, or 2 celery stalks, sliced
1 (6-1/2-oz.) can water-packed tuna, drained
1/3 cup Italian Dressing, page 151
1 tablespoon capers

Combine pasta, broccoli, cucumber or zucchini, bell pepper, carrot, fennel or celery and tuna. Pour about 1/3 cup Italian Dressing over all. Toss to coat. Scatter capers on top. Chill before serving. Makes 6 servings.

Variation: Omit tuna, substitute 3 oz. chopped, skinned, cooked chicken breast.

Each Serving Contains:							
Calories	202.9	Fiber	3.8g	Trans-fatty acids	0.1g
Protein	11.9g	Total Fat	9.3g	Cholesterol	12.9mg
Carbohydrates	18.8g	Saturated Fat	1.4g	Sodium	220.7mg

DRESSINGS, RELISHES, SAUCES & VINEGARS

Our dressings are quick and easy to prepare. Keep several in the refrigerator at all times, ready for use without any fuss. Make your own vinegars. It's simple and can give that personal touch to a tossed green salad.

If you enjoy sharing foods, make Tomato Relish or Fresh Cranberry Chutney for that special friend.

Poppy-Seed Dressing

2 tablespoons Dijon-style
  mustard
2 tablespoons olive oil
1/4 cup red-wine vinegar
1/2 cup orange juice
1/4 cup crushed pineapple,
  drained

1/3 cup honey
2 teaspoons poppy seeds
1/4 cup finely chopped
  red onion

In a blender, combine mustard, oil, vinegar, orange juice, pineapple and honey. Add poppy seeds and onion. Use at once or store in a container with a tight-fitting lid. Makes about 1-3/4 cups.

Variation: For use with Spinach Salad, page 136, omit orange juice and pineapple.

Each 1-Tablespoon Serving Contains:					
Calories	27.0	Fiber	0.1g	Trans-fatty acids	0g
Protein	0.2g	Total Fat	1.2g	Cholesterol	0mg
Carbohydrates	4.5g	Saturated Fat	0.1g	Sodium	27.3mg

Spicy Salad Dressing

6 tablespoons fat-free
  plain yogurt
1 teaspoon minced fresh
  horseradish

1 teaspoon Dijon-style mustard
1/4 teaspoon Worcestershire
  sauce
2 teaspoons lowfat mayonnaise

In a small bowl, beat ingredients until smooth. Chill and serve. Refrigerate in a container with a tight-fitting lid. Makes about 1/2 cup.

Each 1-Tablespoon Serving Contains:					
Calories	10.6	Fiber	0g	Trans-fatty acids	0g
Protein	0.7g	Total Fat	0.3g	Cholesterol	0.5mg
Carbohydrates	1.3g	Saturated Fat	0g	Sodium	33.4mg

Dill Sauce

1/4 cup fat-free cottage cheese
1 tablespoon fat-free
 mayonnaise
1 teaspoon lemon juice
1 to 2 tablespoons chopped
 fresh or dried dill weed

1 teaspoon blended herb
 mixture seasoning
1 tablespoon chopped pimiento
1/2 cup fat-free plain yogurt
Salt and pepper

In a blender or food processor, mix together cottage cheese, mayonnaise, lemon juice, dill and seasoning. Blend or process until smooth. Scoop mixture into a bowl; fold in pimiento and yogurt until thoroughly mixed. Season with salt and pepper to taste. Serve as a sauce for seafood or vegetable dip. Refrigerate in a container with a tight-fitting lid. Makes 1 cup.

Each 1-Tablespoon Serving Contains:

Calories	9.3	Fiber	0g	Trans-fatty acids	0g
Protein	0.9g	Total Fat	0.2g	Cholesterol	0.7mg
Carbohydrates	0.9g	Saturated Fat	0g	Sodium	39.0mg

Creamy Herb Dressing

1/2 cup lowfat buttermilk
1/2 cup fat-free plain yogurt
1 teaspoon each dried-leaf
 basil, oregano, dill weed,
 parsley

1 teaspoon dry or prepared
 mustard
1 tablespoon finely diced
 red onion
Salt and pepper

In a small bowl, combine buttermilk and yogurt. Stir until smooth. Add basil, oregano, dill weed, parsley, mustard and onion. Season with salt and pepper to taste. Chill several hours before serving. Refrigerate in a container with a tight-fitting lid. Makes about 1 cup.

Each 1-Tablespoon Serving Contains:

Calories	8.6	Fiber	0.1g	Trans-fatty acids	0g
Protein	0.8g	Total Fat	0.1g	Cholesterol	0.4mg
Carbohydrates	1.2g	Saturated Fat	0g	Sodium	34.9mg

Cocktail Sauce

1/2 cup bottled chili sauce or
    Fresh Salsa, page 116
1/3 cup catsup
1-1/2 teaspoons Worcestershire
    sauce

2 tablespoons prepared
    horseradish
2 tablespoons lemon juice
Tabasco® sauce, if desired
Pepper

Mix ingredients and chill. For a sharper flavor add more Tabasco sauce or horseradish. Makes about 1 cup.

Each 1-Tablespoon Serving Contains:							
Calories	11.3	Fiber	0.2g	Trans-fatty acids	0g
Protein	0.2g	Total Fat	0.1g	Cholesterol	0mg
Carbohydrates	2.6g	Saturated Fat	0g	Sodium	80.3mg

Sweet & Sour Sauce

3/4 cup vinegar
1/2 cup pineapple juice
1/2 cup water
1 tablespoon catsup

2 tablespoons soy sauce
1 tablespoon cornstarch
1/4 cup water
3/4 cup sugar

Combine vinegar, pineapple juice, 1/2 cup water, catsup and soy sauce. Dissolve cornstarch in 1/4 cup of water; stir in sugar. Add to pineapple-juice mixture. Stir over medium heat until sugar is completely dissolved and mixture is slightly thickened, 7 to 10 minutes. Serve on chicken or seafood, or use as a dip. Makes 3 cups.

Each 1-Tablespoon Serving Contains:							
Calories	15.4	Fiber	0g	Trans-fatty acids	0g
Protein	0.1g	Total Fat	0g	Cholesterol	0mg
Carbohydrates	4.0g	Saturated Fat	0g	Sodium	58.8mg

Garlic-Herb Vinegar

5 garlic cloves
3/4 teaspoon peppercorns
2 or 3 sprigs fresh basil,
    tarragon, marjoram,
    oregano, rosemary or sage

2 cups red-wine or
    cider vinegar

Add garlic, peppercorns and herb sprigs to vinegar in a glass container. Cover tightly; place in a dark cool area for a minimum of 3 weeks. Longer aging increases flavor. Strain mixture into a glass container; discard garlic and peppercorns. Makes 2 cups.

Each 1-Tablespoon Serving Contains:							
Calories	5.7	Fiber	0g	Trans fatty acids	0g
Protein	0g	Total Fat	0g	Cholesterol	0mg
Carbohydrates	2.2g	Saturated Fat	0g	Sodium	0.1mg

Lemon Vinegar

1 lemon
2 cups white vinegar

1/4 teaspoon lemon pepper
Lemon juice

With a sharp knife, remove thin colored layer of lemon peel without any white membrane. Place peel in a glass container with vinegar, lemon pepper and juice from lemon. Cover tightly; place in a dark cool area for a minimum of 3 weeks. Longer aging increases the flavor. Strain mixture into a glass container; discard lemon peel. Makes 2 cups.

Variation: Omit lemon and lemon pepper; substitute 1 cup very ripe raspberries, strawberries, blackberries or fresh pineapple. Proceed as directed above.

Each 1-Tablespoon Serving Contains:							
Calories	5.5	Fiber	0g	Trans-fatty acids	0g
Protein	0g	Total Fat	0g	Cholesterol	0mg
Carbohydrates	1.2g	Saturated Fat	0g	Sodium	0mg

Buttermilk Salad Dressing

1/2 small cucumber, seeded, chopped
1/4 cup lowfat buttermilk
1/4 cup fat-free cream cheese
2 green onions or 2 table-spoons chopped onion
1 parsley sprig or 1/2 teaspoon parsley flakes

4 teaspoons lemon juice
1 teaspoon dill weed
1 teaspoon chives
1/2 teaspoon garlic powder
Salt and pepper

Place cucumber and buttermilk in a blender or food processor. Blend or process briefly, do not over blend. Pour into a small bowl; stir in remaining ingredients. Refrigerate in a container with a tight-fitting lid. Makes about 1 cup.

Each 1-Tablespoon Serving Contains:							
Calories	7.9	Fiber	0.1g	Trans-fatty acids	0g
Protein	0.7g	Total Fat	0g	Cholesterol	0.3mg
Carbohydrates	1.3g	Saturated Fat	0g	Sodium	27.1mg

Tomato-Cream Dressing

1/2 cup lowfat buttermilk
1 tomato, peeled, chopped
2 teaspoons tomato paste
1 green onion

Paprika
Chives
Salt and pepper

Combine buttermilk, tomato, tomato paste and onion in a blender or food processor. Blend or process to desired consistency. Season to taste with paprika, chives, salt and pepper. Refrigerate in container with a tight-fitting lid. Makes about 1 cup.

Each 1-Tablespoon Serving Contains:							
Calories	5.4	Fiber	0.1g	Trans-fatty acids	0g
Protein	0.4g	Total Fat	0.1g	Cholesterol	0.3mg
Carbohydrates	0.9g	Saturated Fat	0g	Sodium	30.8mg

Fruit Dressing

1 cup fruit juice	Sugar, as desired
1 teaspoon lemon juice	Lemon or orange peel,
1 tablespoon cornstarch	if desired

Combine all ingredients in a small saucepan. Stir over medium heat 7 to 10 minutes. Cook until mixture becomes clear and slightly thickened. Makes about 1 cup.

Each 1-Tablespoon Serving Contains:					
Calories	12.6	Fiber	0g	Trans-fatty acids	0g
Protein	0g	Total Fat	0g	Cholesterol	0mg
Carbohydrates	3.2g	Saturated Fat	0g	Sodium	0.4mg

Italian Dressing

2/3 cup olive oil	1 teaspoon chopped chives
1/3 cup wine vinegar	1/2 teaspoon paprika
1 teaspoon chopped parsley	1 garlic clove
1 teaspoon fresh chopped basil,	Salt and pepper
or oregano	

Combine all ingredients in a jar with a tight-fitting lid. Shake vigorously before using. Store in a covered container. Makes about 1 cup.

Each 1-Tablespoon Serving Contains:					
Calories	81.2	Fiber	0g	Trans-fatty acids	0g
Protein	0g	Total Fat	9.0g	Cholesterol	0mg
Carbohydrates	0.4g	Saturated Fat	1.2g	Sodium	16.8mg

Pepper Relish

4 cups chopped tomatoes

2 cups chopped green bell peppers

1 red bell pepper, chopped

2 onions, chopped

1/4 cup shredded cabbage

1/4 teaspoon ground cloves

1/4 teaspoon ground allspice

1/4 teaspoon pepper

1/4 teaspoon mustard seed

1/8 teaspoon celery seed

1/8 teaspoon turmeric

1 cup sugar

3/4 cup cider vinegar

In a Dutch oven or heavy pot, combine all ingredients. Simmer about 2 hours. Chill before serving. Refrigerate in a container with tight-fitting lid. Makes about 6 cups.

Each 1/4-Cup Serving Contains:					
Calories	46.8	Fiber	0.2g	Trans-fatty acids	0g
Protein	0.5g	Total Fat	0.2g	Cholesterol	0mg
Carbohydrates	11.8g	Saturated Fat	0g	Sodium	3.6mg

Tomato Relish

4 cups chopped, peeled tomatoes

1 small onion, chopped

1/2 green bell pepper, chopped

1 mild green chile, chopped

1/4 teaspoon ground cloves

1/4 teaspoon ground allspice

1/4 teaspoon ground cinnamon

1-1/2 cups vinegar

Combine all ingredients in a large saucepan or Dutch oven. Cook over medium heat, stirring occasionally, about 40 minutes. Serve either hot or cold. Refrigerate in a container with a tight-fitting lid. This is especially good with beef or chicken. Makes about 6 cups.

Each 1/4-Cup Serving Contains:					
Calories	10.9	Fiber	0.4g	Trans-fatty acids	0g
Protein	0.3g	Total Fat	0.1g	Cholesterol	0mg
Carbohydrates	2.9g	Saturated Fat	0g	Sodium	3.2mg

Corn-Raisin Relish

1 (17-oz.) can whole-kernel
   corn, drained
1 cup raisins
1/4 cup chopped red bell
   pepper
1/2 onion, chopped

1/4 cup chopped celery
1 cup brown sugar
1 cup cider vinegar
1/2 teaspoon turmeric
1 teaspoon dry mustard
1 (3- to 4-inch) cinnamon stick

Combine all ingredients in a large saucepan. Cook over medium heat, stirring occasionally, about 20 minutes. Remove cinnamon stick. Serve either hot or cold. Refrigerate in a container with a tight-fitting lid. Makes about 4 cups.

Each 1/4-Cup Serving Contains:					
Calories	91.1	Fiber	1.1g	Trans fatty acids	0g
Protein	1.2g	Total Fat	0.4g	Cholesterol	0mg
Carbohydrates	23.1g	Saturated Fat	0g	Sodium	103.8mg

Fresh Cranberry Chutney

4 cups fresh or frozen
   cranberries
2 cups water
1 cup white sugar
2 cups brown sugar
1 onion, chopped
6 (4-inch) cinnamon sticks

1/2 cup currants or raisins
6 tablespoons chopped
   crystallized ginger
1 cup cider vinegar
1/2 cup chopped dates
2 firm green apples, peeled,
   cored, chopped

Combine all ingredients in a large saucepan. Cook over medium heat, stirring occasionally, about 25 minutes. Remove cinnamon sticks. Serve either hot or cold. Refrigerate in a container with a tight-fitting lid. Makes about 6 cups.

Each 1/4-Cup Serving Contains:					
Calories	125.2	Fiber	1.4g	Trans-fatty acids	0g
Protein	0.3g	Total Fat	0.1g	Cholesterol	0mg
Carbohydrates	32.6g	Saturated Fat	0g	Sodium	16.4mg

Peach Chutney

5 or 6 large fresh peaches, peeled, or canned peaches, sliced
1/2 cup raisins
1/3 cup raspberry or cider vinegar
3/4 cup brown sugar
1 tablespoon ground ginger

2 green onions, chopped
1 teaspoon dry mustard
1 tablespoon grated orange peel
1/2 teaspoon red-pepper flakes
4 or 5 whole cloves
1 cinnamon stick
1/2 cup water

In a large heavy pot, combine all ingredients. Simmer uncovered 30 to 35 minutes, stirring often, until desired consistency. Serve at once or spoon into a container with a tight-fitting lid. May be stored in the refrigerator for several months. Makes about 2-1/2 cups.

Variation: Omit peaches and substitute any firm near-ripe fruit. Try apples, apricots, pears or a combination of fruits, both fresh and dried. For a milder chutney, omit pepper flakes and cloves.

Each 1/4-Cup Serving Contains:							
Calories	91.8	Fiber	1.4g	Trans-fatty acids	0g
Protein	0.8g	Total Fat	0.3g	Cholesterol	0mg
Carbohydrates	23.6g	Saturated Fat	0g	Sodium	6.7mg

Basic White Sauce

1 tablespoon mono-unsaturated oil
2 tablespoons all-purpose flour
1 cup nonfat milk or fat-free broth

1/2 teaspoon onion powder
Salt and pepper

In a small saucepan, blend together oil and flour. Slowly stir in milk or broth. Combine until smooth. Add onion powder. Heat, stirring, over medium heat until thickened. Season to taste with salt and pepper. Makes about 1 cup.

Each 1/4-Cup Serving Contains:							
Calories	66.6	Fiber	0.1g	Trans-fatty acids	0g
Protein	2.5g	Total Fat	3.6g	Cholesterol	1.1mg
Carbohydrates	6.18g	Saturated Fat	0.3g	Sodium	38.4mg

BREADS

IS ANYTHING MORE INVITING THAN THE AROMA OF FRESH BAKED BREAD?

That delightful aroma entices everyone into the kitchen immediately. You, too, can create this special atmosphere by baking any one of our breads.

We have a Classic French Bread, which is wonderful. If time is a problem, our muffins can be made quickly.

In an effort to appeal to your tastes, we offer Almond, Raisin, Applesauce, Zucchini and Old-Country Bran Muffins. Try them all and select your favorite.

Pancakes make a wonderful light supper. Made with yogurt, they are delightfully tender. Top with fresh fruit.

Almond-Bran Muffins

1/4 cup egg substitute
1/4 cup canola oil
1 cup lowfat buttermilk
6 tablespoons brown sugar
3 tablespoons dark molasses
2 tablespoons honey
1/2 teaspoon ground
    cardamom

2-1/2 cups raisin-bran cereal
1 cup plus 2 tablespoons
    all-purpose flour
1/2 teaspoon baking soda
1-1/2 teaspoons baking powder
1/2 cup chopped almonds

Preheat oven to 400F (205C). Line muffin-pan cups with paper baking cups or spray with vegetable cooking spray; set aside. In a large bowl, beat egg substitute until light. Stir in oil, buttermilk, brown sugar, molasses, honey and cardamom. Fold in cereal, flour, baking soda, baking powder and almonds. Spoon batter into prepared muffin cups. Bake 25 minutes or until a wooden pick inserted into center of a muffin comes out clean. Remove from pan; cool 5 minutes and serve. Makes 12 muffins.

Each Muffin Contains:					
Calories	204.6	Fiber	2.2g	Trans-fatty acids	0g
Protein	4.9g	Total Fat	8.1g	Cholesterol	0.8mg
Carbohydrates	30.9g	Saturated Fat	0.8g	Sodium	214.0mg

Raisin-Oat Muffins

1-1/2 cups lowfat buttermilk
1-1/2 cups rolled oats
1-1/2 cups all-purpose flour
1 tablespoon baking powder
1/2 teaspoon baking soda
2 teaspoons ground cinnamon

1/2 cup egg substitute
1/2 cup brown sugar
1/3 cup canola oil
1 teaspoon maple flavoring
1 cup raisins

Preheat oven to 400F (205C). Line muffin-pan cups with paper baking cups or spray with vegetable cooking spray; set aside. In a medium bowl, pour buttermilk over oats. In a small bowl, stir together flour, baking powder, baking soda and cinnamon; add mixture to soaked oats. In a small bowl, combine egg substitute, brown sugar, oil and maple flavoring. Pour into flour mixture; add raisins. Gently fold together until flour is moistened, batter will be lumpy. Spoon batter into prepared muffin cups. Bake 20 to 25 minutes or until a wooden pick inserted into center of a muffin comes out clean. Remove from pan; cool 5 minutes and serve. Makes 12 large muffins.

Cherry-Almond Muffins: Omit raisins, cinnamon and maple flavoring. Substitute 1 cup chopped cherries and 1 teaspoon almond extract.

Apricot-Orange Muffins: Omit raisins, cinnamon and maple flavoring. Substitute 1 cup chopped dried apricots, 1 tablespoon grated orange peel and 1 teaspoon vanilla extract.

Apple-Date Muffins: Omit raisins and maple flavoring. Substitute 2/3 cup chopped apple and 1/3 cup chopped dates. Reduce cinnamon to 1 teaspoon, add 1/2 teaspoon ground cardamom.

Each Muffin Contains:					
Calories	231.0	Fiber	2.2g	Trans-fatty acids	0g
Protein	5.9g	Total Fat	7.5g	Cholesterol	1.2mg
Carbohydrates	36.3g	Saturated Fat	0.8g	Sodium	229.6mg

Applesauce-Bran Muffins

2 cups unprocessed bran
1 cup oat bran
1/2 cup egg substitute
3/4 cup unsweetened
    applesauce
1/2 cup brown sugar

3/4 cup chopped dried apricots
    or raisins
1/2 teaspoon almond extract
1 teaspoon ground cinnamon
3 tablespoons canola oil
1 tablespoon baking powder

Preheat oven to 425F(220C). Line muffin pan cups with paper baking cups or spray with vegetable cooking spray; set aside. In a large bowl, combine all ingredients. Gently fold together until dry ingredients are moistened, batter will be lumpy. Spoon batter into prepared muffin cups. Bake 17 to 20 minutes or until a wooden pick inserted into center of a muffin comes out clean. Remove from pan; cool 5 minutes and serve. Makes 12 large muffins.

Each Muffin Contains:					
Calories	129.5	Fiber	6.3g	Trans-fatty acids	0g
Protein	4.5g	Total Fat	4.8g	Cholesterol	0.1mg
Carbohydrates	24.8g	Saturated Fat	0.5g	Sodium	144.4mg

Zucchini Muffins

1/2 cup egg substitute
1/3 cup nonfat milk
1/3 cup canola oil
1/2 cup grated zucchini
1-1/2 tablespoons unsweetened
   cocoa powder
1 cup all-purpose flour

1/2 cup sugar
1/2 teaspoon baking soda
1/2 teaspoon baking powder
1 teaspoon ground cinnamon
1/2 teaspoon ground ginger
1/2 teaspoon chocolate
   flavoring

Preheat oven to 375F (190C). Line muffin pan cups with paper baking cups or spray with vegetable cooking spray; set aside. In a large bowl, thoroughly mix egg substitute, milk, oil and zucchini. Add remaining ingredients. Gently fold together until dry ingredients are moistened, batter will be lumpy. Spoon batter into prepared muffin cups. Bake 15 to 18 minutes or until a wooden pick inserted into center of a muffin comes out clean. Remove from pan; cool 5 minutes and serve. Makes 12 large muffins.

Each Muffin Contains:						
Calories	138.0	Fiber	0.7g	Trans-fatty acids	0g
Protein	2.8g	Total Fat	6.6g	Cholesterol	0.2mg
Carbohydrates	17.4g	Saturated Fat	0.6g	Sodium	95.4mg

Old-Country Muffins

1-2/3 cups oat bran
1 cup whole-wheat flour
1 cup brown sugar
2 tablespoons unsweetened
  cocoa powder
5 teaspoons baking powder
1-1/2 teaspoons baking soda
1/2 cup bran flakes cereal

1/4 cup honey
5 tablespoons dark molasses
3 tablespoons mono-
  unsaturated oil
1 cup lowfat buttermilk
1 teaspoon vanilla extract
2 egg whites, beaten
1-1/2 cups raisins

Preheat oven to 375F (190C). Line muffin-pan cups with paper baking cups or spray with vegetable cooking spray; set aside. In a large bowl, combine oat bran, flour, sugar, cocoa powder, baking powder, baking soda and cereal. In a small bowl, stir together honey, molasses, oil, buttermilk and vanilla. Stir mixture into dry ingredients. Fold in beaten egg whites and raisins. Spoon batter into prepared muffin cups. Bake 20 to 25 minutes, or until a wooden pick inserted into center of a muffin comes out clean; cool 5 minutes and serve. Makes 24 large muffins.

Each Muffin Contains:					
Calories	129.2	Fiber	2.2g	Trans-fatty acids	0g
Protein	2.9g	Total Fat	2.5g	Cholesterol	0.4mg
Carbohydrates	28.5g	Saturated Fat	0.3g	Sodium	208.1mg

Whole-Wheat Pancakes

1 cup nonfat milk
3/4 cup all-purpose flour
3/4 cup whole-wheat flour
3/4 cup egg substitute
1 tablespoon sugar

1 tablespoon brown sugar
1/4 cup melted soft margarine
1/2 teaspoon baking soda
1 tablespoon baking powder
1/2 cup currants or raisins

Pour milk into a blender or food processor; add flours, thoroughly blend. Add egg substitute, sugars, melted margarine, baking soda and baking powder. Blend or process briefly, until batter is smooth. Spray a non-stick griddle with vegetable cooking spray. Preheat griddle. Pour about 1/4 cup batter for each pancake. When bubbles appear and edges look dry, turn and cook other side. Makes 16 (4-inch) pancakes or 4 servings. Serve with jam, maple syrup, honey or fruit syrup.

Note: If margarine is used on pancakes, it increases the amount of saturated fat.

Each 4-Pancake Serving Contains:					
Calories	344.9	Fiber	4.0g	Trans fatty acids	0.0g
Protein	14.0g	Total Fat	7.9g	Cholesterol	1.6mg
Carbohydrates	57.2g	Saturated Fat	1.4g	Sodium	691.8mg

Quaker Oats® Pancakes

1 cup all-purpose flour
1/2 cup Quaker Oats, quick or
   old-fashioned, uncooked
1 tablespoon baking powder

1 cup nonfat milk
1/4 cup egg substitute or
   2 egg whites, beaten
2 tablespoons canola oil

Spray a non-stick griddle or electric fry pan with vegetable cooking spray. Preheat griddle. In a large bowl, combine flour, oats and baking powder. Add milk, egg substitute or beaten egg whites and oil. Pour about 1/4 cup batter for each pancake. When bubbles appear and edges look dry, turn and cook other side. Serve with syrup and fruit. Makes 12 pancakes.

Each 3-Pancake Serving Contains:

Calories	249.3	Fiber	2.0g	Trans-fatty acids	0g
Protein	8.8g	Total Fat	8.4g	Cholesterol	1.3mg
Carbohydrates	34.7g	Saturated Fat	0.8g	Sodium	426.0mg

(Courtesy of The Quaker Oats Company)

Cornmeal Pancakes

1 tablespoon lemon juice or
   vinegar
1-1/4 cups nonfat milk
1/2 cup cornmeal
1/2 cup all-purpose flour

1/2 teaspoon baking soda
1 tablespoon baking powder
1 tablespoon sugar, if desired
1/2 cup egg substitute

Spray a non-stick griddle or electric fry pan with vegetable cooking spray. Preheat griddle. Add lemon juice or vinegar to milk; set aside for 5 minutes. In a mixing bowl, stir together cornmeal, flour, baking soda and baking powder. Add sugar, if desired. Add milk mixture and egg substitute, stir to blend. Pour about 1/4 cup batter for each pancake. When bubbles appear and edges look dry, turn and cook other side. Serve with syrup on fruit. Makes 12 pancakes.

Each 3-Pancake Serving Contains:

Calories	175.9	Fiber	1.8g	Trans-fatty acids	0g
Protein	9.5g	Total Fat	1.6g	Cholesterol	1.7mg
Carbohydrates	30.5g	Saturated Fat	0.4g	Sodium	618.9mg

Orange-Yogurt Pancakes

2 egg whites
3/4 cup egg substitute
1 (8-oz.) container fat-free
    mandarin-orange yogurt

1 cup all-purpose flour
3/4 teaspoon baking soda
1 (11-oz.) can mandarin
    oranges

Spray a non-stick griddle or electric fry pan with vegetable cooking spray. Preheat griddle. In a mixer bowl, beat egg whites until soft peaks form. Add egg substitute and beat at low speed to blend. Continue beating and add yogurt, flour and baking soda. Pour about 1/4 cup batter for each pancake. When bubbles appear and edges look dry, turn and cook other side. Top pancakes with mandarin oranges. Makes 12 pancakes.

Variation: Substitute any other fruit flavor for orange yogurt. Top with the same fruit, fresh or canned.

Each 3-Pancake Serving Contains:						
Calories	243.9	Fiber	1.3g	Trans-fatty acids	0g
Protein	13.8g	Total Fat	1.9g	Cholesterol	2.1mg
Carbohydrates	42.8g	Saturated Fat	0.4g	Sodium	386.2mg

Classic French Bread

6 to 6-1/2 cups bread flour
(divided)
1 (1/4-oz.) pkg. active dry yeast
1 teaspoon salt

1 teaspoon sugar, if desired
2-1/4 cups warm water
1 tablespoon water
Cornmeal

In a large mixer bowl, using a dough hook, combine 2 cups flour, yeast, salt and sugar. Gradually add water. Continue to mix 1-1/2 to 2 minutes; add an additional 2 cups flour. Mix until thoroughly blended. Beat in more flour, making a stiff and manageable dough. Turn out on a floured board; knead about 10 minutes. Dough should be smooth and elastic. Place dough in a large oiled bowl, turning dough to coat top. Place bowl in a draft-free area. Let dough rise until doubled, 1-1/2 to 2 hours. Punch dough down, cover and let rise again until doubled.

Spray a baking sheet with vegetable cooking spray; sprinkle with cornmeal. Place dough on floured surface. Cover and let rest about 10 minutes. Divide dough in half. Pat or roll each piece into a 15 x 10-inch rectangle. Starting from the long side, roll dough up tightly; gently press loaf with each turn. Gently roll dough between hands to seal edges and taper ends. Place loaves seam-side down, on baking sheet. Brush with water. Cover and let rise about 1 hour.

Heat oven to 450F (205C). With a sharp knife, make slashes on the top, about 2 inches apart and 1/4 inch deep. Brush with water. Bake in upper third of oven. Brush with water every 3 minutes during first 10 minutes of baking. Bake another 15 to 20 minutes, until bread is brown. Remove from oven; lightly brush with water, set on a rack and cool. Makes 2 loaves.

Variation: For a glazed crust, combine 1 egg white and 1 tablespoon water. Bake 10 minutes, brush with egg glaze; bake 10 more minutes, brush again. Continue baking 15 to 20 minutes.

Each Slice Contains:

Calories	69.7	Fiber	0.6g	Trans-fatty acids	0g
Protein	2.4g	Total Fat	0.5g	Cholesterol	0mg
Carbohydrates	13.8g	Saturated Fat	0.1g	Sodium	55.2mg

Light Oatmeal Bread

3 cups lukewarm water
2 (1/4-oz.) pkgs. or 2 table-
    spoons active dry yeast
1/2 cup honey
1/4 cup canola oil
3 cups whole-wheat flour

1 cup cracked wheat
3 to 5 cups all-purpose flour
1 cup oat bran
1 egg white
1 tablespoon water

In a large mixer bowl, combine water, yeast, honey, oil and whole-wheat flour. Let rise until double in bulk. Stir down. Beat at medium speed; add cracked wheat and about 2 cups all-purpose flour and oat bran. Mix thoroughly for about 10 minutes or by hand 12 to 15 minutes. Add some remaining flour and mix until dough pulls away from sides of bowl. Turn out dough onto a lightly floured board. Knead about 15 minutes. Place dough in a large greased bowl; turn dough to coat all sides. Cover with a dry cloth towel or plastic wrap. Place bowl in a warm draft-free area and let dough rise until double in bulk, 1 1/2 to 2 hours. Punch dough down. Form into loaves or rolls. Place in pans sprayed with vegetable cooking spray. Let rise again until doubled in bulk, 45 to 60 minutes. Preheat oven to 375F (190C). Combine egg white and water. Brush tops with egg mixture. Bake 30 to 40 minutes. Remove from pans, and cool. Makes 2 loaves (12 slices each.)

Each Large Slice Contains:					
Calories	216.3	Fiber	4.0g	Trans-fatty acids	0g
Protein	6.5g	Total Fat	3.2g	Cholesterol	0mg
Carbohydrates	43.1g	Saturated Fat	0.3g	Sodium	5.5mg

Onion-Caraway Bread

1/2 cup finely chopped onion	1 teaspoon salt
2 cups (16 oz.) large-curd fat-free cottage cheese, room temperature	1/2 teaspoon baking soda
	3-1/2 cups all-purpose flour
	1/2 cup egg substitute
1/4 cup sugar	2 (1/4-oz.) pkgs. active dry yeast
3 tablespoons melted soft margarine	1 cup quick or rolled oats
	2 tablespoons caraway seeds

In a large mixer bowl, beat onion, cottage cheese, sugar, margarine, salt and baking soda until well combined. Stir in 2 cups flour, egg substitute and yeast; beat 2 minutes. Stir in oats, caraway seeds and remaining flour. Cover with a dry cloth towel or plastic wrap. Place bowl in a warm draft-free area and let dough rise until double in bulk; about 1 hour. Stir batter down. Spray 2 deep 1-1/2-quart casseroles or soufflé dishes with vegetable cooking spray. Place batter in prepared dishes. Brush with melted margarine. Let rise, uncovered in a draft-free area until doubled, about 45 minutes. Preheat oven to 350F (175C). Bake 35 to 40 minutes or until golden brown. Remove pans and cool. Makes 2 loaves (12 slices each).

Each Large Slice Contains:					
Calories	116.1	Fiber	1.4g	Trans-fatty acids	0.1g
Protein	5.9g	Total Fat	1.4g	Cholesterol	1.7mg
Carbohydrates	19.8g	Saturated Fat	0.2g	Sodium	193.2mg

166

Mixed-Fruit Bread

1 cup chopped dried figs
1 cup chopped dates
1 cup raisins
2 cups hot apple juice
2 teaspoons baking soda
1/2 cup egg substitute
1 egg white

1-1/2 cups sugar
4 tablespoons melted soft
   margarine
4 cups all-purpose flour
1/2 teaspoon ground allspice
1 teaspoon vanilla extract

In a large bowl, combine figs, dates and raisins with hot apple juice. Set aside for 10 minutes. In a mixer bowl, beat together egg substitute, egg white, sugar and margarine. Alternately add fruit mixture and flour, blending well after each addition. Add allspice and vanilla. Spray 2 9 x 5-inch) baking pans with vegetable cooking spray. Spoon batter into prepared pans. Bake 35 to 40 minutes at 350F (190C), until a wooden pick inserted into center of a loaf comes out clean. Remove from pans and cool. Makes 2 loaves (12 slices each).

Each Slice Contains:						
Calories	200.0	Fiber	2.0g	Trans-fatty acids	0.1g
Protein	3.5g	Total Fat	1.4g	Cholesterol	0.1mg
Carbohydrates	44.7g	Saturated Fat	0.3g	Sodium	127.5mg

Cornbread

1 cup corn meal
1/2 cup all-purpose flour
1/2 cup oat bran
3 tablespoons sugar
2 teaspoons baking powder

1 teaspoon baking soda
1/4 teaspoon salt
1/2 cup plain fat-free yogurt
3 egg whites, beaten

Preheat oven to 400F (205C). Spray a 9-inch pie pan with vegetable cooking spray; set aside. In a medium bowl, thoroughly combine corn meal, flour, oat bran, sugar, baking powder, baking soda and salt. Stir in yogurt. Fold in egg whites. Pour into prepared pan. Bake 20 to 25 minutes. Makes 8 servings.

Each Serving Contains:						
Calories	139.6	Fiber	2.4g	Trans-fatty acids	0g
Protein	5.5g	Total Fat	0.8g	Cholesterol	0.3mg
Carbohydrates	29.6g	Saturated Fat	0.1g	Sodium	379.0mg

Golden Herbed Rolls

1 (1/4-oz.) pkg. active dry yeast
1/2 cup sugar
1 cup warm skim milk
3 tablespoons canola oil
1/2 teaspoon salt, if desired
1 cup pureed, cooked yellow
    squash or pumpkin

1 tablespoon dried-leaf
    oregano
1 tablespoon dill weed
1/4 teaspoon lemon pepper
5 cups all-purpose flour,
    divided

In a mixer bowl, sprinkle yeast and sugar into warm, not hot, milk and oil. Let stand about 5 minutes. Turn mixer to low; gradually add salt, squash, oregano, dill weed, lemon pepper and about 2 cups flour. Beat until well blended. Remove beaters and gradually beat in remaining flour by hand. Cover with a dry cloth towel or plastic wrap. Place bowl in a warm draft-free area and let dough rise until double in bulk, 1 to 1-1/2 hours. Turn dough out onto a floured board or pastry cloth. Knead gently about 2 minutes. Roll out dough to 1-inch thickness. Cut into rolls using 3-inch cutter. Place on baking sheet or 13 x 9-inch pan sprayed with vegetable cooking spray. Cover and let rise until doubled in bulk. Preheat oven to 400F (205C). Uncover rolls and bake 20 to 25 minutes until golden brown. Makes 12 large rolls.

Each Roll Contains:					
Calories	266.7	Fiber	2.2g	Trans-fatty acids	0g
Protein	6.5g	Total Fat	4.0g	Cholesterol	0.4mg
Carbohydrates	50.7g	Saturated Fat	0.4g	Sodium	12.7mg

BEANS & OTHER LEGUMES

*BEANS AND RICE ARE A VITAL PART OF COOKING
FOR THE HEALTHY HEART.*

We are all relearning the simple truth that plain, wholesome foods are good for us. In this chapter we help you explore new recipes with a variety of grains, legumes and beans.

It is easy to work these into your diet, with just a little thought. Here's a great combination for entertaining: easy-to-prepare and delicious Jamaican Bean Pot served with a tossed salad, Classic French Bread, page 164, and Buttermilk Sherbet, page 224.

Brown rice has a distinct flavor that complements other foods. Brown Rice with Vegetables is a good example. Spanish Rice & Bean Pie gives a different look to basic ingredients. This is a taste-award winner.

Black-Eyed Peas

2 cups dried or 1 (16-oz.) pkg.
  frozen black-eyed peas
3 quarts water
1/2 small onion, chopped

1 garlic clove, chopped
1/2 teaspoon salt
Coarse pepper to taste

Presoak dried black-eyed peas; drain. In a large pot, place peas and remaining ingredients. Bring to a boil, reduce heat and simmer until tender, 1-1/2 to 2 hours. If using frozen peas, thawing is not necessary. Place all ingredients in a large pot. Bring to a boil, reduce heat and simmer until tender, 45 to 50 minutes.

Each 1-Cup Serving Contains:

Calories	110.1	Fiber	3.5g	Trans-fatty acids	0g
Protein	7.7g	Total Fat	0.4g	Cholesterol	0mg
Carbohydrates	19.7g	Saturated Fat	0.2g	Sodium	87.5mg

Wild Rice Stir-Fry

1/2 (10-oz.) can beef consommé
1 tablespoon canola oil
2 teaspoons grated fresh ginger
  or 1/4 teaspoon ground
  ginger
1 medium onion, sliced
1/2 cup fresh or canned sliced
  mushrooms, drained

1 (8-oz.) can water chestnuts,
  drained
1/2 cup Chinese pea pods
3 teaspoons chopped pimiento
2 cups cooked wild rice
1/2 cup fresh bean sprouts
Soy sauce

Chill consommé. Remove fat that rises to top. Heat oil in a wok or large skillet. Add ginger and onion, stir-fry about 1 minute. Add remaining ingredients, stirring after each addition. Continue stirring until liquid is absorbed. Serve at once. Season with soy sauce to taste. Makes 4 servings.

Each Serving Contains:

Calories	189.1	Fiber	5.5g	Trans-fatty acids	0g
Protein	8.8g	Total Fat	4.1g	Cholesterol	0mg
Carbohydrates	31.6g	Saturated Fat	0.5g	Sodium	491.4mg

Brown Rice with Vegetables

1 tablespoon olive or canola oil
1 onion, chopped
3 carrots, sliced
3 celery stalks, sliced
1 cup brown rice

2 cups Chicken Broth, page 129
1 tablespoon chopped parsley
1/2 cup fresh mushrooms, sliced
Salt and pepper

In a 2-quart pan or Dutch oven, heat oil. Sauté onion, carrots and celery. Add rice and stir to coat. Add chicken broth and parsley. Cover and cook over low heat about 40 minutes. Add mushrooms and continue cooking about 5 minutes. Season with salt and pepper to taste. Makes 6 servings.

Each Serving Contains:

Calories	177.6	Fiber	2.9g	Trans-fatty acids	0g
Protein	5.3g	Total Fat	3.8g	Cholesterol	0mg
Carbohydrates	31.0g	Saturated Fat	0.6g	Sodium	336.9mg

Brown Rice in Tomato Sauce

2 tablespoons olive or
  canola oil
2 medium onions, chopped
2 garlic cloves
1 cup brown rice
1 cup water
2 cups tomato juice

1/2 teaspoon pepper
1 cup sliced mushrooms
1 teaspoon fresh parsley
1 cup peas
Salt and pepper
Tabasco sauce

Heat oil in a Dutch oven or heavy pot. Sauté onions and garlic. Add rice and stir to coat. Pour in water, tomato juice and pepper. Bring to a boil; cover and reduce heat to a simmer. Continue cooking 40 to 45 minutes. Add mushrooms, parsley and peas; cook about 10 minutes more. Season with salt, pepper and Tabasco sauce to taste. Makes 6 to 8 servings.

Each Serving Contains:

Calories	212.2	Fiber	3.8g	Trans-fatty acids	0g
Protein	5.7g	Total Fat	5.8g	Cholesterol	0mg
Carbohydrates	36.0g	Saturated Fat	0.8g	Sodium	346.1mg

171

Barbecued Beans

2 quarts water
2 cups dried navy beans
1 onion, diced
1 (6-oz.) can tomato sauce
1/4 cup sweet relish
1 tablespoon vinegar

1 teaspoon dry mustard
1 teaspoon ground pepper
2 tablespoons Worcestershire
  sauce
5 tablespoons brown sugar
Salt and pepper

In a large pot, bring 2 quarts water to a boil. Rinse beans thoroughly, add to hot water. Boil 2 minutes. Turn off heat and let beans sit covered, 1 hour. Or soak beans in water overnight. Drain; add fresh water to beans. Bring to a boil, reduce heat and cook about 1 hour, until beans are soft and tender. Spray a small non-stick skillet with vegetable cooking spray. Sauté onion. Add remaining ingredients; cook about 5 minutes to blend. Drain liquid from beans. Add tomato mixture to beans. Season to taste with salt and pepper. Mix thoroughly. Preheat oven to 350F (175C). Pour beans into a 2-quart baking dish or bean pot and bake uncovered about 1 hour. Makes about 8 servings.

Each 1-Cup Serving Contains:							
Calories	139.3	Fiber	6.3g	Trans-fatty acids	0g
Protein	6.2g	Total Fat	0.6g	Cholesterol	0mg
Carbohydrates	28.6g	Saturated Fat	0.1g	Sodium	268.5mg

Easy Bean Bake

1 (15-oz.) can pinto beans,
    drained
1 (15-oz.) can kidney beans,
    drained
1 (15-oz.) can garbanzo beans,
    drained
1 (8-oz.) can tomato sauce
1/2 cup chopped onion
2 teaspoons Italian herbs
2 teaspoons chopped fresh
    parsley

1 teaspoon garlic powder
1 fennel bulb, sliced or 2 celery
    stalks, sliced
1 green bell pepper, chopped
1 red or yellow bell pepper,
    chopped
2 medium tomatoes, chopped
3 tablespoons grated Parmesan
    cheese

In a large bowl, combine all beans, tomato sauce, onion, Italian herbs, parsley, garlic powder, fennel or celery and bell peppers. Spray a 13 x 9-inch baking dish with vegetable cooking spray. Pour in bean mixture. Top with chopped tomato. Bake in a 350F (175C) oven 35 to 40 minutes. To serve, sprinkle with Parmesan cheese. Makes 8 servings.

Each Serving Contains:						
Calories	201.7	Fiber	12.9g	Trans-fatty acids	0g
Protein	11.1g	Total Fat	2.7g	Cholesterol	1.8mg
Carbohydrates	35.1g	Saturated Fat	0.5g	Sodium	450.9mg

Jamaican Bean Pot

1 lb. dried black beans
10 cups water
1/2 cup chopped onion
1 garlic clove, minced
1/2 cup sliced celery
1/2 cup sliced carrot
2 tablespoons olive or
    canola oil

1 bay leaf
1-1/2 teaspoons salt
1/4 cup dark molasses
1/4 cup packed brown sugar
1/4 cup dark Jamaican rum
1 teaspoon dry mustard
Pinch of dried-leaf thyme

Rinse beans in sieve under running water. In a large pot, combine beans and 10 cups water. In a skillet, sauté onion, garlic, celery and carrot in oil until onion softens. Add vegetables, bay leaf and salt to beans. Bring to a boil; reduce heat. Cover and simmer until beans are almost tender, 1-1/2 to 2 hours. Add hot water as needed to keep beans just covered while cooking. Drain beans, reserving liquid. Discard bay leaf. Preheat oven to 300F (150C). In a small bowl, combine molasses, brown sugar, rum, dry mustard and thyme; mix well. Put beans in a 2-1/2-quart bean pot or casserole with cover. Pour molasses mixture over beans; stir. Add enough reserved cooking liquid to just cover beans, about 1-1/2 cups. Cover and bake 2 hours. Uncover; bake 30 minutes longer or until beans are tender. Serve bubbling hot. Makes 8 (1/2-cup) servings.

Each Serving Contains:							
Calories	188.6	Fiber	5.4g	Trans-fatty acids	0g
Protein	5.4g	Total Fat	3.9g	Cholesterol	0mg
Carbohydrates	27.0g	Saturated Fat	0.6g	Sodium	425.4mg

Spanish Rice & Bean Pie

1 cup dried pinto, red or
   pink beans
Water for soaking
2-1/2 cups water
1 garlic clove, minced
1/3 cup chopped onion
2 teaspoons imitation
   bacon bits
1/2 teaspoon salt
1/8 teaspoon pepper
1 cup water
1 chicken bouillon cube

1/2 cup uncooked rice
1/2 cup chopped onion
1/2 cup chopped green
   bell pepper
1 tablespoon olive or canola oil
2 tablespoons chopped
   pimiento
2 tablespoons egg substitute
1 cup fat-free cottage cheese
1/2 cup (2 oz.) shredded lowfat
   Cheddar cheese

Place beans in a saucepan with water to cover by more than 2 inches. Bring to a boil. Boil 2 minutes. Remove from heat; cover. Set aside 1 hour. Drain. In a saucepan, combine beans, 2-1/2 cups water, garlic, 1/3 cup onion, bacon bits, salt and pepper. Bring to a boil; reduce heat. Cover; simmer until beans are tender, 1 to 1-1/2 hours. In a small saucepan, bring 1 cup water and bouillon cube to a boil. Stir to dissolve bouillon. Add rice. Reduce heat to lowest setting. Cover and simmer 20 minutes. Preheat oven to 325F (165C). In a small skillet, sauté 1/2 cup onion and 1/2 cup green pepper in oil until onion is limp. Stir in pimiento. Add onion mixture and egg substitute to cooked rice; mix well. Spray a 9-inch pie pan with vegetable cooking spray. Press rice mixture into pie pan to form a crust. Spread cottage cheese over rice crust. Pour beans over cottage cheese. Bake 20 minutes. Sprinkle top with Cheddar cheese; bake another 20 minutes. Remove from oven; let stand 10 minutes before cutting into wedges. Serve with a spatula. Makes 6 servings.

Each Serving Contains:						
Calories	183.9	Fiber	3.8g	Trans-fatty acids	0g
Protein	12.5g	Total Fat	3.1g	Cholesterol	3.5mg
Carbohydrates	26.3g	Saturated Fat	0.5g	Sodium	655.9mg

VEGETABLES

*WE ARE FORTUNATE TO LIVE IN A TIME WHEN
WONDERFUL VEGETABLES ARE AVAILABLE YEAR ROUND.*

Vegetables can be served in a variety of ways: baked, steamed, stir-fried, stewed and, of course, raw. As a side dish or the basis of a main dish, vegetables offer nutrition, fiber, color, texture and—most of all—flavor.

Some of the recipes are super simple, such as Baked Hubbard Squash or Garden Medley. For special occasions, fix Stuffed Tomatoes or Pineapple Yams.

Stuffed Tomatoes

4 tomatoes
4 green onions, chopped
4 tablespoons crushed corn
    flakes
1/4 bunch fresh spinach,
    washed, chopped
1/2 teaspoon dried-leaf basil

1 tablespoon parsley
1 tablespoon crushed corn
    flakes
1 tablespoon grated Parmesan
    cheese
Salt and pepper

Preheat oven to 375F (190C). Slice tops off tomatoes. Scoop out pulp and place tomato shells in a baking dish. Chop tomato pulp. In a small bowl, combine chopped tomato with green onions, 4 tablespoons corn flakes, spinach, basil and parsley. Fill tomato shells with mixture. Sprinkle tops with additional crushed corn flakes, Parmesan cheese and salt and pepper to taste. Bake about 15 minutes. Makes 4 servings.

Variation: Omit corn flakes and spinach; substitute 1/4 cup sliced celery, 2 slices of bread, cubed and 2 tablespoons chopped green bell pepper.

Each Serving Contains:					
Calories	48.5	Fiber	2.1g	Trans-fatty acids	0g
Protein	2.5g	Total Fat	1.0g	Cholesterol	1.2mg
Carbohydrates	9.0g	Saturated Fat	0.4g	Sodium	140.5mg

Broiled Tomatoes

1/2 cup fat-free plain yogurt
1/4 cup shredded-wheat crumbs
1 teaspoon each chives, parsley
   and dill
1/2 teaspoon garlic powder

1/2 teaspoon dry mustard
Salt and pepper
2 teaspoons capers, if desired
4 tomatoes

Preheat broiler. In a small bowl, mix fat-free yogurt with shredded-wheat crumbs, chives, parsley, dill, garlic powder, mustard, salt and pepper to taste and capers, if desired. Cut tomatoes into 1/2-inch slices; place on a broiler pan or baking sheet. Spread mixture evenly on tomato slices. Broil until topping begins to brown. Remove from oven and serve at once. Makes 4 to 6 servings.

Each Serving Contains:					
Calories	56.1	Fiber	1.6g	Trans-fatty acids	0g
Protein	3.3g	Total Fat	0.7g	Cholesterol	0.6mg
Carbohydrates	10.7g	Saturated Fat	0.1g	Sodium	101.7mg

Honey-Glazed Carrots

2 cups mini carrots
3 tablespoons water
2 tablespoons honey
1 tablespoon soft margarine

1/4 teaspoon ground cinnamon
1/4 teaspoon ground nutmeg
2 tablespoons orange juice

In a saucepan, cook carrots with water to cover about 15 minutes. Drain water. Return carrots to heat. Add remaining ingredients; stir until honey mixture is hot and all carrots are well coated. Makes 4 servings.

Each Serving Contains:					
Calories	72.7	Fiber	1.6g	Trans-fatty acids	0.2g
Protein	0.7g	Total Fat	1.5g	Cholesterol	0mg
Carbohydrates	15.3g	Saturated Fat	0.3g	Sodium	32.6mg

Baked-Zucchini Casserole

4 zucchini, trimmed, sliced
3 tomatoes
1 (12-oz.) can whole-kernel
    corn, drained
3 chopped green onions

1/4 cup breadcrumbs
1/2 teaspoon garlic powder
1 teaspoon dried-leaf oregano
1 teaspoon dried-leaf basil
Salt and lemon pepper

Preheat oven to 350F (175C). Spray a 2-quart casserole with vegetable cooking spray. Alternate layers of zucchini, tomatoes, corn and green onions. Repeat. Cover and bake 20 minutes. Mix together breadcrumbs, garlic powder, oregano and basil. Sprinkle on top. Bake uncovered 10 to 12 minutes. Season to taste with salt and lemon pepper. Makes 6 servings.

Each Serving Contains:					
Calories	97.8	Fiber	3.8g	Trans-fatty acids	0g
Protein	4.3g	Total Fat	1.2g	Cholesterol	0mg
Carbohydrates	21.2g	Saturated Fat	0.2g	Sodium	274.0mg

Corn Fritters

1 cup all-purpose flour
3/4 teaspoon baking powder
1/2 cup egg substitute
1/4 cup nonfat milk
1 pkg. imitation butter granules

1-1/2 cups creamed corn,
    drained
1/2 teaspoon sugar
1 to 2 teaspoons canola oil

In a medium bowl, stir flour and baking powder together. Add remaining ingredients; stir well to blend. Spray a non-stick skillet with vegetable cooking spray. For each fritter, drop 2 spoonfuls mixture, adding oil to skillet if needed. Makes 4 to 6 servings. Turn once to brown, both sides.

Each Serving Contains:					
Calories	246.3	Fiber	2.2g	Trans-fatty acids	0g
Protein	9.2g	Total Fat	4.1g	Cholesterol	0.6mg
Carbohydrates	45.1g	Saturated Fat	0.7g	Sodium	459.1mg

Creamed Green Beans

1 lb. fresh green beans
2 green onions, chopped
1 pkg. imitation butter granules,
   if desired
3/4 cup Chicken Broth,
   page 129
1 teaspoon caraway seeds

2 tablespoons all-purpose flour
4 tablespoons fat-free
   plain yogurt
1/2 teaspoon sugar
2 tablespoons vinegar
1 tablespoon chopped pimiento
Chopped parsley

Rinse beans; cut or break into 2-inch pieces. In a saucepan, simmer green beans, onions, butter granules, if desired, chicken broth and caraway seeds about 20 minutes. Mix flour, yogurt and sugar together. Add to beans, cook stirring constantly for several minutes, until thickened. Stir in vinegar and pimiento; sprinkle with parsley. Serve at once. Makes 6 servings.

Each Serving Contains:							
Calories	49.0	Fiber	3.0g	Trans-fatty acids	0g
Protein	3.1g	Total Fat	0.4g	Cholesterol	0.2mg
Carbohydrates	9.6g	Saturated Fat	0.1g	Sodium	111.2mg

Baked Hubbard Squash

1 lb. hubbard or banana
  squash, peeled
Water
3 tablespoons melted, soft
  margarine

1/3 cup light-brown sugar
Ground nutmeg

Preheat oven to 400F (205C). Cut squash into serving-size pieces.
Place in baking dish cut-side up; add water until 1/4 inch deep. Cover
and bake about 30 minutes, until tender when pierced with a fork.
Drizzle margarine over pieces. Sprinkle brown sugar and nutmeg to
taste on top. Return to oven for 5 minutes or until sugar is melted.
Makes 6 servings.

Each Serving Contains:							
Calories	93.1	Fiber	2.0g	Trans-fatty acids	0.3g
Protein	1.9g	Total Fat	3.3g	Cholesterol	0mg
Carbohydrates	16.1g	Saturated Fat	0.6g	Sodium	35.4mg

Garden Medley

1 tablespoon olive oil
1 garlic clove, crushed
1 large onion, sliced
1 green bell pepper, sliced

1 yellow bell pepper, sliced
4 large tomatoes, cut in eighths
Dill weed

In a large skillet, heat oil. Sauté garlic and onion for about 2 minutes.
Add bell peppers and tomatoes. Continue stirring and cooking
another 4 to 5 minutes, until peppers are tender-crisp. Sprinkle with
dill weed. Serve at once. Makes 6 servings.

Each Serving Contains:							
Calories	62.4	Fiber	2.1g	Trans-fatty acids	0g
Protein	1.6g	Total Fat	2.7g	Cholesterol	0mg
Carbohydrates	9.6g	Saturated Fat	0.4g	Sodium	12.4mg

Pineapple Yams

1 (8-oz.) can pineapple slices, drained
1 (20-oz.) can yams, sliced, drained
1/3 cup raisins

1/2 cup orange juice
1/2 cup pineapple-orange preserves
2 teaspoons rum flavoring

Preheat oven to 350F (175C). Spray a shallow baking dish with vegetable cooking spray. Arrange alternate slices of pineapple and yams in prepared baking dish. In a small saucepan, combine raisins, orange juice and pineapple-orange preserves. Stir over low heat about 5 minutes. Remove from heat, add rum flavoring. Pour mixture over pineapple and yams. Bake uncovered about 25 minutes, until heated. Serve either hot or cold. Makes 6 servings.

Each Serving Contains:					
Calories	217.2	Fiber	2.0g	Trans-fatty acids	0g
Protein	2.5g	Total Fat	0.3g	Cholesterol	0mg
Carbohydrates	54.2g	Saturated Fat	0.1g	Sodium	87.4mg

Marinated Broccoli

2 lb. fresh or 2 (10-oz.) pkgs. frozen broccoli spears
1 (8-oz.) can water chestnuts, drained

2 tablespoons chopped pimiento
6 tablespoons Italian Dressing, page 151

Trim ends and peel stems of fresh broccoli. Cook with water to cover 10 to 12 minutes, until tender-crisp. If using frozen, cook according to package directions, drain. Combine broccoli, water chestnuts and pimiento in a shallow bowl. Pour Italian Dressing over broccoli mixture. Cover and refrigerate at least 1 hour. Stir twice while chilling. Makes 6 servings.

Each Serving with 1 Tablespoon of Dressing Contains:					
Calories	144.0	Fiber	6.6g	Trans-fatty acids	0.1g
Protein	4.9g	Total Fat	9.7g	Cholesterol	0mg
Carbohydrates	13.2g	Saturated Fat	1.3g	Sodium	62.7mg

Hash Browns with Onions

2 teaspoons olive oil
1 teaspoon soft margarine
1/2 teaspoon paprika
1/2 teaspoon garlic salt

1/4 teaspoon pepper
1 small onion, chopped
1/2 green bell pepper, chopped
4 cooked, grated potatoes

Spray a large, non-stick skillet with vegetable cooking spray. Add oil
and margarine, stir in paprika, garlic salt and pepper. Add onion and
bell pepper; cook about 1 minute. Add potatoes; stir to blend. Cover
and reduce heat. Cook 2 to 3 minutes, until crisp and brown underneath. Carefully turn and brown other side. Serve at once. Makes 6
servings.

Each Serving Contains:

Calories	100.4	Fiber	1.5g	Trans-fatty acids	0g
Protein	1.8g	Total Fat	2.0g	Cholesterol	0mg
Carbohydrates	19.6g	Saturated Fat	0.3g	Sodium	96.7mg

Hot German Cabbage

1 large red cabbage, shredded
1 cup water
1 teaspoon salt
1 cup vinegar

1 teaspoon ground cloves
1/2 teaspoon ground
　coarse pepper

Place all ingredients in a pot and simmer for one hour. If time permits,
let stand for another hour, reheat, and serve.

Makes 6 servings.

Each Serving Contains:

Calories	37.8	Fiber	2.4g	Trans-fatty acids	0g
Protein	1.2g	Total Fat	0.3g	Cholesterol	0mg
Carbohydrates	10.7g	Saturated Fat	50mg	Sodium	398.4mg

FISH

SHORT ON TIME AND LONG ON APPETITE?
FISH OR SEAFOOD IS THE ANSWER FOR YOU.

Ease of preparation and short cooking time make fish or seafood an ideal choice. And don't overlook the benefits of omega-3 oils gained by eating these foods. What a great combination — good and good for you.

Enjoy the Easy Seafood Platter if you are in the mood for something cold. Or there's the opposite side, with Hot Crab Salad or Baked Orange Roughy. Tender Scallops in Wine tastes so great no one will suspect it was prepared in minutes. If you are a salmon lover, several recipes will satisfy your tastes.

When purchasing tuna remember: Use water-packed tuna. If it is not available, place oil-packed tuna in a strainer and rinse with water. Drain well before using. This helps to eliminate the excess oil.

Blackened Fish

2 teaspoons Cajun Pepper Mix, below
1 (6-oz.) fillet orange roughy or Icelandic cod

1 to 2 teaspoons olive or canola oil
Lemon or lime slices or Barbecue Sauce, page 201

Shake Cajun Pepper Mix on both sides of fillets. Preheat an iron skillet; add oil and carefully place fillets in hot oiled skillet. Cook uncovered about 2 to 3 minutes. Turn fillets over and continue cooking 3 to 4 minutes more until fish is flaky. Serve immediately with lemon or lime slices or Barbecue Sauce. Makes 1 serving.

Each 6-oz. Fillet Contains:					
Calories	241.8	Fiber	0.9g	Trans-fatty acids	0.1g
Protein	30.8g	Total Fat	10.6g	Cholesterol	73.1mg
Carbohydrates	5.2g	Saturated Fat	1.5g	Sodium	692.8mg

Cajun Pepper Mix

2 tablespoons paprika
2 teaspoons salt
4 teaspoons cayenne pepper
2 teaspoons coarse black pepper
1/2 teaspoon white pepper
1/2 teaspoon crushed red-chili-pepper flakes

1/4 teaspoon onion powder
1/4 teaspoon garlic powder
1 teaspoon crushed dried chives
1 teaspoon dried-leaf basil

In a small bowl, thoroughly blend all ingredients together. For a finer mix, place ingredients in a blender or food processor and process briefly. Store unused mix in a shaker or small container with a tight-fitting lid. Makes about 1/3 cup.

Each Teaspoon Contains:					
Calories	4.7	Fiber	0.3g	Trans-fatty acids	0g
Protein	0.2g	Total Fat	0.2g	Cholesterol	0mg
Carbohydrates	0.9g	Saturated Fat	0g	Sodium	267.7mg

Classic Broiled Salmon

1 (6-oz.) salmon steak, skin
   removed
Coarse pepper

1 lemon or lime
Chopped fresh parsley
   or dill

Sprinkle coarse pepper on salmon steak. Preheat broiler or grill; lightly spray broiler pan or grill with vegetable cooking spray. Place salmon on prepared surface and cook 4 inches from heat 7 to 10 minutes. Turn salmon and continue cooking 5 to 7 minutes until fish flakes easily. Cooking time may vary depending on thickness of salmon steak. Remove from heat. Squeeze on fresh lemon or lime juice, sprinkle with chopped parsley or dill and serve immediately. Makes 1 serving.

Each 6-oz. Serving Contains:

Calories	246.7	Fiber	0.2g	Trans-fatty acids	0g
Protein	33.8g	Total Fat	10.9g	Cholesterol	93.7mg
Carbohydrates	1.6g	Saturated Fat	1.7g	Sodium	77.1mg

Tuna Salad

1/2 (6-oz.) can water-packed
   tuna, drained
1 cup shredded cabbage
1 carrot, grated
1 green onion, chopped
2 tomatoes, chopped
1 teaspoon fat-free mayonnaise

2 tablespoons fat-free
   plain yogurt
1 tablespoon lemon juice
Lemon pepper
Salt and pepper
Blended herb mixture, if desired

In a medium bowl, combine tuna, cabbage, carrot, green onion and tomatoes. In a small bowl or cup, blend mayonnaise with yogurt; add lemon juice, lemon pepper, salt and pepper to taste and blended herb mixture, if desired. Stir mayonnaise mixture into tuna, thoroughly combine. Chill. Makes 4 servings.

Each Serving Contains:

Calories	58.9	Fiber	1.6g	Trans-fatty acids	0g
Protein	6.9g	Total Fat	0.7g	Cholesterol	6.8mg
Carbohydrates	7.0g	Saturated Fat	0.1g	Sodium	166.3mg

Linguini with Clam Sauce

1 tablespoon olive oil
1 medium onion, diced
1 garlic clove, diced
1 (8–oz.) can minced clams
   or oysters
1/4 cup white wine or cider
1/2 teaspoon pepper

Juice of 1 lemon
2 tablespoons chopped
   pimiento
1/4 lb. linguini or spaghetti
1/4 cup chopped fresh parsley,
   basil or oregano

Heat oil in a medium skillet; sauté onion and garlic. Stir while cooking about 2 to 3 minutes. Add juice from clams or oysters and wine or cider. Continue cooking over medium heat until the total volume is reduced to almost half. This will take about 15 minutes. Add clams or oysters, pepper and lemon juice. Cover, reduce heat and simmer 5 minutes; add chopped pimiento. Cook pasta according to package directions. Drain; return pasta to skillet. Pour clam mixture and parsley into pasta and cook about 5 to 8 minutes more. Or combine clam mixture and pasta in a 1-1/2-quart casserole and bake at 350F (175C) 15 minutes. Makes 4 servings.

Each Serving Contains:							
Calories	142.7	Fiber	1.3g	Trans-fatty acids	0g
Protein	9.8g	Total Fat	4.3g	Cholesterol	20.1mg
Carbohydrates	14.2g	Saturated Fat	0.6g	Sodium	95.7mg

Easy Seafood Platter

6 oz. smoked or baked salmon,
    sliced
6 oz. cooked shrimp
Lettuce leaves
6 pineapple spears

1 orange, segmented
1 banana, sliced
1 tablespoon lemon juice
2 teaspoons sesame seeds

Arrange chilled salmon slices and shrimp on a lettuce-lined plate. Make an attractive arrangement of pineapple spears, orange segments and banana slices. Drizzle lemon juice over bananas; sprinkle with sesame seeds. Makes 2 servings.

Variation: Substitute any fresh fruit. Try apples, apricots, grapes, papaya or peaches. Or omit fruit and substitute celery sticks, chilled cooked peas and carrots, sliced radishes and sweet red onion rings. Top with capers.

Each 3-oz. Serving Contains:						
Calories	416.7	Fiber	6.2g	Trans-fatty acids	0g
Protein	36.8g	Total Fat	7.7g	Cholesterol	185.4mg
Carbohydrates	55.1g	Saturated Fat	1.5g	Sodium	864.4mg

Hot Crab Salad

12 oz. precooked frozen crab or imitation crab

1 cup bottled chili or seafood sauce

1 teaspoon minced fresh ginger root

1/3 cup brown sugar

1 tablespoon vinegar

1 teaspoon prepared horseradish

1/2 lb. pasta, fettuccine or spaghetti, broken into 2-inch pieces

2 tablespoons olive oil

1 carrot, julienned

1 small zucchini, julienned

1/2 red or green bell pepper, julienned

1 tomato, chopped

1 green onion, chopped

Salt and pepper

Thaw seafood and cut into bite-size pieces. In a small saucepan, combine chili sauce, ginger root, brown sugar, vinegar and horseradish; simmer over low heat about 10 minutes. Set aside. Pour chili sauce over thawed crab pieces and marinate at least 1 hour. Cook pasta according to package instructions, drain and set aside. Heat oil in a large skillet; sauté carrot, zucchini and pepper. Add tomatoes, green onions and cooked pasta. Lightly toss together, cover and set aside. Preheat broiler, spray rack with vegetable cooking spray. Place crab pieces on prepared rack and broil 5 minutes; turn and brush pieces with additional sauce; broil 3 minutes more. Combine warm pasta mixture and broiled crab. Season to taste with salt and pepper. Makes 4 servings.

Each Serving Contains:					
Calories	308.2	Fiber	2.4g	Trans-fatty acids	0.1g
Protein	21.4g	Total Fat	9.2g	Cholesterol	85.1mg
Carbohydrates	35.6g	Saturated Fat	1.2g	Sodium	336.4mg

Poached Salmon

1 cup chopped onions
2 celery stalks with leaves
2 carrots
1 bunch parsley
2 bay leaves

2 quarts water
2 tablespoons lemon juice
1 cup white wine, if desired
1/2 or 1 whole salmon
Lemon wedges

In a fish poacher or roasting pan, combine onions, celery, carrots, parsley, bay leaves and water. Bring to a boil, reduce the heat and simmer uncovered 20 minutes. Remove vegetables and add lemon juice and wine, if desired. Rinse fish and pat dry with paper towels. Place fish on a rack so it is covered by liquid. If the fish is large, add hot water to cover. Bring liquid to a simmer; cover and reduce heat so water quivers, but does not bubble. Cook about 45 minutes or just until the fish flakes easily with a fork. Another method is to bring the liquid to a boil and immediately turn off heat. Cover and let stand until liquid is cold. Serve immediately or chilled. Top with freshly squeezed lemon juice.

Each 3-oz. Serving Contains:

Calories	206.1	Fiber	2.1g	Trans-fatty acids	0g
Protein	22.5g	Total Fat	8.8g	Cholesterol	68.0mg
Carbohydrates	8.8g	Saturated Fat	1.5g	Sodium	85.0mg

Salmon Loaf

1 (6-oz.) can salmon or
    water-packed tuna
1-1/2 cups fresh French
    bread cubes
1 cup nonfat milk
1/2 cup egg substitute
3 tablespoons lemon juice or
    vinegar
1 pkg. imitation butter granules
1/2 teaspoon paprika

1/2 teaspoon dry mustard
1/2 onion, chopped
1/4 teaspoon coarse pepper
2 tablespoons chopped chives
1/4 cup sliced fresh mushrooms
1 tablespoon chopped pimiento
1/2 cup fat-free plain yogurt
2 tablespoons lemon juice
2 teaspoons dried-leaf tarragon

Preheat oven to 350F (175C). Drain salmon or tuna; place in a mixing bowl and flake. Add the remaining ingredients except yogurt, lemon juice and tarragon; thoroughly combine. Spray a 9 x 5-in. loaf pan with vegetable cooking spray. Turn fish mixture into prepared pan and smooth top. Bake in preheated oven 30 to 35 minutes. In a small bowl, blend yogurt, lemon juice and tarragon. Serve loaf from pan or place on a serving dish. Top with yogurt mixture. Makes 4 servings.

Each Serving Contains:						
Calories	189.6	Fiber	1.0g	Trans-fatty acids		0g
Protein	18.3g	Total Fat	5.1g	Cholesterol		21.1mg
Carbohydrates	17.9g	Saturated Fat	1.1g	Sodium		428.2mg

Baked Orange Roughy

2 teaspoons soft diet margarine
2 (6-oz.) orange-roughy fillets
3 tablespoons lemon juice
1/4 cup orange juice
1 orange, thinly sliced

2 teaspoons grated orange peel
1 teaspoon chopped cilantro
  (Chinese parsley) or parsley
1/2 teaspoon dried-leaf thyme
Salt and pepper

Spread margarine in non-stick baking dish, add fillets. In a cup, combine lemon and orange juices with orange peel. Pour juice over fillets. Top with layer of orange slices and sprinkle with chopped cilantro or parsley and thyme. Bake uncovered at 375F (190C) about 10 minutes until fish flakes with a fork. Season to taste with salt and pepper. Makes 2 servings.

Each 6-oz. Serving Contains:					
Calories	220.9	Fiber	1.5g	Trans-fatty acids	0.2g
Protein	33.2g	Total Fat	3.5g	Cholesterol	44.2mg
Carbohydrates	13.8g	Saturated Fat	0.4g	Sodium	288.5mg

Tuna Casserole

1 (7-oz.) can water-packed tuna,
  drained
2 green onions, chopped
1/4 cup chopped pimiento
  stuffed olives
1/4 cup chopped green bell
  pepper

1/4 cup chopped celery
White Sauce, page 154
1/2 teaspoon prepared mustard
1/4 cup white wine, if desired
2 cups cooked pasta
Salt and pepper

Preheat oven to 350F (175C). Spray a 2-quart baking dish with vegetable cooking spray. In a medium bowl, mix all ingredients. Pour into prepared baking dish. Cover and bake about 20 minutes. Uncover; bake 10 minutes longer. Makes 6 servings.

Each Serving Contains:					
Calories	151.2	Fiber	0.9g	Trans-fatty acids	0g
Protein	12.6g	Total Fat	3.9g	Cholesterol	14.6mg
Carbohydrates	15.8g	Saturated Fat	0.5g	Sodium	333.2mg

Stuffed Fish Fillets

3 tablespoons fat-free
 plain yogurt
1 tablespoon nonfat milk
3 slices fresh French
 bread cubes
2 tablespoons wine vinegar or
 lemon juice
2 tablespoons finely chopped
 onion

2 tablespoons finely chopped
 green bell pepper
2 tablespoons sliced pimiento-
 stuffed olives
2 (6-oz.) fillets orange roughy,
 cod or sole
Salt and coarse pepper
Paprika
Dill weed

Preheat oven to 350F (175C). Spray an 8-inch round baking dish with vegetable cooking spray. In a small bowl, combine yogurt, milk, bread cubes, wine vinegar or lemon juice, onion, bell pepper and olives; mix well. Sprinkle both sides of fillets with salt, pepper and paprika. Place 1 fillet in prepared dish. Spread stuffing evenly over fillet; place second fillet on top of stuffing like a sandwich. Cut in half; sprinkle tops with paprika and dill weed. Bake 20 to 25 minutes. Makes 2 servings.

Each 6-oz. Fillet Contains:					
Calories	302.0	Fiber	1.7g	Trans-fatty acids	0g
Protein	37.8g	Total Fat	3.6g	Cholesterol	44.8mg
Carbohydrates	27.0g	Saturated Fat	0.4g	Sodium	676.5mg

Barbecue Shrimp

1 tablespoon olive or canola oil
1/2 onion, chopped
2 tablespoons vinegar
2 tablespoons brown sugar
1 cup catsup
2 tablespoons dry mustard
1/2 teaspoon garlic powder

5 to 6 drops Tabasco sauce
2 tablespoons dried-leaf
  oregano
24 large raw shrimp, peeled,
  deveined
1 lime or lemon

In a small saucepan, heat oil; sauté onion briefly. Add vinegar, brown sugar, catsup, mustard, garlic powder, Tabasco sauce and oregano. Stir to combine; cook over low heat about 5 minutes. Set aside to cool. Place shrimp in a bowl; pour cooled sauce over. Turn shrimp, coating well with sauce. Cover tightly and refrigerate at least 4 hours or overnight. Preheat broiler or grill. Thread shrimp on skewers. Broil 3 to 4 minutes on each side. To serve, squeeze fresh lime or lemon juice over shrimp. Makes 6 servings.

Each Serving Contains:							
Calories	126.9	Fiber	1.2g	Trans-fatty acids	0g
Protein	6.9g	Total Fat	3.9g	Cholesterol	46.8mg
Carbohydrates	18.1g	Saturated Fat	0.5g	Sodium	540.6mg

Scallops in Wine

1 tablespoon olive oil
1/3 cup chopped onions
1-1/2 tablespoons minced
  shallots or green onions
1-1/2 lb. scallops, washed, sliced
1/2 cup all-purpose flour
1 tablespoon soft margarine
1 tablespoon olive oil

1 garlic clove, crushed
3/4 cup dry white wine
1/2 cup vermouth
1 bay leaf
4 tomatoes, chopped
1 teaspoon dried-leaf oregano
1 teaspoon chopped parsley
Salt and pepper

In a skillet, heat oil and sauté onions and shallots. Toss scallops with flour to coat. Shake off excess flour. Add scallops to onions. Stir quickly 2 to 3 minutes to combine. In another skillet, heat margarine, olive oil and garlic. Add wine, vermouth, bay leaf, tomatoes, oregano and parsley. Cook about 2 minutes; add scallops. Stir to combine and cook about 4 to 5 minutes. Season to taste with salt and pepper. Serve at once. Makes 6 servings.

Each Serving Contains:							
Calories	274.4	Fiber	1.4g	Trans-fatty acids	0.1g		
Protein	20.4g	Total Fat	9.4g	Cholesterol	36.1mg		
Carbohydrates	17.2g	Saturated Fat	1.5g	Sodium	530.9mg		

POULTRY & MEATS

REMEMBER CHICKEN ON SUNDAY?

Years ago we ate chicken on Sunday. Now that we know the health benefits of eating poultry, we are encouraged to eat it three or four times a week.

White meat is preferred over dark because it contains less fat. And be sure to remove skin and all visible fat when preparing any poultry dish. White meat tends to dry out if overcooked, so we suggest shorter-than-usual cooking times. Chicken and turkey can easily be substituted for other meats in many recipes.

Enjoy beef in smaller amounts and purchase select lean beef which has a lower proportion of fat. Two rabbit dishes are included because rabbit is readily available and similar to poultry in fat content. It, too, is a good source of protein.

We also include fruits and vegetables with many poultry and meat recipes to give added fiber as well as flavor. Some of the combinations may be new to you. Try the Cranberry Chicken. Perhaps Brunswick Stew or Chili Mac Casserole will be your choice. Personalize the recipes as you choose.

Savory Crepes

3/4 cup egg substitute
2 egg whites
2 cups nonfat milk

1-1/2 cups all-purpose flour
1/2 teaspoon salt
1/2 teaspoon white pepper

In a mixer bowl, beat egg substitute and egg whites. Add milk and flour alternately; continue beating until smooth. Add salt and pepper. Batter can rest for an hour before making crepes. Use either a non-stick crepe pan or a skillet sprayed with vegetable cooking spray. Heat pan; add about 1/4 cup batter. Quickly tilt pan to evenly spread batter. When batter surface appears dry and begins to bubble, turn crepe. Repeat with remaining batter. Fill cooked crepes; either roll or fold as desired. Makes 12 crepes.

Each Crepe Contains:						
Calories	87.1	Fiber	0.5g	Trans-fatty acids	0g
Protein	5,5g	Total Fat	0.7g	Cholesterol	0.9mg
Carbohydrates	14.1g	Saturated Fat	0.2g	Sodium	147.1mg

Lemon-Broiled Chicken Breasts

Chicken or turkey breasts,
    boned, skinned
Lemon juice
Lemon pepper

Fresh spinach leaves
Lemon or lime wedges
Salt and pepper

Remove all visible fat from breasts; cut into fillets. Sprinkle with lemon juice and lemon pepper. Broil about 10 minutes, turning often, until meat is no longer pink. Serve on a spinach-lined platter. Season with additional fresh lemon juice or lime juice. Season with salt and pepper to taste.

Each 3-oz. Serving Contains:						
Calories	256.0	Fiber	0.6g	Trans-fatty acids	0g
Protein	30.9g	Total Fat	13.5g	Cholesterol	92.8mg
Carbohydrates	1.4g	Saturated Fat	3.9g	Sodium	174.8mg

Chicken Florentine Crepes

1 recipe Savory Crepes,
    page 198
1 tablespoon canola oil
1/4 cup chopped onion
1/4 cup chopped celery
1/2 cup sliced mushrooms
2 tablespoons all-purpose flour
1 cup Chicken Broth, page 129

2 cups (10 oz.) cooked chicken
    breast, cubed
1/2 cup chopped spinach,
    cooked, drained
1 teaspoon sweet paprika
1 teaspoon poultry seasoning
1/4 cup fat-free plain yogurt
Dill weed

Prepare crepes. Heat oil in a skillet; sauté onion, celery and mush-rooms. Mix flour with chicken broth and stir into onion mixture. Continue stirring; cook 3 to 4 minutes until thickened and smooth. Add chicken, well-drained spinach, paprika and poultry seasoning. Cook until chicken is heated. Place 2 to 3 tablespoons filling on cen-ter of crepe. Roll up and place seam-side down. Top with dollop of yogurt; sprinkle with dill weed. Bake in 350F (175C) oven for 15 min-utes. Serve at once. Makes 12 crepes.

Each Crepe Contains:

Calories	156.8	Fiber	0.9g	Trans-fatty acids	0g
Protein	13.2g	Total Fat	3.9g	Cholesterol	18.7mg
Carbohydrates	16.6g	Saturated Fat	0.9g	Sodium	234.9mg

Turkey & Wild-Rice Crepes

1 recipe Savory Crepes,
    page 198
1 tablespoon olive or canola oil
2 tablespoons chopped onion
1 teaspoon dried-leaf tarragon
1/4 cup all-purpose flour
1 cup nonfat milk
1/2 cup Chicken Broth,
    page 129
1/2 cup vermouth or dry
    white wine

2 tablespoons chopped
    pimiento
1/4 cup raisins
1-1/2 cups (7-1/2-oz.) cooked
    turkey breast, cubed
1/2 cup cooked carrots, sliced
2/3 cup cooked wild rice or
    long-grain and wild rice
1 cup whole cranberry

Prepare crepes. Heat oil in a skillet; sauté onions. Add tarragon. Mix flour with milk and broth; stir into onion mixture. Continue stirring; cook 3 to 4 minutes until thickened and smooth. Add vermouth or wine, pimiento, raisins, turkey, carrots and rice. Cook until all ingredients are heated. Spray a 13 x 14-inch baking dish with vegetable cooking spray. Place 2 to 3 tablespoons filling on center of crepe. Roll up and place seam side down. Place in prepared baking dish. Spoon cranberry sauce over filled crepes. Bake in oven at 350F (175C), about 15 minutes until heated. Serve at once. Makes 12 crepes.

Each Crepe Contains:					
Calories	178.0	Fiber	1.3g	Trans-fatty acids	0g
Protein	11.0g	Total Fat	3.1g	Cholesterol	10.6mg
Carbohydrates	23.7g	Saturated Fat	0.7g	Sodium	201.9mg

Barbecued Chicken

4 chicken breasts, skinned
   and boned
Lemon juice

Barbecue Sauce, see below

Place chicken or turkey in a single layer in a baking dish. Brush with lemon juice. Pour 1 cup Barbecue Sauce over all; turn to coat both sides. Cover and let stand at least 1 hour. Place chicken or turkey on grill; cook about 10 minutes, brushing with additional sauce as needed. Turn pieces often; continue grilling until meat is no longer pink when cut. Makes 4 servings.

Each 3-oz. Serving Contains:					
Calories	230.1	Fiber	0.9g	Trans-fatty acids	0g
Protein	20.9g	Total Fat	9.1g	Cholesterol	61.9mg
Carbohydrates	16.2g	Saturated Fat	2.6g	Sodium	364.2mg

Barbecue Sauce

1 onion, chopped
1 (6-oz.) can tomato sauce
1/4 cup sweet relish
1 tablespoon vinegar

1 teaspoon pepper
2 tablespoons Worcestershire
   sauce
5 tablespoons brown sugar

Sauté onion in a small non-stick coated skillet or saucepan. Add tomato sauce, relish, vinegar, pepper, Worcestershire sauce and brown sugar. Cook over low heat about 5 to 7 minutes. Makes about 1-3/4 cups.

Each 1/4-Cup Serving Contains:					
Calories	53.6	Fiber	0.8g	Trans-fatty acids	0g
Protein	0.6g	Total Fat	0.1g	Cholesterol	0mg
Carbohydrates	13.5g	Saturated Fat	0g	Sodium	259.9mg

Baked Orange–Chicken Breasts

4 chicken breasts, skinned,
    boned
1/2 cup corn-flake crumbs
1-1/2 teaspoons paprika
1/2 teaspoon grated orange
    peel
2 teaspoons dried-leaf mint
    or basil

1/4 cup egg substitute
2 tablespoons soy sauce
1 teaspoon water
1 pkg. imitation butter granules
1/3 cup orange-juice
    concentrate, thawed

Remove all visible fat from chicken breasts. Combine crumbs, paprika, orange peel and mint or basil in a pie plate or small paper bag. In
another pie plate, blend egg substitute, soy sauce, water, butter granules and orange-juice concentrate. Spray a baking sheet with vegetable
cooking spray. Preheat oven to 375F (190C). Dip each chicken piece
into egg mixture and then into crumb mixture. Place coated pieces on
prepared baking pan. Bake 30 to 40 minutes. Makes 4 servings.

Each 3-oz. Serving of Chicken Contains:					
Calories	212.0	Fiber	0.6g	Trans-fatty acids	0g
Protein	31.0g	Total Fat	2.2g	Cholesterol	68.6mg
Carbohydrates	15.7g	Saturated Fat	0.5g	Sodium	825.5mg

Cranberry Chicken

2 tablespoons honey
2 tablespoons orange juice
1 teaspoon grated orange peel
1/2 teaspoon ground allspice

1 (16-oz.) can whole cranberry
   sauce
4 chicken breasts, boned,
   skinned

Preheat oven to 375F (190C). Mix honey, orange juice, orange peel, allspice and cranberry sauce in a small bowl. Remove all visible fat from chicken breasts. Pour 1/2 of mixture over chicken breasts. Bake 15 minutes. Turn chicken pieces; pour on remaining sauce. Continue baking another 30 to 35 minutes. Makes 4 servings.

Each 3-oz. Serving of Chicken Contains:					
Calories	225.2	Fiber	0.8g	Trans-fatty acids	0g
Protein	18.4g	Total Fat	1.1g	Cholesterol	45.6mg
Carbohydrates	36.0g	Saturated Fat	0.3g	Sodium	73.5mg

Chicken à la King

2 teaspoons canola oil
1 cup sliced mushrooms
1/2 cup diced green bell pepper
1/2 cup all-purpose flour
2 cups nonfat milk
1 cup Chicken Broth, page 129

2 cups (10 oz.) cooked, skinned,
   cubed chicken breast
1 (4-oz.) jar chopped pimiento
Salt and pepper
Toast, rice or pasta

Heat oil in a large non-stick skillet or saucepan. Cook and stir mushrooms and green bell peppers 5 minutes. Blend in the flour. Cook over low heat; stir until mixture is bubbly. Remove from heat and stir in the milk and broth. Heat to boiling, stirring constantly. Add chicken and pimiento. Season with salt and pepper to taste. Serve hot over toast, cooked rice or pasta. Makes 4 servings.

Each Serving Contains:					
Calories	350.2	Fiber	3.0g	Trans-fatty acids	0g
Protein	33.3g	Total Fat	6.2g	Cholesterol	62.4mg
Carbohydrates	39.0g	Saturated Fat	1.4g	Sodium	383.5mg

Chicken Stir-Fry

2 tablespoons canola oil
1 teaspoon grated ginger root
    or 1/2 teaspoon ground
    ginger
2 chicken breasts, skinned,
    boned, cut into 1/2-inch
    strips
2 green bell peppers, sliced
4 green onions including tops,
    cut in 1-1/2-inch lengths

1 zucchini, cut in 1-1/2-inch
    lengths
1 (6-oz.) can water chestnuts,
    drained
2 medium tomatoes, cut in
    eighths
2 teaspoons cornstarch
1 teaspoon sugar
3 tablespoons soy sauce
1/4 teaspoon five-spice powder

Preheat a wok or large fry pan. Add oil and ginger; add chicken pieces. Stir-fry chicken until white. Remove chicken, cover and set aside. Add bell peppers, green onions and zucchini. Stir-fry until vegetables are tender crisp. Return chicken to wok; add drained chestnuts and tomatoes. Gently stir to combine. In a cup or small bowl, blend cornstarch, sugar, soy sauce and five-spice powder. Pour mixture over chicken and vegetables. Stir-fry, turning to coat all ingredients until sauce thickens. Serve at once. Makes 4 servings.

Variation: Add 1 cup walnuts and 1/4 cup sliced mushrooms with the vegetables.

Each Serving Contains:					
Calories	198.2	Fiber	4.4g	Trans-fatty acids	0.1g
Protein	16.8g	Total Fat	8.0g	Cholesterol	34.2mg
Carbohydrates	16.2g	Saturated Fat	1.2g	Sodium	1040.2mg

With Walnuts & Mushrooms:					
Calories	388.9	Fiber	5.9g	Trans-fatty acids	0.1g
Protein	24.5g	Total Fat	25.7g	Cholesterol	34.2mg
Carbohydrates	20.2g	Saturated Fat	2.3g	Sodium	1040.7mg

Chicken-Almond Casserole

1/3 cup minced onions
1-1/4 cups nonfat milk
1/2 teaspoon salt
1/4 teaspoon pepper
1 pkg. imitation butter granules
1/4 cup all-purpose flour

4 cups (20-oz.) cooked chicken
  breast, cubed
1/2 lb. fresh mushrooms, sliced
1 cup blanched sliced almonds
1 (10-1/2-oz.) pkg. frozen
  chopped broccoli, thawed

In a non-stick fry pan sprayed with vegetable cooking spray, sauté onions. In a small saucepan, combine milk, salt, pepper, butter granules and flour. Stir to blend; cook, stirring, over medium heat until sauce thickens; add sautéed onions. Preheat oven to 350F (175C). Spray a 2-quart baking dish with vegetable cooking spray. Place chicken cubes, mushrooms, almonds and chopped broccoli in baking dish. Pour sauce over chicken mixture; stir to combine. Bake uncovered 30 minutes. Makes 6 servings.

Each Serving Contains:					
Calories	326.7	Fiber	3.8g	Trans-fatty acids	0g
Protein	37.5g	Total Fat	13.0g	Cholesterol	81.3mg
Carbohydrates	16.1g	Saturated Fat	1.9g	Sodium	308.1mg

Hearty Chicken & Rice Casserole

1 recipe Brown Rice with
  Vegetables, page 171
2 cups (10 oz.) cooked, skinned,
  chopped chicken breast
1/2 cup peas

2 tablespoons chopped
  pimiento
1/2 cup Chicken Broth,
  page 129

Preheat oven to 350F (175C). Spray a 2-1/2-quart baking dish with vegetable cooking spray; set aside. Prepare Brown Rice with Vegetables mixture; combine with chicken, peas. pimiento and broth. Spoon into prepared baking dish. Bake about 15 minutes, until heated through. Makes 8 servings.

Each Serving Contains:					
Calories	202.1	Fiber	2.7g	Trans-fatty acids	0g
Protein	15.8g	Total Fat	4.3g	Cholesterol	30.1mg
Carbohydrates	24.8g	Saturated Fat	0.9g	Sodium	328.2mg

Enchiladas

2 teaspoons olive or canola oil
1/2 cup chopped onions
1/2 cup cooked pinto beans,
    drained
2 cups (10 oz.) cubed cooked,
    skinned, chicken breast
1/2 cup chopped green chiles
1 teaspoon dried-leaf oregano
1 large tomato, chopped

1/4 teaspoon chili powder
1/4 teaspoon ground cumin
1 (12-oz.) can tomato sauce
12 corn tortillas
1 cup salsa
3/4 cup (3 oz.) grated lowfat
    mozzarella cheese

Heat oil in a saucepan, add onions and cook until softened. Stir in pinto beans, chicken, chilies, oregano and tomato. Heat mixture and set aside. In a small skillet, blend chili powder and cumin with tomato sauce; simmer 2 minutes. Remove from heat. Dip each tortilla in tomato sauce; set aside on a plate. Fill each tortilla with 3 tablespoons chicken mixture in a 13 x 9-inch baking dish. Roll and place seam side down. Pour about 1 cup salsa over filled enchiladas. Sprinkle with cheese. Bake in a 350F (175C) oven about 20 minutes. Makes 12 enchiladas.

Each Enchilada Contains:							
Calories	162.5	Fiber	3.1g	Trans-fatty acids	0g
Protein	12.5g	Total Fat	3.8g	Cholesterol	23.9mg
Carbohydrates	20.6g	Saturated Fat	1.2g	Sodium	376.0mg

Teriyaki Chicken

1 tablespoon fresh grated
  ginger or 1 teaspoon
  ground ginger
4 green onions, chopped
1/4 cup soy sauce
3 tablespoons sugar

1/4 cup rice wine or dry sherry
1 garlic clove, crushed
6 chicken breasts, skinned,
  cubed
Sesame seeds

In a bowl, combine ginger, green onions, soy sauce, sugar, rice wine or sherry and garlic. Add chicken cubes; turn to coat all pieces. Cover and refrigerate at least 2 hours. Occasionally turn chicken. Thread chicken cubes on 6 skewers. Brush with additional soy mixture, as needed. Broil 4 to 5 minutes, turning frequently. Brush with soy mixture again and sprinkle with sesame seeds. Broil 3 to 4 minutes longer. Serve at once. Makes 6 servings.

Each 4-oz. Serving Contains:

Calories	180.9	Fiber	0.4g	Trans-fatty acids	0g
Protein	28.7g	Total Fat	2.3g	Cholesterol	68.4mg
Carbohydrates	8.5g	Saturated Fat	0.5g	Sodium	956.2mg

Cajun Chicken Bake

4 (4-oz.) chicken breasts boned,
  skinned
1 (8-oz.) can tomato sauce

1 (4-oz.) can sliced mushrooms,
  drained
Cajun Pepper Mix, page 186

Preheat oven to 350F (175C). Spray a baking dish or pie pan with vegetable cooking spray; set aside. Place chicken breasts in prepared dish. Combine tomato sauce and mushrooms. Spoon over chicken. Sprinkle with Cajun Pepper Mix to taste. Bake uncovered 40 to 45 minutes. Makes 4 servings.

Each Serving Contains:

Calories	167.2	Fiber	2.9g	Trans-fatty acids	0g
Protein	28.4g	Total Fat	2.4g	Cholesterol	65.8mg
Carbohydrates	9.1g	Saturated Fat	0.5g	Sodium	1609.3mg

Chicken & Shrimp Oriental

3/4 lb. chicken breast, boned, skinned

1/2 lb. raw shrimp, shelled, deveined

3 tablespoons canola oil

3 green onions, cut in 1-inch lengths

1 tablespoon chopped fresh ginger

1/2 cup sliced bamboo shoots

1/2 cup pea pods or 1/2 cup peas

1/2 cup sliced mushrooms

1/4 cup sliced blanched almonds

Marinade

1 egg white

1 teaspoon grated fresh ginger

1 teaspoon cornstarch

Seasoning Sauce

4 tablespoons soy sauce

2 tablespoons sugar

2 tablespoons rice wine or dry sherry

1 tablespoon cornstarch

Slice chicken into 1/2-inch strips. Cut each shrimp into thirds. Blend Marinade ingredients in a bowl. Add chicken and shrimp to marinade, mix to coat. Set aside for 20 minutes. Heat wok or large fry pan, add oil, green onions and ginger. Stir and add shrimp and chicken pieces. Stir-fry about 1 minute. Remove from wok. Add bamboo shoots, pea pods or peas and mushrooms. Stir-fry 1 to 2 minutes. In a small bowl, combine Seasoning Sauce ingredients and add to wok. Bring to a boil. Add chicken, shrimp and almonds; continue to stir-fry about 1 minute. Serve at once. Makes 6 servings.

Each Serving with Sauce Contains:					
Calories	227.6	Fiber	1.4g	Trans-fatty acids	0g
Protein	22.5g	Total Fat	10.3g	Cholesterol	86.7mg
Carbohydrates	10.6g	Saturated Fat	1.0g	Sodium	988.6mg

Golden Turkey Curry

1 tablespoon olive or canola oil
1 onion, chopped
1/2 green bell pepper, chopped
1 garlic clove, crushed
3 tablespoons all-purpose flour
1 cup Chicken Broth, page 129
1/4 teaspoon ground cinnamon
1/4 teaspoon ground cloves
2 teaspoons curry powder

1 tablespoon chopped
   crystallized ginger
1/4 cup raisins
2 cups (10 oz.) cubed, skinned
   turkey breast
Hot cooked rice
1/4 cup chopped peanuts
1/4 cup imitation bacon bits
Peach Chutney, page 154

In a saucepan, heat oil; add onion, bell pepper and garlic. Stir in flour and chicken broth. Simmer 5 minutes, stirring constantly. Add cinnamon, cloves, curry powder, ginger, raisins and turkey. Cook about 15 minutes, stirring occasionally. Mound hot cooked rice on a serving platter. Spoon turkey curry over rice. Top with chopped peanuts and bacon bits. Serve with Peach Chutney. Makes 6 servings.

Each Serving Contains:					
Calories	427.3	Fiber	4.4g	Trans-fatty acids	0g
Protein	16.9g	Total Fat	9.3g	Cholesterol	24.8mg
Carbohydrates	72.5g	Saturated Fat	1.8g	Sodium	217.1mg

Tomato-Curry Chicken

1 tablespoon olive or canola oil
4 cups (20 oz.) boned, skinned,
    cubed chicken breasts
1/2 onion, chopped
1/4 cup chopped celery
1 teaspoon curry powder
1/2 teaspoon chili powder
1 tablespoon all-purpose flour

1 tablespoon tomato paste
1 cup Chicken Broth, page 129
1/2 cup dry white wine or water
1 apple, peeled, chopped
1 tomato, chopped
2 cups cooked rice
1/2 cup fat-free plain yogurt
Ground cinnamon

Heat oil in a heavy skillet. Add chicken, onion and celery. Stir-fry about 2 minutes. Stir in curry and chili powders. In a cup, blend flour, tomato paste and chicken broth. Add to chicken with white wine or water. Cover, reduce heat and simmer, stirring occasionally, about 20 minutes. Add apple and tomato; continue cooking another 7 to 10 minutes. To serve, spoon chicken curry over hot rice. Top with a dollop of yogurt. Sprinkle cinnamon to taste on top. Makes 6 servings.

Each Serving Contains:							
Calories	273.8	Fiber	1.7g	Trans-fatty acids	0g
Protein	26.4g	Total Fat	4.2g	Cholesterol	55.2mg
Carbohydrates	28.2g	Saturated Fat	0.8g	Sodium	238.3mg

Oven-Baked Chicken

1 cup fat-free plain yogurt
1/2 teaspoon ground cumin
2 teaspoons chopped chives
6 (4-1/2-oz.) boned, skinned
    chicken breasts
1-1/2 cups shredded-wheat
    crumbs

1/2 cup oat bran
1 teaspoon parsley
1 teaspoon dried-leaf marjoram
1 teaspoon paprika

Blend yogurt with cumin and chives. Pour into a flat baking dish.
Place chicken breasts in yogurt, turning to coat. Cover and refrigerate
24 hours, turning chicken several times. Preheat oven to 375F (190C).
Combine shredded wheat, oat bran, parsley, marjoram and paprika.
Dip chicken breasts into crumb mixture, turning and pressing to coat.
Spray a baking sheet with vegetable cooking spray. Place chicken on
prepared baking sheet. Bake 35 minutes. Makes 6 servings.

Each Serving Contains:					
Calories	222.8	Fiber	2.4g	Trans fatty acids	0g
Protein	34.5g	Total Fat	2.6g	Cholesterol	74.7mg
Carbohydrates	17.2g	Saturated Fat	0.6g	Sodium	116.2mg

Brunswick Stew

3 (4-1/2-oz.) boned, skinned
   chicken breasts
4 cups water
1 large onion, sliced
2 chicken bouillon cubes
1/8 teaspoon cayenne pepper
2 teaspoons Worcestershire
   sauce
1/4 teaspoon dried-leaf thyme
1/2 teaspoon dried-leaf
   oregano

2 medium potatoes, peeled,
   diced
1 (10-oz.) pkg. frozen baby
   lima beans
1 (16-oz.) can diced tomatoes,
   undrained
1 (10-oz.) pkg. frozen
   whole-kernel corn
1 teaspoon salt
2 slices white bread

Remove visible fat from chicken breasts. Cut breasts in half. In a 4-quart pot, combine chicken, water, onion, bouillon, cayenne pepper, Worcestershire sauce, thyme and oregano. Bring to a boil; reduce heat. Cover and simmer until chicken is tender, about 20 minutes. Remove chicken; set aside. Add potatoes and lima beans to broth in pot. Cover and simmer until potatoes are tender, about 20 minutes. Add tomatoes with juice, corn, salt and chicken pieces. Cover and simmer 10 minutes longer. Break bread into bite-size pieces. Add to stew; stir constantly until stew has thickened. For each serving, put a piece of chicken in a large soup bowl. Surround with stew. Makes 6 (1-1/2-cup) servings.

Each Serving Contains:							
Calories	258.9	Fiber	6.2g	Trans-fatty acids	0g
Protein	22.4g	Total Fat	2.0g	Cholesterol	37.7mg
Carbohydrates	39.7g	Saturated Fat	0.5g	Sodium	988.4mg

Rabbit Stew

1 rabbit, cut up or 1 pkg. frozen rabbit, thawed	2 carrots, sliced
1/4 cup vinegar or lemon juice	1/2 cup white wine
2 tablespoons olive or canola oil	1/2 cup tomato juice
	4 whole cloves
1 (10-oz.) pkg. frozen boiling onions	Peel of 1 orange
	Salt and pepper
	Hot cooked pasta or brown rice

Sprinkle rabbit with vinegar or lemon. Heat oil in a Dutch oven or heavy saucepan. Brown rabbit in oil. Add remaining ingredients except pasta or rice. Cover, reduce heat; cook until rabbit is tender, 30 to 40 minutes. Remove cloves. Season with salt and pepper to taste. Serve with hot cooked pasta or brown rice. Makes 4 servings.

Each 3-oz. Serving Contains:

Calories	616.8	Fiber	2.7g	Trans-fatty acids	0.1g
Protein	54.5g	Total Fat	20.9g	Cholesterol	134.3mg
Carbohydrates	44.4g	Saturated Fat	5.0g	Sodium	278.8mg

Rabbit Italian Style

2 tablespoons olive oil	2 tablespoons tomato paste
1 rabbit, cut up or 1 pkg. frozen rabbit, thawed	1 tablespoon dried-leaf basil
	1 tablespoon oregano
1 onion, sliced	1 cup sliced mushrooms
2 garlic cloves	1 tablespoon capers
1 green bell pepper, sliced	1/2 cup red wine or Chicken
1/2 cup sliced celery	Broth, page 129
1 (14-1/2-oz.) can tomatoes, including juice	Salt and pepper
	Hot cooked pasta

Heat oil in a Dutch oven or heavy saucepan. Brown rabbit in oil. Add remaining ingredients. Cover, reduce heat; cook until rabbit is tender, 30 to 40 minutes. Season with salt and pepper to taste. Serve with hot cooked pasta. Makes 4 servings.

Each 3-oz. Serving Contains:

Calories	311.0	Fiber	4.8g	Trans-fatty acids	0.1g
Protein	9.0g	Total Fat	8.3g	Cholesterol	0mg
Carbohydrates	47.7g	Saturated Fat	1.2g	Sodium	397.5mg

Chili Mac Casserole

2 teaspoons olive or canola oil
3/4 lb. select extra-lean
   ground beef
1 onion, chopped
2 garlic cloves, crushed
1 green bell pepper, chopped
2 celery stalks, sliced
1 (8-oz.) can tomato sauce
1 (16-oz.) can whole tomatoes,
   or 4 fresh tomatoes,
   chopped

1 teaspoon dried-leaf oregano
1/2 teaspoon Italian seasoning
1 (16-oz.) can kidney beans,
   drained
1-1/2 cups cooked macaroni
Salt and pepper

In a large non-stick fry pan, heat oil. Add beef and stir to brown; add onion, garlic, pepper and celery. Cook about 3 minutes, stirring often. Add tomato sauce, tomatoes, including juice, oregano and Italian seasoning. Cover, reduce heat and cook about 20 minutes. Add beans and macaroni. Cook 4 to 5 minutes until heated through. Season to taste with salt and pepper. Makes 6 servings.

Each Serving Contains:					
Calories	288.8	Fiber	9.1g	Trans-fatty acids	0g
Protein	20.5g	Total Fat	7.5g	Cholesterol	20.6mg
Carbohydrates	35.6g	Saturated Fat	2.3g	Sodium	450.3mg

Beef with Peppers & Tomato

3/4 lb. select flank or
  round steak
2 tablespoons canola oil
1 teaspoon chopped
  ginger root
2 garlic cloves
1/2 onion, sliced
1 green bell pepper, sliced
2 tomatoes, cut in eighths
1/2 cup Beef Broth, page 130
1 teaspoon cornstarch
1 tablespoon soy sauce

Marinade
1 teaspoon sugar
1 teaspoon cornstarch
2 tablespoons soy sauce
1 tablespoon rice wine or
  vinegar
1 green onion, chopped
1 teaspoon chopped
  ginger root or 1/4 teaspoon
  ground ginger

Chill or partially freeze steak for easier slicing. Remove all visible fat.
Slice chilled steak into 1/2 x 2-inch strips. In a bowl, combine all
ingredients for marinade. Add steak strips; stir to combine. Let stand
at least 15 minutes. Heat oil in a wok or large non-stick fry pan. Add
ginger and garlic; sauté until golden. Add steak strips, stir-fry until
lightly browned. Remove and set aside. Add onion and bell peppers;
stir-fry about 2 minutes. Add tomatoes and steak; continue stirring.
Combine broth, cornstarch and soy sauce. Pour over beef mixture.
Quickly stir-fry about 1 minute to coat all ingredients. Serve at once.
Makes 4 servings.

Each Serving Contains:					
Calories	242.0	Fiber	1.3g	Trans-fatty acids	0.1g
Protein	20.2g	Total Fat	13.7g	Cholesterol	43.9mg
Carbohydrates	9.5g	Saturated Fat	3.9g	Sodium	1146.1mg

Veal Stew

1 lb. veal stew meat
2 tablespoons all-purpose flour
1 tablespoon olive or canola oil
1 to 2 tablespoons sweet
   paprika
1 onion, chopped
5 carrots, sliced
1-1/2 cups Chicken Broth,
   page 129

4 potatoes, peeled, cubed
1-1/2 cups fresh or frozen
   green beans
1 tablespoon all-purpose flour
1/2 cup fat-free plain yogurt
Dill weed

Trim all visible fat from stew meat; cut into bite-size pieces. Toss with 2 tablespoons flour to coat. In a Dutch oven or heavy pot, heat oil. Add meat; stir to brown all sides evenly. Add paprika, onion, carrots and broth. Cover and simmer about 45 minutes. Add potatoes and green beans. Continue cooking until vegetables are tender. Stir 1 tablespoon flour into yogurt. Remove meat and vegetables to a serving bowl and cover. Stir yogurt mixture into remaining stew liquid. Heat, stirring, until blended. Pour over meat and vegetables, sprinkle with dill weed. Serve at once. Makes 6 servings.

Each Serving Contains:							
Calories	269.6	Fiber	4.6g	Trans-fatty acids	0g
Protein	20.0g	Total Fat	6.6g	Cholesterol	56.2mg
Carbohydrates	33.4g	Saturated Fat	1.8g	Sodium	285.9mg

Oven Meatballs

1/2 cup rolled or quick oatmeal
1/2 cup soft breadcrumbs
1/2 lb. select extra-lean
    ground beef
1/4 cup egg substitute
1/4 cup nonfat milk
1/4 teaspoon ground nutmeg
1/2 teaspoon celery seed

1/2 teaspoon chopped parsley
1 tablespoon Worcestershire
    sauce
2 green onions, chopped
2 tablespoons chopped
    mushrooms
Salt and pepper
Red-currant or raspberry jelly

Preheat oven to 400F (205C). In a bowl, combine all ingredients except jelly. Shape into 12 (2-inch) balls. Place on an ungreased baking sheet. Bake 15 to 20 minutes, until browned. Heat red-currant or raspberry jelly. Place meatballs in a serving dish. Either pour jelly over meatballs or serve separately. Makes 4 servings.

Each Serving Contains:					
Calories	233.0	Fiber	1.6g	Trans-fatty acids	0g
Protein	16.7g	Total Fat	6.7g	Cholesterol	21.2mg
Carbohydrate	36.6g	Saturated Fat	2.4g	Sodium	218.2mg

Fruited Meatloaf

18 dried or canned apricot
   halves
1 cup hot water
1/2 lb. skinned turkey breast,
   ground
1/2 lb. fat-free round steak,
   ground
1 cup rolled oats
1/4 cup egg substitute or
   2 egg whites

3 tablespoons tomato paste
1 celery stalk, chopped
1 medium onion, chopped
1 tablespoon chopped fresh
   parsley
1/2 teaspoon Fine Herbes
Salt and pepper
8 pitted prunes

Preheat oven to 350F(175C). Spray a 9 x 5-inch pan with vegetable cooking spray. Place dried apricots in a small bowl. Cover with 1 cup hot water. If using canned apricots, drain; set aside. In a large bowl, thoroughly combine turkey, steak, oats, egg substitute or egg whites, tomato paste, celery, onion, parsley and herbs. Season with salt and pepper to taste. Pat mixture into prepared pan. Drain apricots. Press prunes in a single row down center of meat loaf. Press apricots cut side down on either side of prunes. Cover with foil and bake 30 minutes. Uncover and continue baking another 25 to 30 minutes. Let stand about 10 minutes before slicing. Makes 8 servings.

Each Serving Contains:							
Calories	190.3	Fiber	3.0g	Trans-fatty acids	0g
Protein	14.3g	Total Fat	6.6g	Cholesterol	33.7mg
Carbohydrates	19.5g	Saturated Fat	2.0g	Sodium	158.7mg

DESSERTS

*EVEN WITH FAT AND CHOLESTEROL COUNTS IN MIND,
WE OFFER A GREAT GROUP OF DESSERTS.*

Crepes can be filled with any number of fillings that are tasty, yet contain little or no fat. Frozen desserts seem to be the most popular, so don't feel denied. Our suggestions are delicious.

Along with homemade sorbet or sherbet, serve one of our cookies. Homey Bread Pudding becomes a special treat when topped with one of the fruit sauces. Chilled Melon Soup is a delightful way to end a summer meal.

Or create your own yogurt combination. Start with plain fat-free yogurt, add applesauce, cinnamon and nutmeg, and you have the choice of eating it as is or freezing it for later.

Dessert Crepes

3/4 cup egg substitute   2 tablespoons sugar
1-1/2 cups nonfat milk   1 teaspoon vanilla extract
1 cup all-purpose flour

In a small bowl, beat egg substitute until frothy; continue beating while adding nonfat milk. Gradually add flour, sugar and vanilla. Use either a non-stick crepe pan or a skillet sprayed with vegetable cooking spray. Heat pan; add about 1/4 cup batter. Quickly tilt pan to evenly spread batter. When batter surface appears dry and begins to bubble, turn crepe. Repeat with remaining batter. Use any of the fillings below, and either roll or fold as desired. Makes about 20 (8-inch) crepes.

Fillings: Spread cooked crepes with your favorite berries. Fold, roll or stack and top with jam or additional fruit. Dust with powdered sugar.

Fruit Crepes: Combine 1-1/2 cups cooked apples, apricots or peaches with 1/3 cup raisins or currants and 1/2 teaspoon pumpkin-pie spice.

Cheese Crepes: Combine 1 cup fat-free cottage cheese with 2 tablespoons sugar and 1 teaspoon vanilla.

Each Plain Crepe Contains:							
Calories	42.4	Fiber	0.2g	Trans-fatty acids	0g
Protein	2.4g	Total Fat	0.4g	Cholesterol	0.4mg
Carbohydrates	7.0g	Saturated Fat	0.1g	Sodium	26.3mg

Raspberry Sorbet

1/3 cup sugar
2 teaspoons lemon peel
1 cup water

3 cups fresh or frozen
    raspberries
1 orange, peeled, sectioned

In a small saucepan combine sugar, lemon peel and water. Bring to a boil; simmer until sugar is dissolved. Set aside to cool. Combine lemon syrup, raspberries and orange in a blender or food processor. Blend until smooth; pour into an ice-cream maker and freeze according to manufacturer's instructions. If you do not have an ice-cream maker, pour mixture into a freezer container, cover surface with plastic wrap. Freeze until firm. Remove, break into chunks. Beat in a mixer or food processor until fluffy, but not thawed. Spoon back into freezer container, cover with plastic wrap, return to freezer until firm. Makes about 1 quart.

Variation: For a smoother sorbet, substitute 1 (10-oz.) can frozen raspberry-juice concentrate and 1 cup strained orange juice.

Strawberry Gelatin: Dissolve 1 (3 oz.) pkg. strawberry gelatin in 1-1/2 cups boiling water; add 3 ice cubes. Stir until ice is melted. Pour into blender or food processor with 2 cups strawberries. Blend until smooth. Proceed according to instructions above.

Each Serving Contains:							
Calories	125.4	Fiber	4.4g	Trans-fatty acids	0g
Protein	1.2g	Total Fat	0.5g	Cholesterol	0mg
Carbohydrates	31.4g	Saturated Fat	0g	Sodium	2.0mg

Peaches & Cream Frozen Yogurt

This will become a summertime favorite with a new twist.

1 lb. fresh or 1 (1-lb.) pkg.
   frozen peaches, thawed
1 tablespoon cream sherry,
   if desired
1/2 cup honey

1 cup fat-free plain yogurt
1 cup evaporated skimmed milk
8 strawberries for garnish
Mint leaf for garnish

In a blender or food processor, purée peaches with cream sherry and honey. Stir in yogurt and evaporated milk. Freeze in ice-cream maker according to manufacturer's directions. Serve cold with garnish of strawberries or mint leaf.

Makes 8 servings.

Each Serving Contains:					
Calories	138.6	Fiber	1.5g	Trans-fatty acids	0g
Protein	3.7g	Total Fat	0.2g	Cholesterol	1.3mg
Carbohydrates	32.8g	Saturated Fat	50mg	Sodium	47.9mg

Frozen Yogurt

2 cups fat-free plain yogurt
1/4 cup light corn syrup
1/4 cup egg substitute

1 banana
1 (10-oz.) pkg. frozen berries
  or fruit

Combine all ingredients in blender or food processor. Pour into a freezer container. For individual servings, pour into 8 (4-oz.) paper cups. Cover and freeze until firm. For a smoother texture, break into pieces and place in a mixer bowl, blender or food processor. Blend until fluffy. Makes 1 quart. Serves 4.

Variation: Omit corn syrup, banana and fruit. Increase egg substitute to 1 cup, add 3/4 cup sugar, 1/3 cup lemon juice and 1 (12-oz.) can frozen juice concentrate.

Peach Melba: Omit egg substitute and banana. Substitute 1-1/2 cups puréed peaches and use frozen raspberries.

Each 1-Cup Serving Contains:					
Calories	210.9	Fiber	4.4g	Trans Fatty Acids	0g
Protein	10.1g	Total Fat	1.2g	Cholesterol	2.4mg
Carbohydrates	43.0g	Saturated Fat	0.4g	Sodium	147.3mg

Strawberry-Banana Frozen Yogurt

Treat yourself: Use any fresh or frozen fruit that you like.

1 cup fat-free plain yogurt
1 cup fat-free milk
1/4 cup light corn syrup
1/2 cup egg substitute

1 banana
1 (10-oz.) pkg. frozen
  strawberries

Combine all ingredients in blender or food processor. Pour into a freezer container. For individual servings, pour into 8 (4-oz.) paper cups. Cover and freeze until firm. For a smoother texture, break into pieces and place in a mixer bowl, blender or food processor. Blend until fluffy. Makes 1 quart.

Variations:

Lemon Supreme: Omit corn syrup, banana and strawberries; increase egg substitute to 1 cup, add 3/4 cup sugar, 1 tablespoon lemon peel, 1/3 cup lemon juice and 1 (12-oz.) can frozen orange-juice or lemonade concentrate.

Peach Melba: Omit egg substitute and banana. Substitute 1-1/2 cups puréed peaches and replace strawberries with frozen raspberries.

Each Serving Contains:					
Calories	98	Fiber	1.2g	Trans-fatty acids	10mg
Protein	3.3g	Total Fat	0.5g	Cholesterol	0.7mg
Carbohydrates	22.1g	Saturated Fat	0.1g	Sodium	56.2mg

Apricot Cookies

2 cups rolled or quick oats
1 cup oat bran
1/2 cup brown sugar
1/2 cup granulated sugar
1/2 teaspoon baking powder
1 tablespoon canola oil
1/4 cup nonfat milk
1/2 cup egg substitute

1 cup unsweetened applesauce
2 teaspoons vanilla extract
1-1/2 cups or 1 (6-oz.) pkg.
   chopped dried apricots
Glaze
1 cup powdered sugar
2 tablespoons lemon juice
1 teaspoon grated lemon peel

Preheat oven to 375F (190C). Spray a 9 x 13-inch baking pan with vegetable cooking spray; set aside. In a large bowl, combine oats, bran, sugars and baking powder; stir to blend. In a separate bowl, combine oil, milk, egg substitute, applesauce, vanilla and apricots. Stir together. Pour into oat mixture. Thoroughly mix together. Pour into prepared pan. Bake 25 to 30 minutes. Combine ingredients for Glaze; spread on warm cookies. Cut into 2 x 2-inch bars. Let cool completely before serving. Makes 24 cookies.

1 Cookie Contains:					
Calories	114.4	Fiber	2.1g	Trans-fatty acids	0g
Protein	2.8g	Total Fat	1.5g	Cholesterol	0.1mg
Carbohydrates	24.9g	Saturated Fat	0.2g	Sodium	23.5mg

Lace Cookies

3 tablespoons all-purpose flour
2 teaspoons unsweetened
  cocoa powder
1/2 cup oats, rolled or
  quick-cooking
2 tablespoons canola oil

2 tablespoons soft diet
  margarine
1/4 cup light-brown sugar
2 tablespoons light corn syrup
1/2 teaspoon vanilla extract

Preheat oven to 375F (190C). Line 2 cookie sheets with foil. In a small bowl, stir together flour, cocoa and oats. In a saucepan, heat together oil, margarine, sugar and corn syrup. Stir over medium heat until mixture is well blended. Remove from heat; add vanilla. Pour oat mixture into hot mixture. Quickly stir to blend. Drop by half-teaspoonfuls onto prepared cookie sheets. Place 3 inches apart. Bake about 8 minutes. Cool about 5 minutes. Carefully remove cookies. Makes 20 cookies.

1 Cookie Contains:					
Calories	42.2	Fiber	0.3g	Trans-fatty acids	0.1g
Protein	0.5g	Total Fat	2.1g	Cholesterol	0mg
Carbohydrates	5.7g	Saturated Fat	0.2g	Sodium	8.3mg

Raisin-Rum Sauce

2 tablespoons cornstarch
2 tablespoons sugar
1-1/2 cups cider or apple juice

3/4 cup raisins
2 tablespoons rum or
  rum flavoring

In a small saucepan, stir cornstarch and sugar into cider or apple juice. Add raisins. Stir over medium heat until mixture begins to thicken. Remove from heat; stir in rum or rum flavoring. Serve at once. Makes about 2 cups.

Each 1/4-Cup Serving Contains:					
Calories	97.8	Fiber	0.5g	Trans-fatty acids	0g
Protein	0.5g	Total Fat	0.1g	Cholesterol	0mg
Carbohydrates	21.1g	Saturated Fat	0g	Sodium	3.3mg

Delicious Oatmeal Cookies

1-1/2 cups quick or instant oats
1/2 cup oat bran
1/2 cup all-purpose flour
2 tablespoons unsweetened
   cocoa powder
1 teaspoon baking soda

1 cup brown sugar
2 tablespoons peanut butter
1/3 cup nonfat milk
1 teaspoon vanilla extract
1 cup finely chopped apples
1/2 cup chopped dates

Preheat oven to 375F (190C). Spray cookie sheets with vegetable cooking spray. In a large mixer bowl, combine oats, oat bran, flour, cocoa powder, baking soda and sugar. In a cup, combine peanut butter, milk and vanilla. Stir into dry mixture; thoroughly combine. Add apples and dates. Batter will be stiff. Drop by tablespoonfuls onto prepared cookie sheets. Bake 15 to 17 minutes. Makes 48 cookies.

1 Cookie Contains:						
Calories	39.9	Fiber	0.7g	Trans fatty acids	0g
Protein	1.0g	Total Fat	0.6g	Cholesterol	0mg
Carbohydrates	8.3g	Saturated Fat	0.1g	Sodium	31.7mg

Lemon Sauce

2 tablespoons cornstarch
1/2 cup sugar
1/4 cup lemon juice

1-1/2 cups orange juice
2 teaspoons grated lemon peel

In a small saucepan, stir cornstarch and sugar into juices. Add lemon peel. Stir over medium heat until mixture begins to thicken. Remove from heat. Serve at once. Makes about 1-3/4 cups.

Each 1/4-Cup Serving Contains:						
Calories	90.4	Fiber	0.2g	Trans-fatty acids	0g
Protein	0.4g	Total Fat	0g	Cholesterol	0mg
Carbohydrates	22.9g	Saturated Fat	0g	Sodium	1.0mg

Bread Pudding

1/2 cup egg substitute
1/4 cup nonfat plain yogurt
2 cups nonfat milk
1 teaspoon vanilla extract
3/4 teaspoon ground cinnamon
1/4 teaspoon nutmeg
1/2 cup brown sugar

3 cups bread cubes
1/3 cup raisins

Meringue
4 egg whites
1/2 cup sugar
1/2 teaspoon vanilla extract

Preheat oven to 325F (165C). Spray a 2-quart baking dish with vegetable cooking spray. In a mixer bowl, beat egg substitute; blend in yogurt and milk. Add vanilla, cinnamon, nutmeg and sugar. Add bread and raisins, stir to completely coat bread cubes. Pour into prepared baking dish. Place a shallow pan on lowest oven rack. Pour in about 1-inch water. Place baking dish on rack above. Bake 45 minutes. To make Meringue, beat egg whites until foamy, continue beating and slowly add sugar and vanilla. Beat until mixture forms stiff peaks. Remove pan with water. Spread meringue over bread pudding and return to oven. Bake 12 to 15 minutes, until meringue is golden brown. Serve warm. Makes about 8 servings.

Variations: Omit meringue and top with Raisin-Rum Sauce, page 226 or Apricot-Orange Sauce, page 236.

Date Bread Pudding: Omit raisins and substitute 1 chopped banana and 1/3 cup chopped dates.

Each Serving Contains:					
Calories	180.7	Fiber	0.6g	Trans-fatty acids	0g
Protein	7.4g	Total Fat	1.1g	Cholesterol	1.7mg
Carbohydrates	35.8g	Saturated Fat	0.3g	Sodium	153.7mg

Meringue

3/4 cup sugar
2 teaspoons cornstarch
4 egg whites

1/2 teaspoon cream of tartar
1/2 teaspoon vanilla extract

Blend sugar and cornstarch. In a large bowl, whip egg whites and cream of tartar until soft peaks form. Continue whipping gradually adding sugar and cornstarch. Mixture should be very stiff.

Pie Shell: Spray a 9-inch pie plate with vegetable cooking spray. Spread meringue evenly on bottom and sides. Bake at 300F (165C) for an hour. Turn off heat; prop oven door open about 1 inch. Meringue crust should be left in oven until cool. Fill with fresh sliced fruit. Makes 1 pie shell.

Cookies: Spray a cookie sheet with vegetable cooking spray. Fill a piping bag with meringue. Pipe circular mounds about 2 inches apart. Or spoon a mound of mixture for each cookie. Bake as above. Makes about 48 cookies.

Almond Meringue Cookies: Fold in 1/2 cup finely chopped almonds to whipped meringue. Omit vanilla, substitute 1/2 teaspoon almond extract.

Currant or Date: Fold in 1/2 cup currants and 1/4 cup chopped dates. Omit vanilla, substitute 1 teaspoon orange flavoring.

Mocha: Blend 3 tablespoons decaffeinated coffee granules with sugar and cornstarch. Omit vanilla, add 1/2 teaspoon chocolate flavoring.

Each 1/6 Pie Shell Serving Contains:

Calories	84.2	Fiber	0g	Trans-fatty acids	0g
Protein	2.3g	Total Fat	0g	Cholesterol	0mg
Carbohydrates	18.9g	Saturated Fat	0g	Sodium	43.8mg

1 Cookie Contains:

Calories	10.5	Fiber	0g	Trans-fatty acids	0g
Protein	0.3g	Total Fat	0g	Cholesterol	0mg
Carbohydrates	2.4g	Saturated Fat	0g	Sodium	5.5mg

1 Cookie with Almonds Contains:

Calories	18.5	Fiber	0.1g	Trans-fatty acids	0g
Protein	0.6g	Total Fat	0.7g	Cholesterol	0mg
Carbohydrates	2.6g	Saturated Fat	0.1g	Sodium	5.6mg

Cantaloupe Pie Supreme

1 single-crust Basic Pastry,
  page 231
1/2 cup apricot preserves
1 tablespoon brandy flavoring,
  if desired
2 teaspoons sugar or sweetener

1/2 cup fat-free cream cheese
1 to 2 ripe cantaloupes, cut in
  half, lengthwise, peeled,
  sliced
Powdered sugar
3/4 cup blueberries

Prepare and bake pie shell. Heat apricot preserves in a small saucepan. Remove from heat and stir in brandy flavoring, if desired. Brush over pie shell; set aside. Stir sugar or sweetener into cream cheese. Spread mixture on bottom of coated pie shell. Arrange cantaloupe slices in a pinwheel design, starting from center. Overlap pieces on second layer. If melon is not sweet, sprinkle with powdered sugar. Cover with plastic wrap and refrigerate until serving. Top with blueberries when serving. Makes 6 servings.

Each Serving Contains:					
Calories	408.6	Fiber	3.0g	Trans-fatty acids	0g
Protein	7.3g	Total Fat	14.6g	Cholesterol	0.7mg
Carbohydrates	65.6g	Saturated Fat	1.1g	Sodium	153.0mg

Chilled Melon Soup

1 large cantaloupe or crenshaw
  melon, peeled, chopped
1 peach, peeled, pitted

1 cup fat-free plain yogurt
1 cup lowfat peach yogurt
Grated nutmeg

Purée melon and peach in a blender or food processor. Pour into a large bowl; whisk in plain and peach yogurt. Chill before serving. Sprinkle with grated nutmeg. Makes 4 servings.

Each 1-Cup Serving Contains:					
Calories	156.8	Fiber	1.6g	Trans-fatty acids	0g
Protein	7.1g	Total Fat	1.2g	Cholesterol	5.6mg
Carbohydrates	30.8g	Saturated Fat	0.5g	Sodium	88.4mg

Basic Pastry

Single-Crust

1-1/2 cups all-purpose flour   1 teaspoon vinegar
1/4 teaspoon salt   2 to 3 tablespoons ice water
6 tablespoons canola oil

In a small bowl, stir flour and salt. Combine oil, vinegar and water. Add to flour and quickly stir until mixture forms a ball. Place dough between 2 sheets of waxed paper. Roll dough into a 9- to 10-inch circle. Remove top paper. Place dough in pie plate; remove other paper. Fold overhanging edges under evenly; crimp with fork or fingers to make a raised edge. Chill 15 minutes before baking. Bake unfilled pie shell in 475F (245C) oven 8 to 10 minutes. Bake filled pie according to recipes.

Each 1/6 Pie Serving Contains:

Calories	234.3	Fiber	1.0g	Trans-fatty acids	0g
Protein	3.2g	Total Fat	13.9g	Cholesterol	0mg
Carbohydrates	23.9g	Saturated Fat	1.0g	Sodium	89.7

Double-Crust: Prepare as above, doubling ingredients.

Each 1/6 Pie Serving Contains:

Calories	468.6	Fiber	4.0g	Trans-fatty acids	0g
Protein	6.4g	Total Fat	27.9g	Cholesterol	0mg
Carbohydrates	47.8g	Saturated Fat	2.0g	Sodium	179.4mg

Rhubarb Crisp

1/2 cup sugar
2 tablespoons cornstarch
1 cup cranberry juice
1/2 cup sugar
1/3 cup honey
1/2 teaspoon ground cinnamon
1/2 teaspoon ground allspice
2 tablespoons lemon juice

1 teaspoon vanilla extract
1 cup toasted rolled oats,
  see below
1 cup oat-raisin cereal flakes
2-1/2 cups chopped fresh or
  1 (16-oz.) pkg. frozen
  rhubarb, blackberries or
  cherries

Preheat oven to 350F (175C). Spray a 9-inch square pan with vegetable cooking spray. In a small saucepan, stir sugar and cornstarch into cranberry juice. Stir over medium heat until mixture begins to thicken. Remove from heat. Set aside.

In a small saucepan, heat together sugar, honey, cinnamon, allspice and lemon juice. Cook, stirring, until sugar is dissolved. Remove from heat and add vanilla. Pour over oats and cereal; stir to mix. Spoon 1/2 oat mixture into prepared baking dish. Evenly distribute fruit over crumb mixture. Pour juice mixture over fruit; sprinkle remaining crumbs over all. Bake 25 to 30 minutes, until golden brown. Serve warm. Makes 9 servings.

To toast oats: Preheat oven to 350F (175C). Line a cookie sheet with foil. Spread oats on cookie sheet, bake about 10 minutes, stirring 2 or 3 times. Remove when oats are golden brown. Use at once, or store in a covered container for later use.

Variations: Omit rhubarb and cranberry juice, substitute apples, peaches, apricots, or pears and apple or orange juice. Try plums with grape juice; cherries and/or berries with cran-raspberry or cherry juice. Experiment with flavors—use almond, brandy, maple, mint or rum.

Each Serving Contains:					
Calories	210.4	Fiber	2.1g	Trans-fatty acids	0g
Protein	2.4g	Total Fat	0.8g	Cholesterol	0mg
Carbohydrates	50.6g	Saturated Fat	0.1g	Sodium	40.4mg

Mocha-Prune Cake

1 cup pitted prunes, chopped
1 cup coffee or apple juice
2/3 cup sugar
1/4 cup oat bran
1-1/4 cups all-purpose flour
3 tablespoons unsweetened
   cocoa powder
1 teaspoon baking soda

3 tablespoons mono-
   unsaturated oil
1 teaspoon chocolate or
   vanilla extract
3 egg whites, stiffly beaten
Powdered sugar
Cocoa Frosting, page 234

Preheat oven to 350F (175C). Spray a 9-inch square baking pan with vegetable cooking spray; set aside. Place prunes in a small bowl, add coffee or apple juice; set aside. In a medium bowl, stir together, sugar, oat bran, flour, cocoa powder and baking soda. Stir in oil, chocolate or vanilla extract and prunes with coffee or apple juice. Fold in beaten egg whites. Pour into prepared pan. Bake 30 to 35 minutes, until a wooden pick inserted in center comes out clean. Cool. Serve dusted with powdered sugar or frost with Cocoa Frosting. Makes 9 servings.

Each Serving Contains:							
Calories	316.1	Fiber	3.2g	Trans-fatty acids	0.6g
Protein	4.7g	Total Fat	5.0g	Cholesterol	0.2mg
Carbohydrates	66.2g	Saturated Fat	1.3g	Sodium	168.2mg

Cocoa Frosting

3 tablespoons fat-free cream
   cheese
1-1/2 teaspoons unsweetened
   cocoa powder

1/2 teaspoon vanilla extract
2 to 2-1/2 cups powdered sugar
1/2 teaspoon fat-free milk,
   if needed

In a small bowl, stir all ingredients together. If needed, add milk to make desired consistency. Makes about 3/4 cup. Frosts one (9-inch) cake or 12 cupcakes.

Each Serving Contains:

Calories	1034.5	Fiber	0.9g	Trans-fatty acids	0g
Protein	5.8g	Total Fat	0.8g	Cholesterol	1.7mg
Carbohydrates	257.3g	Saturated Fat	0.3g	Sodium	73.4mg

Maple-Walnut Pears

3 firm, ripe pears, peeled,
   cut in half lengthwise, cored
1/2 cup maple syrup
1/2 cup apple juice or water

1/4 teaspoon ground allspice
1 tablespoon low-fat margarine
1/4 cup chopped walnuts

Preheat oven to 400F (205C). Place pear halves, cut side up, in a deep baking dish. Heat syrup, apple juice or water and allspice; stir in margarine until melted. Pour syrup mixture over pears and sprinkle with nuts. Cover and bake 30 to 35 minutes.

Makes 6 servings.

Each Serving Contains:

Calories	167.9	Fiber	2.3g	Trans-fatty acids	0g
Protein	1.6g	Total Fat	4.0g	Cholesterol	0mg
Carbohydrates	33.9g	Saturated Fat	0.4g	Sodium	14.8mg

Orange-Blackberry Dessert

1 cup crushed corn flakes
1/4 cup chopped walnuts
1/2 teaspoon ground nutmeg
3 tablespoons brown sugar
8 oz. silken tofu, drained
2 (8-oz.) pkgs. fat-free
    cream cheese

1/2 cup frozen orange juice
    concentrate
1/2 cup sugar
1 teaspoon vanilla extract
2 cups fresh or frozen black-
    berries, strawberries or
    sliced nectarines

In a small bowl, mix together corn flakes, nuts, nutmeg and brown sugar. Set aside.

In a food processor or blender, combine tofu and cream cheese. Add orange-juice concentrate, sugar and vanilla and thoroughly blend.

In glass dessert dishes or parfait glasses, make two alternating layers of crumbs, filling and berries, ending with crumbs on top.

Makes 6 servings.

Each Serving Contains:						
Calories	297.2	Fiber	3.1g	Trans-fatty acids	0g
Protein	15.2g	Total Fat	5.4g	Cholesterol	6.1mg
Carbohydrates	48.4g	Saturated Fat	1.1g	Sodium	418.7mg

Fruit Compote

1/2 cup pitted prunes
1/4 cup raisins
1 cup apple juice
1 cinnamon stick
1/3 cup honey, if desired
1 teaspoon grated lemon peel
1 cup each sliced apricots,
   apples, pears

1 cup red or green seedless
   grapes
1 (11-oz.) can mandarin
   oranges, drained
1 banana, sliced
1/2 cup rum, if desired
1 cup fat-free plain yogurt

In a medium saucepan, heat together prunes, raisins, apple juice, cinnamon stick, honey, if desired, and lemon peel. Simmer about 15 minutes, until prunes are plump. Set aside; remove cinnamon stick. This can be made ahead and reheated. To serve, heat dried-fruit mixture. Add remaining fruits and rum, if desired. Heat and flame rum before serving. To serve, top fruit with yogurt; spoon juice over all. Makes 10 servings.

Each Serving Contains:					
Calories	104.7	Fiber	2.3g	Trans-fatty acids	0g
Protein	2.4g	Total Fat	0.4g	Cholesterol	0.4mg
Carbohydrates	25.1g	Saturated Fat	0.1g	Sodium	22.3mg

Apricot-Orange Sauce

1 tablespoon cornstarch
1 cup apricot nectar
1/2 cup dried chopped apricots
1 (11-oz.) can mandarin
   oranges, drained

2 tablespoons orange
   marmalade
2 teaspoons rum or rum
   flavoring, if desired

In a small saucepan, stir cornstarch into apricot nectar. Stir over medium heat until mixture begins to thicken. Add apricots, oranges and marmalade. Heat and add rum or rum flavoring, if desired. Serve at once. Makes about 2 cups.

Each 1/4-Cup Serving Contains:					
Calories	67.4	Fiber	1.0g	Trans-fatty acids	0g
Protein	0.7g	Total Fat	0.1g	Cholesterol	0mg
Carbohydrates	17.5g	Saturated Fat	0g	Sodium	6.6mg

Miscellaneous

We always seem to end up with recipes we want to include, but have a difficult time placing them. Thus, the Miscellaneous chapter. These recipes are not in any way less important because they are here.

The sandwiches we've included show possibilities on which you can expand. Drinks can be tailored to your personal choice. Try simple or complex combinations. Remember, the choice is yours.

Pita-Pocket Sandwich Bar

Pita bread, regular or
   whole-wheat
Turkey- or chicken-breast slices
Turkey ham slices
Assorted lettuces
Alfalfa sprouts
Bean sprouts
Lentil sprouts

Sliced tomatoes
Pickles
Garbanzo beans
Radishes
Cucumber slices
Shredded cabbage
Pea pods or peas
Fat-free plain yogurt

Serve fresh pita bread with an assortment of fillings and condiments.
Invite everyone to create their own combinations.

Each 3-oz. Serving of Turkey or Chicken Contains:							
Calories	93.6	Fiber	0g	Trans-fatty acids	0g
Protein	19.1g	Total Fat	1.4g	Cholesterol	34.9mg
Carbohydrates	0g	Saturated Fat	0.4g	Sodium	1217.1mg

Each 3-oz. Serving of Turkey Ham Contains:							
Calories	90.0	Fiber	0g	Trans-fatty acids	0g
Protein	15.0g	Total Fat	3.0g	Cholesterol	60.0mg
Carbohydrates	1.5g	Saturated Fat	1.5g	Sodium	960.0mg

Oriental Pocket Sandwiches

1 cup mung-bean sprouts
1 tablespoon olive or canola oil
1 (3-oz.) boned, skinned chicken
  breast, cut in strips
1 celery stalk, diced
1/2 cup chopped onion
1 cup fresh or frozen snow
  peas, cut in thirds
1/3 cup sliced water chestnuts
1/2 teaspoon salt
2 tablespoons Chicken Broth,
  page 129

1 tablespoon white wine or
  additional Chicken Broth
2 teaspoons soy sauce
1/4 teaspoon sugar
1/8 teaspoon ground ginger
1 teaspoon cornstarch
1 tablespoon cold water
4 pita-bread rounds
2 tablespoons sliced almonds

Rinse bean sprouts in cold water. Drain on paper towels. Heat oil in a wok or large heavy skillet over high heat. Add chicken, celery and onion. Stir until chicken begins to turn white. Add snow peas, water chestnuts and salt. Stir in chicken broth, wine or additional chicken broth, soy sauce, sugar and ginger. Cover and simmer 5 minutes. Stir in bean sprouts. In a small bowl, combine cornstarch and cold water. Stir into chicken mixture. Stir constantly over medium heat until liquid thickens and boils. Cut each pita bread round in half and carefully separate side of bread to make pocket. Spoon chicken mixture into pockets. Sprinkle filling with almonds. Makes 4 servings.

Each Serving Contains:					
Calories	301.3	Fiber	3.8g	Trans-fatty acids	0g
Protein	15.0g	Total Fat	7.5g	Cholesterol	17.9mg
Carbohydrates	43.0g	Saturated Fat	1.2g	Sodium	860.6mg

Reuben Sandwich

Prepared mustard
2 slices rye bread
1/3 cup drained sauerkraut
2 teaspoons grated Parmesan
   cheese

2 (1-oz.) slices smoked
   turkey ham
Salt and pepper

Spread prepared mustard on both pieces of rye bread. On 1 slice, layer half of sauerkraut, half of Parmesan cheese, smoked turkey ham, remaining sauerkraut and cheese. Season with salt and pepper to taste. Top with remaining bread. Spray a non-stick skillet with vegetable cooking spray. Heat and place sandwich in skillet, cook about 1 minute per side. Makes 1 sandwich.

Each Serving Contains:							
Calories	238.6	Fiber	5.4g	Trans-fatty acids	0g
Protein	17.5g	Total Fat	6.3g	Cholesterol	43.3mg
Carbohydrates	28.6g	Saturated Fat	2.2g	Sodium	1985.3mg

Scandinavian Open-Face Sandwich

Prepared mustard
4 slices dark rye, pumpernickel
   or crispbread
4 small lettuce leaves

1 tomato, thinly sliced
1 (3.75-oz.) can sardines,
   drained
1 tablespoon capers

Spread mustard on bread. Layer lettuce, tomato slices and sardines on each slice. Sprinkle with capers. Makes 4 open-face sandwiches.

Each Serving Contains:							
Calories	139.2	Fiber	2.4g	Trans-fatty acids	0g
Protein	9.8g	Total Fat	4.7g	Cholesterol	37.7mg
Carbohydrates	14.7g	Saturated Fat	0.6g	Sodium	576.7mg

Smoked-Salmon Open-Face Sandwich

3 tablespoons fat-free
 plain yogurt
6 slices dark rye, pumpernickel
 or crispbread

Dill weed
6 thin slices smoked salmon
12 thin cucumber slices
Yellow or red bell-pepper strips

Spread yogurt evenly on bread. Sprinkle with dill weed. Top with salmon, cucumber and bell pepper. Makes 6 open-face sandwiches.

Each Serving Contains:

Calories	106.7	Fiber	1.9g	Trans-fatty acids	0g
Protein	7.9g	Total Fat	2.1g	Cholesterol	6.7mg
Carbohydrates	13.7g	Saturated Fat	0.4g	Sodium	393.6mg

Tram Burger

3/4 lb. select extra-lean
 ground beef
2 tablespoons Worcestershire
 sauce
1/2 teaspoon celery salt
1/2 teaspoon dry mustard

Hamburger buns
Onion slices, if desired
Tomato slices
Lettuce
Salt and pepper

In a medium bowl, combine beef, Worcestershire sauce, celery salt and mustard. Thoroughly mix together. Shape into 4 patties. Broil as desired. Serve on hamburger buns, topped with onions, if desired, tomato and lettuce. Season to taste with salt and pepper. Makes 4 burgers.

Variation: The fat content can be reduced almost by half by using equal parts soybean meat substitute and beef.

Each Serving Contains:

Calories	286.0	Fiber	1.5g	Trans-fatty acids	0g
Protein	21.7g	Total Fat	10.2g	Cholesterol	31.0mg
Carbohydrates	25.4g	Saturated Fat	3.6g	Sodium	599.1mg

Sour-Cream Substitute

1/2 cup fat-free plain yogurt   2 teaspoons lemon juice
1/2 cup fat-free cottage cheese

Place ingredients in blender or food processor. Blend until smooth. Refrigerate in container with a tight-fitting lid. Use for recipes calling for sour cream. Makes about 1 cup.

1 Teaspoon Contains:					
Calories	16.8	Fiber	0g	Trans-fatty acids	0g
Protein	2.5g	Total Fat	0g	Cholesterol	1.4mg
Carbohydrates	1.6g	Saturated Fat	0g	Sodium	393.6mg

Joyce's Pineapple Smoothie

Naturally sweetened by the combination of fruits.

1/2 cup pineapple chunks   2 tablespoons fat-free
1/4 cup pineapple juice   plain yogurt
1 small banana   3 ice cubes

Combine all ingredients in a blender or food processor. Blend until thoroughly combined and frothy. Serve at once.

Makes 1 (10-oz.) glass.

Each Glass Contains:					
Calories	167.9	Fiber	2.3g	Trans-fatty acids	0g
Protein	1.6g	Total Fat	4.0g	Cholesterol	0mg
Carbohydrates	33.9g	Saturated Fat	0.4g	Sodium	14.8mg

Yogurt Fruit Shake

2 cups fat-free plain yogurt

2 cups raspberries, strawberries, peaches or apricots

4 tablespoons orange or other fruit juice

Sugar

Combine yogurt, fruit and juice in a blender and process until well blended and frothy. Sweeten to taste. Pour into glasses. Makes 4 servings.

Each Serving Contains:					
Calories	117.6	Fiber	2.5g	Trans-fatty acids	0g
Protein	7.7g	Total Fat	0.6g	Cholesterol	2.2mg
Carbohydrates	21.4g	Saturated Fat	0.2g	Sodium	93.9mg

Orange Freezee

3 oranges, peeled, sectioned

1/4 cup cold water

1/3 cup sugar

Ice cubes to obtain desired consistency

Combine orange sections, water, sugar and ice cubes in a blender or food processor. Add ice cubes until desired consistency is reached. Pour into glasses. Makes 2 servings.

Variations: Omit oranges and substitute 1 cup fresh or frozen berries, grapefruit, pineapple, peaches or your favorite fruit.

Icy Orange Cooler: Add 1 cup fat-free yogurt; use 6 ice cubes. Blend mixture until ice is finely chopped and mixture is frothy.

Makes 2 servings.

Each Serving Contains:					
Calories	258.7	Fiber	6.6g	Trans-fatty acids	0g
Protein	2.6g	Total Fat	0.3g	Cholesterol	0mg
Carbohydrates	65.9g	Saturated Fat	40mg	Sodium	2.5mg

SUBSTITUTIONS & HINTS

Recipe Substitutions

Bacon
Imitation bacon bits

Breadcrumbs, 1 cup
3/4 cup cereal, crackers or rolled oats

Breadcrumbs, 1/4 cup
1 slice bread

Butter
Soft margarine

Butter, 1 tablespoon
2 teaspoons canola or monounsaturated oil

Butter, Shortening or Lard, 1 cup
2/3 cup canola or monounsaturated oil

Buttermilk, 1 cup
1 cup nonfat milk, plus 2 tablespoons lemon juice or vinegar

Cake flour, 1 cup
7/8 cup all-purpose flour, plus 2 tablespoons cornstarch

Chocolate, 1 oz.
1/4 cup cocoa, plus 2 teaspoons oil

Cornstarch, 1 tablespoon
2 tablespoons flour or 4 teaspoons tapioca

Cream cheese
Fat-free cream cheese

Egg, 1
2 egg whites or 1/4 cup egg substitute

Fresh herbs, 1 tablespoon
1 teaspoon dried herbs

Garlic clove, 1
1/8 teaspoon garlic powder

Ground beef
Turkey breast, skinned and ground

Honey, 1 cup
1-1/4 cups sugar, plus 1/4 cup water

Lemon juice, 1 teaspoon
1/2 teaspoon vinegar

Mustard, 1 teaspoon prepared
1/2 teaspoon dry mustard

Onion, 1 medium
1-1/2 tablespoons dehydrated onion flakes

Sugar, 1 cup
3/4 cup honey

Sour cream
Plain fat-free yogurt

Whole milk
Nonfat milk or 1 can evaporated skim milk, plus 1 can water

Appendix

How Much Bad Fat Is In Everyday Food?

For the total amount of bad fat you are adding to your daily budget, add the grams of saturated fat and the grams of trans fatty acids in each serving, being careful to note that many of the serving sizes in these tables are very small. Read the labels of food you buy and ask about the fat content of food you order, especially at fast-food restaurants.

To the credit of many food producers and restaurant chains who reduced the amount of bad fat in their entrees, some foods listed in these tables contain considerably less saturated fat than they did a few years ago. But sometimes the lower-fat items don't sell well enough to keep them in the line and the great new lowfat product disappears. Obviously there continues to be considerable variation in the amount of fat in food products depending on the ingredients used and the means of preparation.

Food	Saturated Fat (grams)	Trans-fatty Acids (grams)	Cholesterol (milligrams)
Fruits	0.0	0.0	0.0
Beans & Other Legumes	trace	0.0	0.0
Grains, Wheat, Corn, Oats, Barley, Rice	trace	0.0	0.0
Vegetables *(most)*	0.0	0.0	0.0
Avocados *(1 medium)*	4.5	0.0	0.0
Olives *(4 medium)*	0.5	0.0	0.0
Breads			
Bagel, plain	0.0	0.1	0.0
Baking powder biscuits	1.0	trace	0.0
French bread	0.2	0.2	0.0
Hamburger &	0.5	0.6	0.0
hot dog buns	0.5	0.5	0.0
White soft bread (slice)	0.4	0.2	0.9
Whole wheat bread (slice)	0.3	0.2	0.0
Meat & Poultry *(3 ounces)*			
Roast beef or steak, marbled	6.8	0.9	58.1
Roast beef or steak, lean	2.3	0.0	57.5
Hamburger, regular	4.8	0.5	57.3
Hamburger, extra lean	3.1	0.0	31.0
Liver (beef)	1.6	0.0	301.1
Chicken, white with skin	1.4	--	49.1
Chicken, white without skin	1.3	--	53.7
Chicken, dark with skin	1.8	--	41.9
Chicken, dark without skin	1.5	--	55.4
Bacon, 3 thin slices	3.3	0.0	16.2
Ham, regular with visible fat	3.9	0.0	39.6
Ham, 96% fat-free	1.3	0.0	32.3
Ham, 97% fat-free	1.5	--	38.0
Pork roast or chop, with fat	3.8	0.0	46.6
Pork roast or chop, lean	3.2	0.0	46.4
Pork loin, extra lean	2.2	0.0	51.1
Hot dog	4.9	0.5	22.5
Hot dog, very lowfat Turkey	2.7	0.1	48.2
Lamb roast or chop, with fat	6.5	0.0	79.1
Lamb roast or chop, lean	2.9	0.0	54.8
Bologna (per slice)	2.8	0.4	13.3
Salami (per slice)	2.1	--	15.0
Sausage (per link)	6.1	0.1	52.3

Food	Saturated Fat (grams)	Trans-fatty Acids (grams)	Cholesterol (milligrams)
Snack Foods (1 oz.)			
Corn chips, regular, 1 oz	1.3	--	0.0
Corn chips, baked, 1 oz	0.8	--	0.9
Potato chips, regular, 1 oz	3.1	0.0	0.0
Potato chips, reduced fat, 1 oz	1.2	--	0.0
Popcorn, air-popped, fat-free tablespray	0.2	--	0.0
Popcorn, oil-cooked & butter	1.4	2.1	0.0
Desserts			
Doughnut, plain	1.8	2.3	17.4
Doughnut, glazed	3.5	3.8	3.6
Danish pastry	3.5	--	27.3
Cake, chocolate, yellow, devil	3.1	1.9	35.2
Fruitcake	0.5	--	2.2
Chocolate chip cookie, 1 homemade	1.3	1.6	5.1
Brownie square, 1 homemade	1.8	--	17.5
Angel food cake, 1 piece	0.0	0.1	0.0
Pie, apple, 1 piece	2.6	--	0.0
Gelatin, 1 cup	0.0	0.0	0.0
Egg custard, 1 cup	6.6	--	245.3
Instant pudding with 2% milk	2.9	--	17.0
Instant pudding with milk, 1 cup	4.9	--	31.2
Candy			
Chocolate candy bar	8.1	0.0	9.7
Caramel, 1 oz	1.9	--	2.0
Chocolate, 1 oz, semisweet chips	5.1	--	0.0
Gum drop, 1 oz	0.0	0.0	0.0
Hard candy	0.0	0.0	0.0
Taffy	0.6	--	2.6
Fast foods			
Burrito, large meat	5.2	--	31.9
Cheeseburger	6.4	--	50.0
Chicken nuggets x 9	8.3	0.1	91.8
Roasted chicken sandwich, skinless, breast	8.5	--	60.1
Enchilada, chicken	3.5	0.0	35.9
Pizza, 1/4 of 12" cheese	7.0	--	20.0
Pizza, 1/4 of 12" pepperoni	7.0	--	15.0
French fries (4 oz)	4.3	6.4	14.7
Fried fish sandwich	3.5	--	45.0
Hamburger, double	12.0	--	103.2
Sausage sandwich with egg	15.0	--	302.4

Food	Saturated Fat (grams)	Trans-fatty Acids (grams)	Cholesterol (milligrams)
Eggs & Substitutes			
Egg, 1 large whole	1.6	0.0	212.5
Egg, 1 yolk	1.6	0.0	212.7
Egg, 1 white	0.0	0.0	0.0
Egg substitutes	0.2	0.0	0.3
Tablespreads *(per tablespoon)*			
Butter – salted	7.0	0.3	30.0
Stick margarine, hydrogenated soybean oil	2.4	3.2	0.0
Stick margarine (light), 40% hydrogenated soybean oil	0.9	0.8	0.0
Soft margarine	1.9	1.7	0.0
Soft diet spread	1.8	– –	0.0
Fat-free sprays (1 spray)	0.0	0.0	0.0
Salad Dressings *(per tablespoon)*			
Bleu Cheese	1.5	– –	2.6
Most regular salad dressings	0.8	– –	5.8
Reduced fat dressings	0.0	0.0	0.0
Fat-free dressings	0.0	0.0	0.0
Mayonnaise, regular	0.7	0.0	3.8
Fat-free mayo	0.0	0.0	0.0
Milk Products			
Homogenized milk, 1 cup	5.1	0.2	33.2
2% milk	2.9	0.1	18.3
1% milk	1.6	0.1	9.8
Fat-free (skim) milk	0.3	0.0	4.4
Buttermilk	1.3	– –	8.6
Cream, heavy, 1 tablespoon	3.4	– –	20.4
Cream, half and half, 1 tablespoon	1.1	– –	5.6
Cream, light, 1 tablespoon	1.8	– –	9.9
Creamer, lowfat	0.0	– –	0.0
Dessert topping, non-dairy (1 oz.)	6.1	– –	0.0
Eggnog, 1 cup	11.3	0.2	149.1
Eggnog, lowfat	3.8	– –	193.6
Sour cream, 1 tablespoon	1.9	– –	6.4
Sour cream imitation, 1 tablespoon	2.6	– –	0.0
Yogurt, creamy 1 cup	5.2	0.2	31.1
Yogurt, lowfat 2%, 1 cup	2.5	0.1	15.0
Yogurt, fat-free, 1 cup	0.2	0.0	8.3

Food	Saturated Fat (grams)	Trans-fatty Acids (grams)	Cholesterol (milligrams)
Cheese *(per ounce)*			
Cheddar	6.0	0.2	29.8
Jack	5.4	– –	25.2
Swiss	5.1	– –	26.0
Mozzarella, plain	3.7	– –	22.2
Mozzarella, part skim	2.9	– –	16.9
Cream cheese	6.2	0.3	31.2
Fat-free cream cheese	0.3	– –	2.3
Cottage cheese, creamed, 1 cup	6.0	0.3	31.3
Cottage cheese, 2%, 1 cup	2.8	0.1	19.0
Cottage cheese, 1%, 1 cup	1.5	0.1	9.9
Cottage cheese, fat-free, 1 cup	0.0	0.0	20.0
Reduced fat cheddar, 1 oz.	3.0	– –	15.2
Ice Cream & Frozen Desserts			
Ice cream, 1 cup	9.0	0.4	58.1
Ice milk, 1 cup	3.5	– –	18.5
Soft ice milk, 1 cup	2.9	– –	21.1
Milk shake, 1 cup	3.1	0.2	18.3
Lowfat yogurt, 1 cup	1.7	0.0	10.2
Fat-free yogurt, 1 cup	0.2	0.0	3.0
Nuts			
Almonds, dry, 1/2 oz.	0.7	0.0	0.0
Almonds, oil roasted, 1/2 oz.	0.8	0.0	0.0
Coconut 1/4 cup (0.7 oz)	6.0	0.0	0.0
Peanut butter, pure, 1 tablespoon	1.1	0.0	0.0
Peanut butter, with hydrogenated oil, 1 tablespoon	1.8	0.0	0.0
Peanut butter, reduced fat, 1 tablespoon	1.0	0.0	0.0
Peanuts, dry, 1/2 oz.	1.2	0.0	0.0
Peanuts, oil roasted, 1/2 oz.	1.0	0.0	0.0
Pecans, 1/2 oz.	0.8	0.0	0.0
Sunflower seeds, 1/2 oz.	0.7	0.0	0.0
Walnuts, 1/2 oz.	0.6	0.0	0.0

Food	Saturated Fat (grams)	Trans-fatty Acids (grams)	Cholesterol (milligrams)
Fish *(3 oz. servings broiled, baked or steamed)*			
Catfish	0.6	0.0	61.2
Cod	0.1	0.0	45.7
Crab	0.1	0.0	64.6
Flounder or Sole	0.3	0.0	51.0
Halibut	3.8	0.0	50.2
Herring	1.9	0.0	65.5
Mackerel	3.9	0.0	63.8
Orange Roughy	0.0	0.0	22.1
Salmon, Red Sockeye	1.6	0.0	74.0
Salmon, Pink	0.6	0.0	57.0
Salmon, Coho	1.4	0.0	48.5
Sardines, oil drained off	1.4	0.0	120.8
Snapper	0.3	0.0	40.0
Trout	1.5	0.0	58.7
Tuna, in oil	1.1	0.0	26.9
Tuna, in water	0.7	0.0	35.7
Shellfish *(3 oz. servings, broiled, baked, steamed or boiled)*			
Clams	0.4	0.0	57.0
Crab	1.0	0.0	79.6
Lobster	1.4	0.0	64.6
Scallops	0.5	0.0	27.1
Shrimp	0.8	0.0	155.8
Shrimp (fried)	1.9	0.0	150.5
Oils and Shortening (1 tablespoon serving)			
Lard	5.1	0.2	12.2
Shortening (solid hydrogenated vegetable oil)	3.3	1.7	0.0
Canola oil	1.0	0.0	0.0
Coconut oil	11.9	0.0	0.0
Corn oil	1.8	--	0.0
Olive oil	1.8	0.1	0.0
Palm oil	6.7	0.0	0.0
Peanut oil	2.5	0.0	0.0
Safflower oil	1.2	--	0.0
Soybean/Cottonseed blend	2.5	--	0.0
Sunflower oil	1.8	--	0.0

Index

251